"Most discipleship books focus entirely on personal discipleship—how I can be a better disciple. While not neglecting the personal aspects of discipleship, Dave Earley and Rod Dempsey go one step further and do an excellent job of placing the local church at the center of making disciples. This is where the emphasis lies in the New Testament—building disciples through missionary church planting. This book will give you a detailed account of what the Bible says about disciple making. The careful biblical exegesis is worth the price of the book. Read this book and learn how to follow the Master in making disciples who make disciples."

Joel Comiskey
President, Joel Comiskey Group

"Jesus said, 'Go therefore and make disciples . . .' in Matthew 28 just before His ascension. These were marching orders for those of us in the trenches of ministry. It's not a suggestion; it's an imperative. Many churches today focus more on big crowds than on developing Christ followers. I believe both are important. Let's reach the world with the gospel and then help them develop and grow into fully committed followers of Christ. This book is a great tool in helping the church develop an effective strategy towards that end. Dave Earley and Rod Dempsey are accomplishing much in training the next generation of church leaders to do that which Christ commanded."

Jonathan Falwell
Pastor, Thomas Road Baptist Church

"This volume is a creative how-to handbook at its best. Not written by beginners who hope to get it right, these two veterans have actually applied these principles for decades in very different situations and have discovered that they change lives. Now they are teaching others to do the same. Its many diagrams, charts, discussion questions, suggestions, and treatments of the relevant biblical passages combine in a remarkable effort to share their results and knowledge. The wealth of details here, all up-to-date, tried and tested in tough situations, can work in the lives of real people."

Gary R. Habermas
Distinguished Research Professor, Liberty University

"Have you grasped the vision of multiplication through disciple making? Dempsey and Earley have given us a carefully thought-through opportunity to rethink everything we know about discipleship. A must read!"

Dennis McCallum
Author, *Organic Discipleship*

"Making disciples is the essence of the Great Commission. This book is a careful analysis of what it means to be a disciple of Jesus and what it means to make disciples for Jesus. Dave Earley and Rod Dempsey have been involved in church planting together and teaching seminary classes together, and now they have taken their experience and their passion and they have written a book together. This book is a culmination of their understanding of God's plan for developing followers of Christ. I recommend that you read, study, and apply the biblical principles of *Disciple Making Is*."

Ed Stetzer
President of LifeWay Research, *www.edstetzer.com*

"I wholeheartedly recommend *Disciple Making Is* because the two authors Rod Dempsey and Dave Earley have effectively done discipleship for twenty years together in a church in Ohio. In October 1985, I went to Gahanna, Ohio, to organize the new church plant by Earley and Dempsey. They had a fresh anointing from God that I had not sensed in other church planters, and I knew that the church would accomplish great things for God. I went back five years later to dedicate their first 400-seat auditorium and then two years later I dedicated their 1,000-seat auditorium. The church attendance reached more than 2,000, and the greatness of the church was not in attendance numbers but in the quality of the disciples who began following Jesus Christ; then a vast number of them became co-laborers in building up the church. Then both Earley and Dempsey earned their doctorates at Liberty and came to the university to teach church planting and disciples to a new generation of future church planters. While many books on discipleship focus just on the disciples, I love this book because it focuses on the church and making disciples through a local assembly. This book can change your life if you read it with an open mind and searching heart."

Elmer Towns
Co-founder, Liberty University

Disciple Making Is...

How to Live the Great Commission with Passion and Confidence

DAVE EARLEY AND ROD DEMPSEY

Disciple Making Is...

How to Live the Great Commission with Passion and Confidence

B&H
ACADEMIC
NASHVILLE, TENNESSEE

Disciple Making Is . . .
How to Live the Great Commission with Passion and Confidence
Copyright © 2013 David Earley and Rod Dempsey

B&H Publishing Group
Nashville, Tennessee

All rights reserved

ISBN: 978-1-4336-7706-9

Dewey Decimal Classification: 248.84
Subject Heading: DISCIPLESHIP \ CHRISTIAN LIFE \ GREAT COMMISSION
(BIBLE)

Printed in the United States of America

1 2 3 4 5 6 7 8 9 10 • 17 16 15 14 13

VP

Contents

Part 3. Disciple-Making Methods: Making a Disciple

Disciple Making Is . . .

Part 4. Disciple-Making Models: Pastoral Leadership and the Local Church

Disciple Making Is . . .

Preface

The book you hold in your hands is all about being a disciple of, and making disciples for, Jesus Christ. Many books have been written about this subject (Amazon lists more than two hundreds books on "discipleship"). So you may ask: why another book on the subject? The reason for writing this book is simple. Rod and I want to share with you some important principles about following Jesus, and developing followers of Jesus, from a local church perspective and from our experiences. Obeying and helping others to obey King Jesus and His commands is our highest goal. To accomplish this goal we will examine key biblical passages and, from these passages, extract key biblical principles. From these principles we will suggest several practices that will help the readers become better disciples and disciple makers.

In this book we are going to explore both what it means to be a disciple (the person) and what it means to make disciples (the process). We firmly believe that the best and most effective way to develop followers of Jesus Christ is in the context of His body (a local church). While it is true that many books have been written on this topic, there are few written from the conviction that the church is the essential environment for being and making disciples of Jesus. With this in mind, Dave will examine the Gospels, noting what Jesus said and did in the realm of developing disciples. Rod will investigate the book of Acts and the Epistles, exploring how the first churches attempted to make disciples.

The book itself has thirty chapters and is divided into four sections. Part 1 will address "Disciple-Making Philosophy," seeking to establish a firm *biblical and theological foundation*. Part 2 will cover "Disciple-Making Basics," highlighting what it means to *be a disciple*. Part 3 outlines key "Disciple-Making Methods," which drive the ministry of *making a disciple*. Part 4 surveys and critiques several "Disciple-Making Models," noting the importance of *pastoral leadership and the local church* in the disciple-making endeavor. We hope that by the end of this book you will not only have an understanding of what it means to be a follower of Christ, but you will also have an understanding of how to go about making disciples of Jesus in the local church.

Rod and I never want to stop living as disciples; we are lifelong learners. Our Bibles are full of underlined verses, highlighted words, and notes in the margins. We also love books. Both of us will tell you that the books that have marked us the most are the books that we have marked up the most. We have read and reread key sections of them. We have lifted powerful quotes from them. We have passed along what we have learned from them to others. With this in mind, below are a few suggestions to increase your learning and retention:

- Read with a pencil or pen in hand.
- Underline the stuff you like.
- Put a star in the margin next to good quotes or challenging thoughts.
- Place question marks in the margin by the stuff that does not make sense.
- Summarize each chapter into one sentence.
- Carefully ponder the questions at the end of each chapter.
- Write down one sentence of application for each chapter.

Other aids for getting the maximum benefit for your money and time invested in this book include:

- Talk with someone about what you just read.
- Teach what you are learning to someone else.
- Put as much as possible of what you are learning into practice in your life and ministry.
- Get a copy of this book for each of the people you are investing in and read it together.

So get a cup of coffee, grab a pen, get your Bible, and dive in.

We pray that this book will become a significant tool the Lord uses to launch you on the adventure of a lifetime. This book has the potential not only to change your life but also to change the lives of the people around you. So, don't be guilty of reading this book about disciple making without *being* a disciple in the process. And don't be guilty of reading this book about discipleship without attempting to make disciples! Determine now to be a doer of the commands of Jesus and fulfill the Great Commission. We pray that this book will be beneficial as you pursue being a disciple of, and making disciples for, the Lord Jesus Christ.

Dave Earley, DMin
Senior Pastor, Grace City Church, Henderson, Nevada
Associate Professor of Pastoral Ministries,
Liberty Baptist Theological Seminary

Rod Dempsey, DMin
Director, School of Life and Leadership,
Thomas Road Baptist Church, Lynchburg, Virginia
Professor of Educational Ministries,
Liberty Baptist Theological Seminary

Introduction

Disciple Making Is . . .

Fulfilling the Great Commission

Dave Earley

The Great Commission has been worshipped, but not obeyed.
The church has tried to get world evangelization without
disciple making.[1]

Counting the Cost of Fulfilling the Great Commission

A few years ago I was in Turkey at an outdoor café having coffee with a missionary. During the previous year, persecution of Christians in Turkey had intensified. The government had been steadily harassing him by kicking him and his family out of the country several times. Three missionaries had been martyred by the Muslims. Two of them were associates of my friend.

As we spoke about the increasing levels of persecution, he shared about counting the cost of following Jesus and fulfilling the Great Commission. He was determined to fulfill the Great Commission no matter what.

That man is a disciple of Jesus Christ.

The book you hold in your hands is a book about discipleship and disciple making. Rod Dempsey and I will share what we know about disciple making out of our experience as small-group leaders, church planters, pastors, consultants, and professors. Before we can get into the nuts and bolts of making disciples, we need to anchor our words on the Great Commission.

The Great Commission

A few days before Jesus ascended into glory, He gave His disciples some final instructions. These words were and still are of utmost significance because they are the last words Jesus ever said to His followers. As His last words, they eloquently express His greatest passion and top priority.

These words are also extremely important because Jesus was essentially saying, "This is the culmination and climax of all I have been teaching you the last three years." In other words, when He spoke them, He was saying, "If you don't remember anything else I said, remember this!"

Beyond that, these final instructions were repeated on three separate occasions and are the only commands of Jesus that are recorded in all four Gospels *and* the book of Acts (Matt 28:18–20; Mark 16:15; Luke 24:46–47; John 20:21; Acts 1:8). It is as if He was telling them, "Look, I keep repeating this one thing because it is the main thing. If you don't do anything else, be sure and do this!"

Today we call this final statement "the Great Commission." The most comprehensive of these five proclamations of the Great Commission is recorded in Matthew's Gospel:

> And Jesus came up and spoke to them, saying, "All authority has been given to Me in heaven and on earth. Go therefore and make disciples of all the nations, baptizing them in the name of the Father and the Son and the Holy Spirit, teaching them to observe all that I commanded you; and lo, I am with you always, even to the end of the age." (28:18–20 NASB)

The Great Commission Is *God's Will for Your Life*

Dempsey and I teach Christian students who are vitally interested in the question, "What is God's will for my life?" The answer to this question is twofold: "Be a Disciple and Make Disciples! Orient your life around the Great Commission." These are the last words of Jesus. This is His definitive command to all of His followers. This is God's will for our lives.

The details of where and how we make disciples may vary from person to person, but the big picture is the same: God's will for the life of every Christ follower is to make disciples. David Platt states,

It makes little sense for us to keep asking, "What do you want me to do, God?" the answer is clear. The will of God is for you and me to give our lives urgently and recklessly to make the gospel and glory of God known among all peoples.[2]

God's will for your life is fulfilling the Great Commission. God's will for your life is making disciples.

The Great Commission Is *Not the Great "Suggestion"*

The Great Commission narrative begins with Jesus setting the context: "All authority has been given to Me in heaven and on earth." In essence He said, *"I have the supreme authority to issue orders. Therefore, take what I am about to say very seriously."*

It is foolish for someone to call themselves a follower of Jesus and refuse to fulfill His final wishes and obey His supreme orders. Since this order to evangelize the world by making disciples was clearly and repeatedly given (Mark 16:15; Luke 24:47; John 20:21; Acts 1:8), it is obvious that it must be obeyed. Since we see both the apostles and non-apostles obeying it (Acts 8:1, 4), we know that it was given to all of us.

Making disciples is not a suggestion to be merely considered or an option to entertain. Making disciples must dominate the life of a Christ follower.

The Great Commission Is *Disciple Making*

The primary term in the Great Commission is the imperative verb "make disciples." The other words "go," "baptize," and "teach" all modify and explain *how* we are to fulfill the primary task: make disciples. In order to make this evident to English readers, I paraphrase Matt 28:18–20 as follows:

I am the Supreme Commander in Chief, and these are the orders I am issuing to you: As you are going into the culture, MAKE DISCIPLES!!!
Make disciples of people from every people group by baptizing them and by staying with them in order to teach them to obey everything I have taught you. Then you will really experience My presence.

The book you are reading is a Great Commission book. It is designed to better equip you to fulfill the Great Commission. Therefore, this book is all about making disciples because fulfilling the Great Commission is making disciples, and making disciples is the only way to fulfill the Great Commission.

The Great Commission Is *Fulfilled by Going, Preaching, Baptizing, and Training*

Going

The Great Commission cannot be fulfilled without intentionally pursuing the lost. Just as He was *sent* by His Father, Jesus has *sent* us out in a deliberate quest to win nonbelievers to faith in Christ (John 20:21, 31). Those who are sent are disobedient until they *go*. Aubrey Malphurs provides insight into the importance of the word "go" and the practice of pursuing the lost:

> The Savior clarifies what He means by this word in such passages as Luke 5:27–32, 15:1–10, and 19:1–10, where He develops the concept of seeking lost people such as Levi the tax-gatherer and his friends, tax-gathers and sinners in general, and Zacchaeus. Far too many churches are waiting for lost people to come to them . . . the church will have to take the initiative and pursue these lost people.[3]

Jesus told several parables to reveal the importance of intentionally seeking the lost. In Luke 14, He speaks of going out "into the streets and alleys" to bring in "the poor, maimed, blind, and lame!" (Luke 14:21). Luke 15 opens with the Pharisees rebuking Jesus for eating with tax collectors and sinners (Luke 15:1–2). Jesus responded by telling them two parables about the need for a passionate pursuit of the lost. The first is about a shepherd who left his flock of ninety-nine sheep to find the one that was lost (Luke 15:3–6). The joy of the shepherd over finding his one lost sheep was compared with the joy in heaven when a lost sinner repents (Luke 15:7). Next, Jesus told of a woman who diligently searched to find one lost coin. Again, this is compared with the great joy in heaven when one lost sinner repents (Luke 15:8–10).

Luke's Gospel tells of Jesus reaching out to a tax collector named Zacchaeus. After inviting Himself to dinner and proclaiming the coming of salvation to Zacchaeus's house, Jesus stated His purpose, "For the Son of Man has come to seek and to save the lost" (Luke 19:1–10).

Preaching

It is not enough to go; we must also *tell*. The second practice needed to fulfill the Great Commission is *evangelism: proclaiming the good news*. Christians are to display the gospel. They must also *tell* nonbelievers the message of Jesus' death, burial, and resurrection for their sins. The Great Commission states, "Repentance and forgiveness of sins will be *preached*" (Luke 24:47 NIV). Believers are to "*preach* the Good News" with the goal of leading others to "believe" (Mark 16:15–16 TLB). The result of preaching or proclaiming the gospel should be "to make disciples" (Matt 28:19).

Baptizing

The third action that must be taken in fulfilling the Great Commission is "baptizing them in the name of the Father and of the Son and of the Holy Spirit" (Matt 28:19). This involves incorporating them into a community of believers who identify themselves by the name of the Father, Son, and Holy Spirit. Since baptism is an ordinance of the local church, it is obvious that the Great Commission cannot be fulfilled without the creation of local churches. Trying to make disciples apart from the local church is not only unproductive, it is also unbiblical.

Training

The fourth action in fulfilling the Great Commission is "teaching them to observe everything" Jesus commanded. This involves more than downloading information. Disciple making is about comprehensive training in obedience leading to reproduction and multiplication.

When many speak of fulfilling the Great Commission, they are talking only about evangelism. Yet, Jesus was quite clear: disciple making is not complete until the disciple is practicing everything Jesus commanded, including the command to make more disciples.

Fulfilling the Great Commission *Naturally Results in Church Planting*

Given our understanding of the Great Commission above, the question remains: How does God expect His followers to implement it? The obvious answer is: by *planting churches*. Church planting involves all the elements of fulfilling the Great Commission. New churches are the result of Christians intentionally pursuing the lost, preaching the gospel, baptizing believers, and training them to live for Christ and make more disciples.

After the disciples were given the Great Commission, what did they do to obey it? The book of Acts reveals that after receiving the Holy Spirit, they started new churches. According Aubrey Malphurs, "A careful reading of Acts reveals that the early church implemented the Great Commission mandate primarily by planting churches."[4] Ed Stetzer of Global Church Advancement has planted churches in New York, Pennsylvania, and Georgia and transitioned declining churches in Indiana and Georgia. He writes, "New Testament Christians acted out these commands as any spiritually healthy, obedient believers would: they planted more New Testament churches."[5] He concludes with the axiom, "The Great Commission *is* church planting."[6]

The way the first followers of Jesus carried out the Great Commission directly resulted in the planting of churches. Peter (and others) preached the gospel (Acts 2:14–36); the people who responded were baptized (Acts 2:37–41); and the baptized believers were immediately incorporated into the church as they began obeying what Jesus had taught (Acts 2:42–47). Their followers, the non-apostles, were also seen going and preaching the gospel (Acts 8:1, 4), resulting in new churches (Acts 11:19–26). The fulfillment of the Great Commission always and ultimately results in church planting.

Fulfilling the Great Commission *Ultimately Leads to Global Church Planting*

Fulfilling the Great Commission requires preaching the gospel *all over the world*: "Go into all the world and preach the gospel to the whole creation" (Mark 16:15). It is making disciples *of every people group* on the planet: "Go, therefore, and make disciples of all nations" (Matt 28:19). Even though it began in Jerusalem, the gospel must *spread to all nations*: "Thus it is written, that the Christ would suffer and rise again from the dead the third day, and that repentance for forgiveness of sins would be proclaimed in His name to all the nations, beginning from Jerusalem" (Luke 24:46–47 NASB).

In the last recorded account of the Great Commission, Jesus stressed the unfolding, ever-expanding focus of the Great Commission: "But you will receive power when the Holy Spirit has come upon you; and you shall be My witnesses both in Jerusalem, and in all Judea and Samaria, and even to the remotest part of the earth" (Acts 1:8 NASB). In fulfilling the Great Commission, we must not be content until we have planted churches all over the whole world.

The Great Commission *Contains a Great Promise*

Jesus concluded this final command with an amazing promise of His manifest presence, "*And remember, I am with you always, to the end of the age*" (Matt 28:20). It is good to stand with our arms lifted high and sing to the Lord with a passion for Him to "be with us." Do not miss the fact that Jesus promised to be with us *as we make disciples*. God's heart is, in a special way, with those who fulfill His command to make disciples. He shows up when we step up to fulfill His commission.

The Great Commission *Must Become Our Great Obsession*

Obviously, God and His glory are to be our greatest obsessions. After all, we were created for His glory (Isa 43:7). We are to declare His glory (1 Chron 16:24; Ps 96:3, 7–8). Everything we do should point to God's glory (1 Cor 10:31). We must reflect His glory (2 Cor 3:18). Our salvation is with the purpose that our lives might bring praise to His glory (Eph 1:12, 14). The goal of our prayers for others is ultimately the glory of God through their lives (Eph 3:14–21; Phil 1:9–11; Heb 13:21). God's glory is to be the ultimate goal of our lives and prayers (Rom 11:36; 16:27; Gal 1:5; Phil 4:20; 2 Pet 3:18; Jude 1:25).

How do we give God the greatest glory? One way to answer that question is by looking at what His first followers did. Immediately after hearing the final giving of the Great Commission (Acts 1:8), they convened a weeklong prayer meeting (Acts 1:12–15). Following Pentecost and the giving of the Holy Spirit (Acts 2), they began to preach the gospel and make disciples by baptizing their converts and incorporating them into a local church where they were taught everything Jesus commanded (Acts 2).

They glorified God by making the Great Commission the focal point of their lives. They forsook all to follow Jesus and fulfill His Great Commission. The Great Commission was such a driving obsession in their lives that it led them to travel the world preaching it, no matter the cost. For example, the deacon named Stephen was preaching the gospel in Jerusalem on the Passover after Christ's crucifixion. He was cast out of the city and stoned to death (Acts 8). James, the son of Zebedee and the elder brother of John, was killed when Herod Agrippa arrived as governor of Judea (Acts 12).

History tells us that Philip suffered martyrdom while taking the gospel to Heliopolis, in Phrygia. He was scourged, thrown into prison, and afterwards crucified (about AD 54). Matthew, the tax collector from Nazareth who later wrote one of the four Gospels, was preaching in Ethiopia when he suffered martyrdom by the sword (about AD 60). Andrew, the brother of Peter, preached the gospel throughout Asia. On his arrival at Edessa, he was arrested and crucified on a cross, two ends of which were fixed transversely in the ground (thus the term, St. Andrew's cross). Bartholomew translated the Gospel of Matthew in India. He was cruelly beaten and crucified. Thomas preached in Parthia and India. He was martyred with a spear.

James, the half-brother of Jesus, led the church in Jerusalem and authored the epistle that bears his name. At the age of ninety-four, because of his commitment to the Great Commission, he was beaten, stoned, and pummeled to death with a fuller's club. Matthias was the apostle who filled the vacant place of Judas. He was stoned at Jerusalem and then beheaded. Mark was converted to Christianity and then transcribed Peter's account of Jesus in his Gospel. Mark was dragged to pieces by the people of Alexandria in front of Serapis, their pagan idol.[7]

Now What?

Disciple making must be understood in the context of the Great Commission. The Great Commission is God's will for your life. It is a command that must be obeyed. It is fulfilled by going, preaching, baptizing, and training, and it results in church planting.

This is a book about disciple making. But before we can tell you *how* to make a disciple, we need to make sure that you understand both the biblical and theological foundations of disciple making as well as the basics of what it means to be a disciple. Unless you have abandoned your life to that type of lifestyle, the methods are just nice words on a page. The goal of reading this chapter has been for you to make a deep commitment to spending the rest of your life fulfilling the Great Commission.

— Questions to Ponder —

1. Have you found God's will for your life?
2. Where and when are you going into the lives of lost people? What can you do to be better at going?
3. When was the last time you proclaimed the gospel to a lost person?
4. Are you willing to leave your comfort zone to make disciples whatever the cost and anywhere God directs?
5. Will you make the commitment to spending the rest of your life fulfilling the Great Commission?

Notes

1. Bill Hull, *The Disciple-Making Pastor* (Old Tappan, NJ: Fleming Revell, 1988), 23, emphasis in original.

2. David Platt, *Radical: Taking Back Your Faith from the American Dream* (Colorado Springs, CO: Multnomah, 2010), 159–60.

3. Aubrey Malphurs, *Planting Growing Churches for the Twenty-First Century* (Grand Rapids: Baker, 1992), 42.

4. Ibid., 43.

5. Ed Stetzer, *Planting New Churches in a Postmodern Age* (Nashville, TN: Broadman & Holman, 2003), 37.

6. Ibid., 35.

7. "Christian Persecution" on the website, All About Following Jesus, http://www.allaboutfollowingjesus.org/christian-persecution.htm (accessed March 23, 2007).

Disciple-Making Philosophy: Biblical and Theological Foundations

Foundations are critically important in most every endeavor known to man. Our government has a foundational document called the Constitution. A successful business leader learns to be successful from good foundational business principles. In education, you need a good foundation at the elementary level. In sports, you need a good foundation to excel at the highest levels.

The same is true when it comes to being a disciple of, and making disciples for, Jesus Christ. In order to accomplish this task, we will need to understand certain biblical and theological underpinnings. With this in mind, part 1 will examine several foundational concepts and priorities from the Scriptures upon which to build a disciple-making system. These chapters seek to answer fundamental questions such as: What is a disciple? Why should we make disciples? And, what is the role of the Spirit and the church in the disciple-making process?

Disciple Making Is . . .

Discovering an Organizing Principle

Rod Dempsey

Let's Begin with a Purpose

Why did God create the universe? Why did He create the earth? Why did He create the animals? Why did He create human beings? Why did God create you? What is God's purpose in creating you and me? We find the answer to that last question in Isa 43:7: ". . . Everyone called by My name and created for My glory. I have formed him; indeed, I have made him." You were created by God to bring Him glory.

John Piper states, "The Scriptures teach throughout that all the works of God have as their ultimate goal the display of God's glory."[1] It is a fact that God created everything to bring Him glory. In Rev 4:11 we read, "Our Lord and God, You are worthy to receive *glory* and honor and power, because You have created all things, and because of Your will they exist and were created." In Isa 6:3 we are told that His glory fills the earth, and in Hab 2:14 we are told that all the earth will be filled with the knowledge of His glory. God's glory is the highest aim in all creation. John Calvin echoed this when he said that "creation is the theater of God's glory."[2] You and I are a part of God's creation and, as such, are designed to bring God glory.

The apostle Paul puts it this way, "And in view of this, we always pray for you that our God will consider you worthy of His calling, and will, by His power, fulfill every desire for goodness and the work of faith, so that the name of our Lord Jesus will be *glorified* by you, and you by Him, according to the grace of our God and the Lord Jesus Christ" (2 Thess 1:11–12). So the apostle Paul affirms . . . God's purpose is for you to bring Him glory.

How Can I Bring Glory to God?

As disciples, bringing glory to God should be present in every facet of our lives. There are several different stages in our development as disciples of Jesus. Yet in all phases we are created to bring God glory: we are saved to bring God glory; we grow spiritually to bring God glory; we serve to bring God glory; in our suffering we bring God glory; we use our gifts, bearing fruit to bring God glory. Every aspect of our lives should be lived to fulfill God's plan for our lives, namely, to bring Him glory. This is the organizing principle for the person who would follow King Jesus. This principle guides our daily decisions and affects the way we organize our lives.

Let's consider these stages of development and how they bring God glory. First, we are *saved* to bring God glory. In Eph 1:12 we understand that the purpose of salvation is "that we who had already put our hope in the Messiah might bring praise to His *glory*." God's plan when He called you to salvation is that His glory would be revealed in your life. Second Thessalonians 2:14 states, "He called you to this through our gospel, so that you might obtain the *glory* of our Lord Jesus Christ." We are saved to share in God's glory and to bring God glory.

Second, we are not only saved to bring God glory, but we also *grow* to bring God glory. In 2 Pet 3:18 we see the motivation for spiritual growth: "But grow in the grace and knowledge of our Lord and Savior Jesus Christ. To Him be the *glory* both now and to the day of eternity. Amen." This organizing principle of bringing glory to God affects every area of our lives. We are saved to bring God glory, and we grow in Christ for the same purpose. Second Corinthians 3:18 puts it this way: "We all, with unveiled faces, are looking as in a mirror at the *glory* of the Lord and are being transformed into the same image from *glory* to *glory*; this is from the Lord who is the Spirit." We grow spiritually to reflect God's glory and thereby bring Him glory.

Third, the apostle Peter says that we *serve* God to bring Him glory. "If anyone speaks, [his speech should be] as one who speaks God's words; if anyone serves, [his service should be] from the strength God provides, so that God may be *glorified* through Jesus Christ in everything. To Him belong the *glory* and the power forever and ever. Amen" (1 Pet 4:11). The author of the book of Hebrews also confirms that we serve God to bring Him glory when he says, "Now may the God of peace, who brought up from the dead our Lord Jesus—the great Shepherd of the sheep—with the blood of the everlasting covenant, *equip you with all that is good to do His will*, working in us what is pleasing in His sight, through Jesus Christ. Glory belongs to Him forever and ever. Amen" (Heb 13:20–21).

Fourth, the apostle Peter also says that in addition to all these things, even our *suffering* is to bring God glory, "so that the genuineness of your faith—more valuable than gold, which perishes though refined by fire—may result in praise, *glory*, and honor at the revelation of Jesus Christ" (1 Pet 1:7). Even in our suffering we can reflect God's purpose in our lives.

Finally, every believer is imbued with spiritual gifts that, when employed, *bear fruit* to the glory of God. John 15:8 states, "My Father is glorified by this: that you produce much *fruit* and *prove to be My disciples*." Jesus says here that God is glorified as we are producing fruit. Furthermore, it is in producing fruit that we prove to be His disciples. There is, then, an important connection between discipleship, fruit bearing, and the glory of God.

In every phase of our existence—salvation, spiritual growth, service, suffering, and bearing fruit—God has created us to bring Him glory. Although that purpose was short-circuited when Adam sinned, nevertheless, that purpose has now been restored. Paul states that "if anyone is in Christ, he is a new creation; old things have passed away, and look, new things have come" (2 Cor 5:17). Part of the "new things" is the restoration of our ability to bring glory to God as the believer progresses in their conformity to the image of Jesus (Rom 8:28–29). When we live and walk like Jesus, we bring glory to God. You were saved to bring God glory. You grow to bring God glory. You serve to bring God glory. You endure suffering to bring God glory. You discover and use your gifts to bring God glory (bear much fruit).

The Organizing Principle and Disciple Making

THE organizing principle, then, is the glory of God. Consider 1 Cor 10:31: "Therefore, whether you eat or drink, or whatever you do, do everything for God's glory." The glory of God is, likewise, the organizing principle for the disciple. The apostle John links the glory of God with being a disciple when he says, "My Father is *glorified* by this: that you produce much fruit and prove to be My disciples" (John 15:8). God's ultimate plan for your life is to bring

glory to His name as a follower of Jesus Christ (a disciple), the fundamental proof of which is bearing fruit, or disciple making. Disciple making in its purest form is helping people find Jesus and then helping them to grow and become all they can be for Christ. In turn, they will become committed to following His commands and obeying the Great Commission. This passionate pursuit enables followers of Jesus to bring the maximum amount of glory to God on an individual basis, and it connects the disciple to God's global mission as well. Bringing glory to God is an individual pursuit and a global plan at the same time. As disciple makers, we have the privilege of sharing the good news of Jesus with everyone and then encouraging those who accept Christ to grow and develop for Christ.

God's will for you and God's glory are inextricably linked. God's will is found in God's Word, and as we have already established, God's will for your life is that you would bring Him glory. In every stage of your growth and development as a disciple, God's will is that you would live your life in such a way that God would be glorified. Yet the question always comes down to *how?* How do I bring glory to God? And similarly: "How do I help others bring glory to God?"

Moving People onto God's Agenda

As we mentioned above, there are several stages in our development as a disciple. Each stage must be connected to God's will and the organizing principle of bringing Him glory. Our goal as disciple makers is for God's name to be glorified. We accomplish this goal by "moving people on to God's agenda."[3] Moving people onto God's agenda involves helping them discover and experience God's will for their lives. As we examine God's will in each stage, we will also discover specific aspects of God's will for the disciple.

In this regard, disciple making is very similar to being a parent. In order to be a physical parent, you must have children. In order to be a spiritual parent, people must receive Jesus as Lord and Savior. Natural parents want to see their children grow and develop. When they grow up, they will most likely marry and become parents in their own right, and they in turn will have children of their own. In a similar manner, spiritual parents want to see their children grow and develop as well.

As new believers mature spiritually, they should grow to the point where they reproduce new spiritual babies. As the new babies are born, the spiritual parents watch out for them and help them to "grow up" to the point where they will have spiritual children of their own. Ultimately our goal as spiritual parents is to see the "kids" grow up and go out! Those children will grow up being a reflection of their parents. They will bring glory to their parents. This is the natural pattern and should be the spiritual pattern as well. Children are the glory of their parents, and grandchildren are the "crown of the elderly" (Prov 17:6).

Where Do I Start?

To review, the first stage of God's will for every person is salvation. He desires that every person would come into a right relationship with Jesus Christ. New birth is the entry point for living a life that brings God glory. Second Peter 3:9 says, "The Lord does not delay His promise, as some understand delay, but is patient with you, not wanting any to perish but all to come to repentance." It is not God's will that any person would die in their sins and perish. That is why God sent His Son to die on the cross. He took our place on the cross. He was our substitute, and as a result, we can be forgiven of our sins and live a life that is glorifying to Him.

The next stage of God's will for the disciple is that he or she would grow spiritually. Consider what Paul says in 1 Thess 4:3–4: "For this is the will of God, your sanctification: that you should abstain from sexual immorality, that each of you should know how to possess his own vessel in sanctification and honor" (NKJV). This verse could not be clearer. It is God's will that you grow in your sanctification. *Sanctification* is a word we do not use very often today, but it simply means coming to the place where you consistently say yes to God and no to sin. Encouraging and empowering the disciple to grow and develop brings glory to God.

The third stage of development for the disciple is the area of serving. Listen to what the apostle Paul says in Eph 2:10, "For we are His creation, created in Christ Jesus for good works, which God prepared ahead of time so that we should walk in them." Ephesians 2:8–9 says that we are not saved *by* works, but verse 10 makes it clear that we are saved *to* work. God has something in mind that He wants His children to do. He has prepared us ahead of time to do something in His kingdom. Have you ever wondered why God has given to every believer at least one spiritual gift? Every Christian has a gift, and that person is to use their gift to bring God glory. We lovingly use our gifts in the body to serve one another and to build up the body of Christ (Eph 4:16). Greg Ogden observes, "It is through our ministry or spiritual gifts that we make our contribution to the health of the whole."[4] If you claim to be a follower of Christ and yet you are not serving Christ, I would seriously question your standing in Christ. In Matt 7:16, Jesus put it this way: "You'll recognize them by their fruit."

The fourth stage of development for a disciple is learning to sacrifice and to endure suffering. Let me remind you what Peter says about our suffering and God's glory: ". . . so that the genuineness of your faith—more valuable than gold, which perishes though refined by fire—may result in praise, *glory*, and honor at the revelation of Jesus Christ" (1 Pet 1:7). Leith Andersen offers this perspective on suffering: "God is always the sovereign boss, and we trust him to give the right answer whether we like that answer or not. When God chooses to perform a miracle and solve our problem, we are deeply grateful. When God says no, we must be faithful and pray that he will give us the strength to make it through, make him look good, and be bold in our words for Jesus."[5]

Jesus gave His disciples this stark message: "If anyone comes to Me and does not hate his own father and mother, wife and children, brothers and sisters— yes, and even his own life—he cannot be My disciple. Whoever does not bear his own cross and come after Me cannot be My disciple" (Luke 14:26–27). Taking up the cross of Jesus means the disciple must be willing to suffer for the King of kings. If we sacrifice and suffer for Jesus patiently, God is glorified.

The fifth stage reflects the ultimate goal for the disciple: God's will is for you to bear much fruit, and when you bear much fruit, God is glorified. Listen again to the words of Jesus in John 15:8: "My Father is glorified by this: that you produce much fruit and prove to be My disciples." The highest goal for disciples is to develop to the point where they are producing fruit to the glory of God.

There are several ways to think of "fruit" in this passage. First, there is the fruit of good Christian character. For example, one might think of the fruit of the Spirit that produces good conduct in our lives, such as "love, joy, peace, patience, kindness, goodness, faith, gentleness, self-control" (Gal 5:22–23). Exhibiting this type of fruit is pleasing to God and brings Him glory. This type of fruit shapes the identity of the disciple, which in turn serves as the foundation for all ministry; being leads to doing. In addition, we can also bear fruit by sharing the gospel and assisting in the process of individuals coming to Christ. We can further bear fruit by using our spiritual gifts and serving those around us. All this produces "fruit" in our lives, and it brings glory to God.

Whatever You Do . . .

Our motivation as disciple makers is to bring the maximum amount of glory to God in our lives and in the lives of those we serve. Ultimately, we desire to hear from Jesus, "Well done good and faithful slave" (Matt 25:21). We desire to hear that in our own lives, but we also desire the people we serve to hear that same message.

This is the starting point and organizing principle for disciple making. The way we go about bringing glory to God follows a progression from salvation, to spiritual growth, to serving, to suffering, and finally, to bearing fruit. The organizing principle for a disciple is to bring God glory!

— Questions to Ponder —

1. What is your purpose in life?
2. From the stages listed above, what stage are you in currently?
3. What do you need to do to go to the next level?
4. Are you bearing much fruit for the King?
5. What changes do you need to make to hear from the Master, "Well done, good and faithful slave" (Matt 25:23)?

Notes

1. http://www.desiringgod.org/resource-library/articles/the-glory-of-god-as-the -goal-of-history (accessed September 27, 2012).

2. John Calvin, *Institutes of the Christian Religion*, ed. John T. McNeill, trans. and indexed by Ford Lewis Battles (Philadelphia, PA: Westminster, 1967), 1:6:2 (72).

3. Henry T. Blackaby and Richard Blackaby, *Spiritual Leadership: Moving People on to God's Agenda* (Nashville: Broadman & Holman, 2001), 20.

4. Greg Ogden, *Unfinished Business: Returning the Ministry to the People of God* (Grand Rapids: Zondervan, 2010), 11.

5. Leith Anderson, *The Jesus Revolution: Learning from Christ's First Followers* (Nashville: Abingdon, 2009), Kindle location 585–87.

Disciple Making Is . . .

Beginning on a Sure Foundation

Rod Dempsey

Solid Foundations

Jesus warned us about the perils of building a house on the sand. He explained that if you build a house on sand, when the rain falls and the rivers rise and the wind blows and pound the house, the house will collapse. The reason for the collapse is because the house was not built upon the rock. It did not have a good foundation (Matt 7:24–27). We have just examined one element of this foundation, suggesting that the motivation for being a disciple and making disciples is the glory of God. This chapter will build on that foundation by creating a simple definition of a follower of Christ.

In so doing, this chapter will serve as a biblical foundation for disciple making within the local church. It is a summary of Jesus' teaching on the subject of disciple making. The starting point for disciple making, inside the local church, is to first understand what a disciple of Jesus looks like. Without this understanding, we cannot possibly hope to create God-honoring disciples. We will examine the Scriptures and consider the characteristics of a first-century disciple, drawing from those passages bedrock principles regarding being a disciple. The passages and principles are the foundation for disciple making, and that foundation is rock solid.

Zig Ziglar has famously noted, "If you aim at nothing, you will hit it every time."[1] Many times churches try to make disciples without a clear understanding of what a disciple actually looks like. As a result, many churches are running, and running very hard, but not making progress in the disciple-making process. Therefore, the starting point for disciple making is to examine carefully what the Master had to say about disciple making. Fortunately, in the Gospels Jesus talked often about what it means to be a disciple, and the word *disciple* appears throughout the New Testament.

Start with Clarity

The word *disciple*, or some variation, appears 266 times in the New Testament, with the vast majority of those occurrences recorded in the Gospels. In those contexts, being a disciple generally means abandoning the things of the world and following Jesus. In addition, to be a disciple requires that a person be disciplined in spiritual habits and purpose (see section 2). The epistles emphasize a relational community where disciples are developed in the context of a body of believers. They discover and use their spiritual gifts to love and serve each other and nonbelievers. Disciples obey the Great Commandment (Matt 22:37), the New Commandment (John 13:34), and the Great Commission (Matt 28:19) and, in so doing, become the hands, feet, and voice for Jesus in their world. The disciples are developed as the body grows in maturity and as each part does its work (Eph 4:16).

This clear call of Jesus to come and follow Him in the Gospels cannot be ignored. Jesus clearly identifies the marks of a disciple in the Gospels, and we need to start there. Here are the main passages related to being a disciple as set forth by Jesus Himself. A disciple is someone:

1. *Who seriously considers the cost before following Christ.* Luke 14:28 states, "For which of you, wanting to build a tower, doesn't first sit down and calculate the cost to see if he has enough to complete it?" This verse makes it clear that before a person decides to follow Jesus, he or she must first sit down and calculate the cost of following Christ. For the true disciple, it will only cost you your life, your body, your possessions, and your future. In short, it will cost you everything. God's plan and God's will cost Jesus His life; it cannot cost His followers anything less.

2. *Who is totally committed to Christ.* Dietrich Bonhoeffer states, "Discipleship is commitment to Christ. Because Christ exists, he

must be followed."[2] Jesus is first! He is the first priority. Consider the following verse from Luke 14:26: "If anyone comes to Me and does not hate his own father and mother, wife and children, brothers and sisters—yes, and even his own life—he cannot be My disciple." Hatred here is a comparative term. Our love for Christ is so great, so consuming that, in comparison, it feels like hatred (disdain) for others. Jesus said it this way in Matt 6:33: "But seek first the kingdom of God and His righteousness, and all these things will be provided for you." The priority of Jesus in one's life is evidenced by a willingness to go anywhere and do anything He asks. Have you come to the place where your first and foremost desire is to follow Him whatever the cost?

3. *Who is willing to carry his or her individual burden to sacrifice for Christ and His cause.* Luke 14:27 states, "Whoever does not bear his own cross and come after Me cannot be My disciple." Much has been written and discussed about what it means to "carry your cross." In a nutshell it simply means that the disciple of Jesus will be called upon to lay down his life (his desire for self-direction and determination) and to surrender his will to the will of the Master. The kingdom of God is not advanced on a 9-to-5 schedule. You cannot serve someone without eventually surrendering your will to the person you serve. Consider Luke 17:10: "In the same way, when you have done all that you were commanded, you should say, 'We are good-for-nothing slaves; we've only done our duty.'" Obedience to the point of sacrifice, if called upon, is part of being a disciple of Jesus.

4. *Who is willing to give up all earthly possessions.* Luke 14:33 maintains, "In the same way, therefore, every one of you who does not say good-bye to all his possessions cannot be My disciple." Again, we see the call to abandon totally any and all ownership to possessions. Jesus put it this way in Matt 6:24: "No one can be a slave of two masters, since either he will hate one and love the other, or be devoted to one and despise the other. You cannot be slaves of God and of money." Earlier in the same passage Jesus said, "For where your treasure is, there your heart will be also" (Matt 6:21). This does not mean that to be a disciple a person must take a vow of poverty, but the disciple must be "poor in spirit" (Matt 5:3) and be willing to surrender all possessions if the Master asks.

5. *Who continues in God's Word and experiences freedom in Christ.* John 8:31–32 states, "So Jesus said to the Jews who had believed Him,

'If you continue in My word, you really are My disciples. You will know the truth, and the truth will set you free.'" The Word of God is "living and active." It has the ability to "transform our minds" and our lives if we will read it, study it, memorize it, and meditate on it consistently. The Word can set us free from the lies of the enemy and empower us to overcome the fiery darts of our adversary. If we do not continue in the Word, then we are wide open to deception, discouragement, and defeat. You cannot be a disciple without an aggressive commitment to consume and obey the Scriptures. As we drink in the Word of God, it has the power to transform our minds, and when our minds are transformed, then we can experience the good, acceptable, and perfect will of God (Rom 12:2).

6. *Who genuinely loves other believers.* John 13:35 maintains, "By this all people will know that you are My disciples, if you have love for one another." If you do not love other believers, then you do not know the God of love. Years ago Burt Bacharach penned the lyrics: "What the world needs now is love, sweet love. No not just for some but for everyone."[3] These lyrics capture the call and the challenge of Jesus in the upper room discourse when He called His disciples together and told them to "love one another" (John 15:17). Francis Schaeffer observed that our love for one another should be so strong that it would unite believers in such a way that the world "would believe" that Jesus was sent by God.[4] The modern-day disciple must be committed to love: loving God, loving our neighbor, and loving our brothers and sisters in Christ. When we love like this, there is no argument that can stand against this force. What is your love level like right now?

7. *Who abides in Christ, prays, bears fruit, and glorifies God.* John 15:5, 7–8 states, "I am the vine; you are the branches. The one who remains in Me and I in him produces much fruit, because you can do nothing without Me. . . . If you remain in Me and My words remain in you, ask whatever you want and it will be done for you. My Father is glorified by this: that you produce much fruit and prove to be My disciples." When we abide in Christ, we will ask for His will and know His will, and it will be done for the disciple. As a result, fruit will be produced and God will be glorified. John 15 is the clearest explanation of life as a follower of Christ. This passage should be the normative experience for the disciple. Pay attention to it. Study it. Obey it.

8. *Who is full of the Holy Spirit.* Acts 13:52 states, "And the disciples were filled with joy and the Holy Spirit." Part of the fruit of abiding in Christ is the fruit of the Spirit, which is love, joy, peace, patience, kindness, goodness, faithfulness, gentleness, and self-control (Gal 5:22–23). The other part of fruitfulness is fruit that comes from serving and using your spiritual gift(s). John 15 says that a disciple should bear much fruit—fruit in your character and fruit in your actions. Being should always lead to doing. The Holy Spirit was sent by Jesus to be with us and to guide us in all things. In order to follow Christ fully, we need to be full of the Holy Spirit. He will guide us into the path of obedience and fruitfulness, and that will ultimately lead to joy. We will address this in depth in the next chapter.

9. *Who obediently follows the desires of the Master.* Matthew 26:19 says, "So the disciples did as Jesus had directed them and prepared the Passover." Immediate and complete obedience is a hallmark of a disciple. It is impossible ever to say, "No, Lord!" because the moment you say "no," He is no longer your "Lord." The Gospels portray following God as being a member in His kingdom. As loyal subjects in His kingdom, our job is to follow the King and go wherever and do whatever He says. Jim Putnam reiterates this point when he says, "To be disciples, we too must recognize and accept who Jesus is, and we must place ourselves under His authority."[5] Many times we approach the kingdom of heaven too casually. The Parable of the Talents (Matt 25:14–30) and the Parable of the Minas (Luke 19:11–27) make it clear that one day the Master will return and call His servants into account. In order to hear from Him, "Well done good and faithful slave," we must understand and assume the role of a servant. You cannot be rewarded by the Master if you have not obeyed the wishes of the Master.

10. *Who is intimately involved in the mission of Jesus to make disciples.* Matthew 28:16, 18–20 states, "The eleven disciples traveled to Galilee, to the mountain where Jesus had directed them. . . . Then Jesus came near and said to them, 'All authority has been given to Me in heaven and on earth. Go, therefore, and make disciples of all nations, baptizing them in the name of the Father and of the Son and of the Holy Spirit, teaching them to observe everything I have commanded you. And remember, I am with you always, to the end of the age.'" These were some of the last words spoken by Jesus to His disciples before He ascended back into heaven. They must be carefully studied and diligently observed. A careful study of the

sentence structure yields: one command, three participles, and one promise. The command verb (in the imperative) is "make disciples." Whatever else we are involved in as followers of Christ, we must be involved in His mission. The disciple cannot respond to the person of Christ without responding to the mission of Christ. We must be going and, as we are going, we must be in the business of developing followers of Christ. In addition, we are to baptize them and teach them to obey all the commands and teachings of Jesus. As we are going and making disciples, Jesus has promised to be with us. I often ask students: "How many of you want Jesus to be with you?" Usually everyone in the room raises their hand. "Well, if you want Jesus to be with you, then you must be in the business of making disciples. If you are obeying Him, He has promised to be with you!"

Extract the Principles

We have just surveyed ten different passages and principles that clearly identify the characteristics of a first-century disciple. Can you imagine the wonder and amazement of the first disciples as they heard the Master identify the cost of following Him? What is your reaction when you read the words of Jesus as He explains the cost of discipleship? We hope that, as you read the verses and the principles, your heart is stirred to accept the simple challenge of Jesus to "follow Me."

Before a church embarks on the process of making disciples, there must be absolute clarity on what a disciple of Jesus looks like. We cannot ignore the importance of starting with the Scriptures. From the Scriptures, we can extract guiding principles that will help us create a definition for a modern-day disciple. The definition must come from the principles in order to capture the image that God has in mind for a Christ follower. With this in mind, I suggest three guiding principles that summarize these passages.

A disciple is someone who is:

1. *Sacrificial.* He or she has made a decision to submit to Christ and surrender their will and to follow Christ no matter what the cost. The starting point of this commitment is salvation. After salvation, this person has seriously examined the cost and is willing to abandon family and possessions for the Master if need be. This disciple is also willing to take up his or her cross and follow Christ to the ends of the earth. Sacrifice of time, energy, body, and future plans

are understood to be part of the commitment to come after Christ. Submission to Christ and His plan is the highest goal for the person who would follow Christ.

2. *Relational.* He or she understands that love is the hallmark of followers of Christ. Love for God, love for neighbor, and love for other disciples is a very important part of the value system of a disciple. He or she will set aside time to be with other Christians for spiritual nourishment and encouragement. Loving my neighbor is a natural outflow of my love for God. In addition, if I love God, then I want to spend time with Him and His children. Christ followers also prioritize serving the body by discovering their spiritual gift and using that gift to serve both Christians and non-Christians. The local church is the focal point for this relational community and service. A church that is biblical will prioritize the development of believers in community. Loving God and loving people is not only a consistent passion, but a consistent practice.

3. *Transformational.* He or she understands that the purpose of spiritual growth is directed toward becoming like Christ in word, thought, attitude, and *action*. Habits like Bible study, journaling, memorization, meditation, silence, solitude, prayer, fasting, and giving are all means to an end. They connect us to the grace of God, and through the grace of God we are transformed into the image of Christ. As we become like Christ in character, we also

Disciple of Jesus Christ

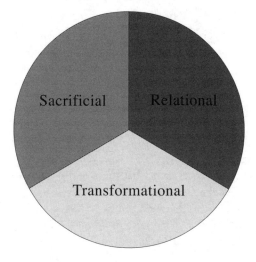

become Christlike and adopt His values. Being leads to doing. The transformation that we are talking about for the disciple connects them not only to the person of Christ but also to the mission of Christ. The disciple discovers, develops, and uses his or her gift for the kingdom of God. You cannot be a follower of the person of Christ without being a follower of the mission of Christ.

Create a Definition

From these three guiding principles—*sacrificial, relational,* and *transformational*—we can create a definition that will help to clarify what a disciple looks like. Only then can we begin to design a simple, relational process for disciple making. From this bedrock foundation, churches can design systems and structures to develop people who think, feel, and act like Jesus. Here is my definition for a person who would follow Jesus:

> A disciple is a person who has trusted Christ for salvation and has *surrendered* completely to Him. He or she is committed to practicing the spiritual disciplines in *community* and *developing to their full potential for Christ and His mission.*

⚊ Questions to Ponder ⚊

1. Have you surrendered everything to Christ?
2. Are you growing spiritually (investing time daily in the spiritual disciplines)?
3. Are you relationally connected to Jesus and other followers of Jesus?
4. Have you discovered and are you using your spiritual gifts?
5. Are you involved in advancing the mission of Christ?

Notes

1. See http://www.goodreads.com/quotes/show/78121 (accessed September 27, 2012).

2. Dietrich Bonhoeffer, *Discipleship*, vol. 4 in *Dietrich Bonhoeffer Works* (Minneapolis, MN: Augsburg: Fortress, 2003), Kindle location 1509.

3. See http://www.metrolyrics.com/what-the-world-needs-now-is-love-lyrics-burt-bacharach.html (accessed September 27, 2012).

4. See http://www.ccel.us/schaeffer.html, p. 15 (accessed September 27, 2012).

5. Jim Putman, *Real-Life Discipleship: Building Churches That Make Disciples* (Colorado Springs: NavPress, 2010), 28.

Cooperating with the Holy Spirit[1]

Dave Earley

In order to become a disciple of Jesus Christ, a person must come to the place where they recognize Jesus as their Lord and Savior. The process that leads to this decision is called "evangelism." Jesus called it fishing "for people" (Matt 4:19). Put another way, "no evangelism . . . no discipleship." The starting point for being a disciple of Jesus, and making disciples for Jesus, is to understand the role of the Holy Spirit in the process of evangelism. Conversion is never a solo operation. There are always at least three persons involved. First, there is the nonbeliever who hears the gospel and receives Jesus by faith and repentance. Second, there is the person who shares the gospel with the nonbeliever. Third, there is the Holy Spirit, who applies the gospel to the understanding of the nonbeliever.

The key to being effective in evangelism is simply learning to cooperate with what the Holy Spirit is already doing and saying to the person we are trying to reach. I am convinced that the times I have been least effective in evangelism have been those times when I either tried to go it alone, without being sensitive to the Holy Spirit or, worse, tried to be the Holy Spirit in the life of the lost person.

Meet the Most Important Person in Your Spiritual Life: The Holy Spirit

Some churches talk a great deal about the Holy Spirit. Others rarely do. While the Bible does speak more often about God the Son and God the Father, it also has much to say about God the Holy Spirit. Let me give you a quick overview.

The Holy Spirit Is God

The Bible teaches the triunity of God. Historically, Christians have believed in one God who expresses Himself in three persons. These three persons are God the Father, God the Son, and God the Holy Spirit. All three are equally God.

When the Bible refers to the Holy Spirit, He is described as having attributes that are only found in God. The Holy Spirit is everywhere present (Ps 139:7). He is all-knowing (1 Cor 2:10–11). He is all-powerful (Gen 1:2; Luke 1:35). He is eternal (Heb 9:14). He is holy (Luke 11:13). Beyond that, the Holy Spirit is frequently referred to as God (Acts 5:3–4; 2 Cor 3:18; Gen 1:1–2; Luke 4:18). He is equated with the Father and the Son (Matt 28:19–20).

The Holy Spirit Is a Person

Some have mistakenly referred to the Holy Spirit as an "it." This could not be more inaccurate. The Holy Spirit is every bit as much a person as is God the Father or God the Son. He has intellect (1 Cor 2:10–11; Eph 1:17; Rom 8:27), emotion (Eph 4:30), and will (1 Cor 12:11). He has creativity (Gen 1:2). He has love (Rom 15:30). Beyond that, He is referred to with a personal pronoun (John 15:26; 16:13–14).

The Holy Spirit is *not* a ghost who will scare the nonbeliever. He is *not* an impersonal force that will zap the nonbeliever. He *is* a person who will lovingly pursue the nonbeliever and speak to his or her heart.

The Holy Spirit Is Primary in God's Work on Earth Today

The gospel is all Jesus—His death, burial, and resurrection for our sins. Yet, the application of the gospel to the heart of the unbeliever is the work of the Holy Spirit. He is the person of the Godhead who is primary in God's work today on earth.

Old Testament Times	Gospel Times	Current Times
1400 BC–4 BC	4 BC–AD 30	AD 30–Today (Tribulation)
God the Father	God the Son	God the Holy Spirit

Billy Graham has noted, "Man has two great spiritual needs. One is forgiveness. The other is for goodness . . . we need this two-sided gift God has offered us: first, the work of God the Son for us; second, the work of God the Spirit in us."[2] Since the day of Pentecost around AD 30, the Holy Spirit has been primary in God's work on earth. The Bible tells us that Jesus sat down because His primary work was finished.

> The Son is the radiance of God's glory and the exact expression of His nature, sustaining all things by His powerful word. After making purification for sins, He sat down at the right hand of the Majesty on high. (Heb 1:3)

Yet, just because Jesus' work on earth was finished, that did not mean God's work was complete. In describing His departure, Jesus explained the turning over of responsibility to the Holy Spirit.

> I am going away to prepare a place for you. (John 14:2)

> And I will ask the Father, and He will give you another Counselor to be with you forever. He is the Spirit of truth. The world is unable to receive Him because it doesn't see Him or know Him. But you do know Him, because He remains with you and will be in you. I will not leave you as orphans; I am coming to you. (John 14:16–18)

The Holy Spirit Is the Primary Player in Bringing a Lost Person to Salvation

I own almost forty books that deal directly with the subject of evangelism. I am shocked that only a handful of them mention the role of the Holy Spirit in effective evangelism. A quick survey of the Bible reveals the essential role of the Holy Spirit in bringing people to Christ.

CONVINCING OF THE NEED

Everyone who is saved has become so as the result of the convincing work of the Holy Spirit. As we share the gospel, the Holy Spirit speaks to the heart of the nonbeliever, convincing and convicting them, pursuing and persuading them. Jesus said that the Holy Spirit convicts them of sin, righteousness, and judgment. Consider John 16:8–11:

> When He comes, He will convict the world about sin, righteousness, and judgment: About sin, because they do not believe in Me; about righteousness, because I am going to the Father and you will no longer see Me; and about judgment, because the ruler of this world has been judged.

Until a nonbeliever is convinced that he or she is lost, he or she has no motivation or desire to be saved. As we share the gospel, the Holy Spirit uses the Word of God to convince the nonbeliever of his sin. Because of the work of the Holy Spirit, the nonbeliever will be persuaded regarding the reality, the weight, and the guilt of his sin.

Yet, the Holy Spirit does not stop there. He also convinces the nonbeliever of righteousness. Only the Holy Spirit can open the eyes of the nonbeliever to see both his own lack of real righteousness and the perfect, sinless righteousness of the Savior, Jesus Christ.

Beyond that, the Holy Spirit also convinces the nonbeliever of judgment. As the Holy Spirit works in the heart of the nonbeliever, he will grasp the severity of his sin and recognize how much the sin deserves to be punished.

Not enough can be said about the supreme importance of the Holy Spirit in convincing and convicting the lost person of sin, righteousness, and judgment. Unless this work occurs, a nonbeliever does not, and cannot, experience salvation. Yet, the work of the Holy Spirit in bringing a lost soul to salvation does not end there.

GIVING NEW LIFE

You may be familiar with the story of Jesus sharing with a seeker named Nicodemus. In that dialogue (John 3:1–8), the passage describes salvation as a new birth. When someone is saved, he is born-again spiritually; a new life is given. Jesus further states that while a physical birth is immediately visible, a spiritual birth is less obvious, yet no less real. The work of the Holy Spirit is compared with the work of the wind. Just as the human eye cannot see wind, we can see its results. So it is with the Holy Spirit. We cannot physically see the Holy Spirit birth a new spiritual baby, but we will no doubt see the results in the life of the new believer. "The wind blows where it pleases, and you hear its sound, but you don't know where it comes from or where it is going. So it is with everyone born of the Spirit" (John 3:8).

ENTERING A LIFE

Often, those who share the gospel encourage a nonbeliever to ask Jesus into his or her heart. While this is not wrong, it is also not completely accurate. When a person calls upon the name of the Lord to save them, Jesus does not enter their hearts. The Spirit of God, or the Holy Spirit, is the one who comes *into* their life. Consider these verses:

> And I will ask the Father, and He will give you another Counselor to be with you forever. He is the Spirit of truth. The world is unable to receive Him because it doesn't see Him or know Him. But you do know Him, because He remains with you and will be in you. (John 14:16–17)

> You, however, are not in the flesh, but in the Spirit, since the Spirit of God lives in you. But if anyone does not have the Spirit of Christ, he does not belong to Him. (Rom 8:9)

It is the Holy Spirit who takes up residence in their lives. In doing so, He makes the new Christian's body His temple, a place where God is to be worshipped: "Don't you know that your body is a sanctuary of the Holy Spirit who is in you . . . ?" (1 Cor 6:19).

The Holy Spirit Is Essential in Helping a Saved Person Grow and Serve

The work of the Holy Spirit does not end when a person gets saved. The Holy Spirit becomes our primary Comforter (John 14:16–17) and Teacher (John 14:26; 1 Cor 2:12; 2 Pet 1:21). As His life flows unhindered through us, He becomes our Life-Changer (Gal 5:22–23). He is our Spiritual Gift-giver (1 Cor 12:4–11). The Holy Spirit is the most important person in your spiritual life.

Beyond that He is described as our Guide (Rom 8:14; 1 Thess 5:19) and Power-giver (Eph 3:16; Luke 24:49; Acts 1:8). In order to lead other people to Christ, we need the spiritual guidance and spiritual power given by the Holy Spirit. The Holy Spirit is the most important person in your ministry life.

The Holy Spirit Partners with a Believer in Effectively Sharing the Gospel

I often ask witnessing Christians: "How many of you have every shared the gospel with a lost person and found yourself saying things that were clearer and more intelligent than you imagined that you could?" They all always nod their heads and answer, yes. Why? The reason is that the Holy Spirit actively partners with us when we share the gospel. Effective evangelism is simply cooperating with Him. Read carefully again the Great Commission promise of Jesus:

> Go therefore and make disciples of all the nations, baptizing them in the name of the Father and of the Son and of the Holy Spirit, teaching them to observe all things that I have commanded you; and lo, I am with you always, even to the end of the age. Amen. (Matt 28:19–20 NKJV)

Think about what Jesus is promising. He says that when we set our lives on making disciples of all types of people, He is *with* us in the process. The Bible tells us that Jesus is seated at the right hand of the Father in heaven (Eph 1:20; Heb 8:1). So how can He be with us when we fulfill the Great Commission? Jesus is with us in the person of the Holy Spirit. If you want to experience the presence of the Spirit, make disciples.

Cooperate with the Holy Spirit

The Holy Spirit wants people saved more than we do. He has supernatural power we do not have to convict lost people of sin, righteousness, and judgment. The Holy Spirit is omniscient. He knows exactly what is going on in lost people's lives and thoughts as we are talking with them. Only the Holy Spirit has the power to regenerate a lost person into a new creation in Jesus Christ. Therefore, it only makes sense that if we hope to evangelize anyone effectively, we should rely on Him.

Effective disciple making is actively cooperating with the Holy Spirit as He works to open the eyes of lost people and bring them to God. When you share the gospel, the Holy Spirit gives you wisdom you did not know you had. He also gives you sensitivity you could not possibly have on your own.

"I Was on My Way to a Drinking Problem"

Prior to giving my life completely to Jesus, I had a problem with drinking alcohol. When I was in middle school, my family was going through some tough times. In order to escape, I began to make wine. I also thought having access to alcohol as a middle school student would increase my popularity. I used the wine to get myself and my friends drunk on weekends. Before long I had a thriving little business going. Speeding down the wrong road and headed in the wrong direction, I was miserable. Because of a nonjudgmental Christian friend and a spiritually passionate youth pastor, I gave my life full out to Jesus a few years later. I was filled with genuine joy and immediately stopped drinking alcohol.

I rarely share this story when I am evangelizing another person, but one day as I was sharing Christ with a businessman, I felt especially prompted by the Holy

Spirit to mention how Jesus had freed me from alcohol. I had no way of knowing that, at the time, the man's wife had just threatened to leave him because of his drinking. When I said, "I was on my way to a real drinking problem," it really caught his attention and gave me the key to his heart. The Holy Spirit used my story of freedom from alcohol to touch this man deeply and bring him to Jesus.

Let us encourage you as you share your faith: do not rely solely on yourself. You cannot convict, or convince, anyone. The Holy Spirit can. You cannot know everything that is going on in another person's life or mind. The Holy Spirit does. You cannot save anyone. The Holy Spirit can. Since the Holy Spirit plays such a key role in bringing a person to salvation, it behooves us to rely on His help.

Jesus Promised the Enabling Empowerment of the Holy Spirit

The last words a person says are often considered the most important. The last words of the most important person who ever lived—Jesus—are certainly to be considered some of the most significant words ever uttered. Interestingly, they involve the promise of the presence of the Holy Spirit in disciple making:

> "But you will receive power when the Holy Spirit has come upon you,
> and you will be My witnesses in Jerusalem, in all Judea and Samaria, and
> to the ends of the earth." (Acts 1:8)

The First Evangelists Relied on the Power of the Holy Spirit

When Jesus promised to give His followers the power of the Holy Spirit as they shared the gospel, He did more than give some nice sounding words. He gave a promise that His followers relied upon and employed effectively. For example, the first message ever given in the first church in history was the detailed proclamation of the gospel by the apostle Peter. As Peter and the others were controlled by the Holy Spirit, they boldly proclaimed the death, burial and resurrection of Jesus for sins. The Holy Spirit so empowered Peter's words that 3,000 were saved and baptized that day (Acts 2:1–41).

Later, Peter and John were arrested for preaching Jesus. Instead of being intimidated into silence, they relied on the power of the Holy Spirit to aid them as they fearlessly proclaimed Christ (Acts 4:1–12). Their boldness stunned the authorities (Acts 4:13). Unsure of what to do, the authorities threatened Peter and John, and released them. Observe the prayer of celebration when Peter and John were reunited with the community of believers:

And now, Lord, consider their threats, and grant that Your slaves may speak Your message with complete boldness, while You stretch out Your hand for healing, signs, and wonders to be performed through the name of Your holy Servant Jesus. When they had prayed, the place where they were assembled was shaken, and they were all filled with the Holy Spirit and began to speak God's message with boldness. (Acts 4:29–31)

The apostles did not retreat from sharing their faith. They did just the opposite. They cried out to God for more boldness to speak God's Word. God's answer came in the form of the Holy Spirit.

— Questions to Ponder —

1. What is the first step in making a disciple of Jesus Christ?
2. Recognize that any time a person gives his or her life to Jesus Christ it is never a solo operation—there are always at least three persons involved: First, there is the nonbeliever who hears the gospel and receives Jesus. Second, there is the person who shares the gospel with the nonbeliever. Third, there is the Holy Spirit, who applies the gospel to the understanding of the nonbeliever. Which of the three concepts above do you need to value more?
3. How important is the Holy Spirit's role in your life right now?
4. What are you doing to cooperate with the Holy Spirit right now?
5. Who are you praying for to come to know Christ right now?

Notes

1. This chapter was adapted from Dave Earley and David Wheeler, *Evangelism Is . . . : How to Share Jesus with Passion and Confidence* (Nashville: B&H Academic, 2010), and used with permission from the publisher.

2. Billy Graham, *The Holy Spirit: Activating God's Power in Your Life* (Nashville: Thomas Nelson, 2000), xi.

4

Knowing the Centrality of the Church

Rod Dempsey

My Story

It was a beautiful spring morning in the month of May when I first understood and acted on the gospel of Jesus Christ. I was nine years old. I had gone to church that morning with my family as usual. We went to Sunday school. After Sunday school we went to the worship service. After church we had a baptism service, after which the pastor mentioned that he believed that the Spirit was moving and there was someone else there that morning who needed to receive Christ. I was that person. Something was different. When he said those words, my heart began to pound in my chest like a freight train. I knew that God was at work in my life. I turned to my friend and asked him to hold my Sunday school material, and he quickly said, "No way." I quickly put the material down and went forward. After talking with the pastor, I confessed Jesus as Savior and Lord (Rom 10:9–10) and was baptized immediately! I felt free and clean and light as a feather. I knew my sins were forgiven and that I was going to heaven.

I was so excited to be a follower of Jesus that I told all my friends. Unfortunately, that excitement soon faded when my friends did not share my newfound faith. Before long, I was not telling them about Christ. I soon learned to keep "my opinions" to myself. I began to miss church whenever I got the chance, and after a few years, you could no longer tell the difference between my life and the lives of my friends who did not know Christ. I went from being totally excited about being a follower of Christ to being afraid of even talking about Jesus. Instead of being a disciple of Jesus, I was a disciple of the world.

During high school, I was very involved in sports and just wanted to fit in with the "in" crowd. You would have been hard pressed to identify me as a believer. Yet looking back on that time, I believe I was saved. However, I was certainly not a "disciple" of Jesus as we have defined in this book. I was a "carnal" believer (1 Cor 3:1–3 NKJV). I was not growing in my walk with Christ. I was a spiritually immature Christian who needed desperately to grow and mature.

Becoming a follower of Jesus means that you intentionally follow Him. The gospels make this clear. You follow His teachings and you follow His mission. You repent of your selfishness and self-rule and surrender to follow the teachings and mission of Jesus Christ. That is what it means to be a disciple. The process of helping Christians grow and develop spiritually is called disciple making.

The Bible teaches us that whenever a Christian first accepts Christ, they are born again (John 3:1–5). They are likened to spiritual babies (Heb 5:13–14) who should "grow up" in all aspects into Christlikeness (Eph 4:14 MSG). That is the normal Christian life. My spiritual growth during my teenage years, however, was hit and—more often than not—miss. I had surrendered to Christ and wanted to follow Him, but I also felt powerless to do so in a consistent manner. In just a few short years, I went from being a passionate follower of Christ to a powerless, confused, and miserable "secret agent Christian."

Painful Lessons

Sadly, in almost thirty years of Christian ministry, I have witnessed stories similar to my testimony many times over—young men and women who made a commitment to Christ in their childhood yet subsequently strayed from Christ during their teen years. In most cases the wandering prodigal returns, but not without some painful scars. Maybe that is similar to your story.

You may ask: why do children, why do people, why does anyone stray from Christ? There are many reasons, but one of the biggest reasons that people stray from Christ is because they have not developed their walk with Christ. I was not working "out [my] salvation with fear and trembling" (Phil 2:12), and the church where I grew up was not helping. The church I grew up in was a country church where the preacher preached and families attended church. Yet, there was not an intentional plan to help young Christians grow and develop. The leaders of the church were good and godly people, but there was no intentional effort to help young believers grow and mature spiritually. This story is not uncommon.

Unfortunately, many churches are not intentional when it comes to focusing on equipping and empowering new believers to grow and develop to their full potential for the King and kingdom. As a result, many new believers stray from their Lord and Savior. The new believer is not strong enough to handle the "triple threat"—lust of the flesh, lust of the eyes, and the pride of life—and they fall away from their Lord and Savior (1 John 2:16).

Fail to Plan . . . Plan to Fail

The church of Jesus Christ needs to have specific plans in place to help everyone grow and develop to reach their full potential in Christ. The main command of the Great Commission is to "make disciples." I am not blaming the church where I grew up. I made those poor decisions. We are all moral free agents. We have the power to choose, and we will ultimately be held accountable for our choices. Nevertheless, I do believe the church needs to be very intentional about helping baby Christians grow and mature into fully devoted followers of Jesus Christ. Aubrey Malphurs, in his book *Strategic Disciple Making*, maintains, "The church's marching orders are very clear . . . we are to make disciples. The church is to pursue and make and mature believers at home and abroad."[1] Young Christians need to advance from the milk of the Word to the meat of the Word. They need to mature from babies to young men and women, and then on to maturity where they can be a part of God's plan of spiritual reproduction to help reach an exponentially growing world.

The Church's Role

The church must be in the absolute middle of God's global plan of making disciples. The word *church* is used eighty-two times in the New Testament, and Jesus first mentions the concept of "church" in Matt 16:18 when He says, "And I also say to you that you are Peter, and on this rock I will build My *church*, and the forces of Hades will not overpower it." We notice from this verse that the church is not yet in existence. It is something in the future. Jesus says, "I will," pointing to the future. We also notice that this new thing is going to be something that He builds. That Jesus is the founder and head of the church

(Eph 1:22; 5:23; Col 1:18) is without question. He further describes the church as a force that will knock down the gates of hell. We see from this first passage that the church is going to be the means for assaulting the kingdom of darkness (Col 1:13).

In the book of Acts, the church bursts on the scene after Peter preaches the first gospel message. Thousands believe, repent, and come together to form the first body of Christ (Acts 2:42–47). The word *church* is used 21 times in the book of Acts. The many and varied references describe this active body of believers who band together for prayer, fellowship, teaching, and intentionally accomplishing the Great Commission. By the time we get to Acts 9:31, Luke describes the church this way: "So the *church* throughout all Judea, Galilee, and Samaria had peace, being built up and walking in the fear of the Lord and in the encouragement of the Holy Spirit, and it increased in numbers." From this passage we begin to see some of the basic elements of church life. There is harmony. People are being built up and growing in their knowledge of the Spirit-filled life. The church is having an impact on the culture throughout all Judea, Galilee, and Samaria, and that impact comes from transformed lives.

What Is the Role of the Pastor?

What, then, is the role of the pastor in a global-minded, disciple-making church? The book of Ephesians is insightful here. Paul wrote Ephesians when he was in prison (Eph 6:20) around AD 62.[2] In Ephesians 4:11–16, Paul gives the clearest and most powerful description of the proper function of the body of Christ. Likewise, he identifies the role and function of pastors and the role and function of the saints:

> And He personally gave some to be apostles, some prophets, some evangelists, some pastors and teachers, for the training of the saints in the work of ministry, to build up the body of Christ, until we all reach unity in the faith and in the knowledge of God's Son, growing into a mature man with a stature measured by Christ's fullness. Then we will no longer be little children, tossed by the waves and blown around by every wind of teaching, by human cunning with cleverness in the techniques of deceit. But speaking the truth in love, let us grow in every way into Him who is the head—Christ. From Him the whole body, fitted and knit together by every supporting ligament, promotes the growth of the body for building up itself in love by the proper working of each individual part.

Pastors are to "train" or "equip" the saints, and the saints are to do the "work of ministry." *Barnes' Notes on the Bible* explains that this "training" (*katartismon*) properly refers to "the restoring of anything to its place. Here [in Ephesians] it means that these various officers were appointed in order that everything in the church might be well arranged, or put into its proper place; or that the church might be 'complete.' "[3] This arranging has to do with helping the saints "grow up in every way into Him," becoming "mature" believers. This maturity is exhibited by the fact that they "will no longer be little children, tossed by the waves and blown around by every wind of teaching." It also involves the body being "fitted and knit together by every supporting ligament, [which] promotes the growth of the body for building up itself in love by the proper working of each individual part." This involves properly connecting the individual inside the body, just as Christ desires.

Spiritual growth involves the disciple discovering and developing his or her gift (see 1 Pet 4:10–11), within the body (community of believers), to its full potential, for Christ and His kingdom. As the individual believer grows and matures, the body becomes healthier. The more parts of the body that are working "properly" (as He intended), the healthier the body becomes. The health of the body of Christ should be a very important consideration for the leaders of a church. Greg Ogden observes, "The church is not a human organization that has contracted by common consent to keep alive the memory of a great man, Jesus Christ. On the contrary, the church is a divine organism mystically fused to the living and reigning Christ who continues to reveal himself in a people whom he has drawn to himself."[4] A healthy church means the body of Christ will be healthy as well.

Let's Get Personal

Let me ask: How many parts of your body do you want to work? Well, if you are like me, I want all the parts of my body working. If I have parts of my body not working then I am definitely not going to feel healthy. If this is true of your physical body, why is it not true of the spiritual body of Christ? Why are we content to limp along with only a very small minority of God's children involved in God's work?

The church must be intentional in developing all of God's children to reach their full potential. Perhaps the greatest challenge in reaching the world is the challenge of developing all of God's children. While the church must be in the business of preaching the gospel, it must also concentrate on the mission of developing the saints.

What Should I Be Doing?

The church is here to help believers grow and develop into maturity. Maturity does not merely seek to understand who Christ is, or even who you are as a believer. Maturity finds its full expression when the believer fulfills their God-given role. Have you ever asked: "Why has God given to every believer at least one spiritual gift?" According to 1 Pet 4:10–11, every believer has at least one supernatural gift:

> Based on the gift each one has received, use it to serve others, as good managers of the varied grace of God. If anyone speaks, [his speech should be] as one who speaks God's words; if anyone serves, [his service should be] from the strength God provides, so that God may be glorified through Jesus Christ in everything. To Him belong the glory and the power forever and ever. Amen.

This passage makes it clear that every believer has at least one spiritual gift, and we are to use the gift in such a way that God will be glorified. First Corinthians 12:7 puts it this way: "A demonstration of the Spirit is *given to each person* to produce what is beneficial." Do you know what your spiritual gift might be? Do you know you are supposed to be using your spiritual gift to serve others? Do you know that you should be using your spiritual gift to bring glory to God? If you know your gift, are you using it on a regular basis to strengthen others?

Let's Go, Church!

The church exists to spread the gospel and develop the believer to the point where they become the missionaries of the movement. Ed Stetzer comments on the mission of the church by saying, "Jesus came to save and to serve and we join Him on His mission."[5] The growth and development of the believer is both internal (becoming like Christ in word, thought, and attitude) and external (becoming like Christ in action). As we grow and mature, we are then to join Christ on His mission to reach the entire world.

The word *church* simply means a gathering of "called out ones."[6] Christians are called out of the world and called to a Savior who calls them to a mission. The church is a fulfillment of the kingdom; the kingdom is a fulfillment of the mission of God; and the mission of God springs from His nature and love. John 3:16 says it best: "For God loved the world in this way: He gave His One and Only Son, so that everyone who believes in Him will not perish but have eternal life." God sent His son on a mission to save the world. He accomplished His mission and now He asks us to finish the mission. John 20:21 explains it this way: "As the father has sent Me, I also send you." The church exists to win people to Christ, help them grow in their walk, and then send them out to participate in the mission of winning the entire world.

It has been 2,000 years since the early church began the task of winning and discipling the world. Over that time span it has had its share of challenges, such as persecution and doctrinal heresies. In addition, the church has, at times, struggled to form a clear understanding of what it is supposed to be doing. Some churches think they should be primarily showing love to the world. Some churches believe they should be condemning and criticizing the world. Some churches believe they should be like the world and, consequently, are hardly distinguishable from the world. Some churches believe the focus should be on preaching. Some churches believe the focus should be on evangelism. Some churches think the focus should be on prayer. Some churches think the focus should be on the Holy Spirit. It is apparent to even the casual observer that the interpretation of what the church should be doing is not as clear as one would like to think.

The Church Is His Body

Let me be clear, the church of Jesus Christ is in the business of preaching the gospel and then helping those people who respond to the gospel grow spiritually strong. As they grow spiritually strong, the leaders of the church are to assist the individual to discover and develop his or her spiritual gift. As the individual uses their gift, in the proper manner, the body grows healthy. As the body grows healthy, it reaches out in love to the unbelieving world with the message of Christ, leading more people to hear and accept God's gracious gift.

The more people grow and develop, the healthier they become. The healthier they become, the healthier the body becomes. Jesus continues to be seen and heard. The visible, strong, and healthy body of Christ continues to go about "[proclaiming] good news to the poor . . . freedom to the captives . . . and to set free the oppressed" (Luke 4:18–19). In the Gospels, Jesus called His disciples to join Him and follow His plan. We discover in the epistles how Jesus' ministry and mission continue through His church! You are a part of His body . . . what is your role in God's global mission?

— Questions to Ponder —

1. When did you come to know Christ?
2. What were the circumstances?
3. Do you know your spiritual gift?
4. Do you know your position/role in the body?
5. What should the church focus on?

Notes

1. Aubrey Malphurs, *Strategic Disciple Making: A Practical Tool for Successful Ministry* (Grand Rapids: Baker, 2009), 21.

2. Charles Ryrie, *The Ryrie Study Bible* (Chicago: Moody, 1978), 1799.

3. See http://bible.cc/ephesians/4-12.htm (accessed December 12, 2012).

4. Greg Ogden, *Unfinished Business: Returning the Ministry to the People of God* (Grand Rapids: Zondervan, 2010), Kindle location 605–7.

5. See http://www.edstetzer.com/2010/02/what-is-a-missional-church.html (accessed December 12, 2012).

6. See http://www.xenos.org/classes/um1-1a.htm (accessed December 12, 2012).

Part 2

Disciple-Making Basics: Being a Disciple

In the previous section we worked to establish a firm biblical and theological foundation. We dis,covered the organizing principle of the glory of God. Then we crafted a working definition of a disciple based on key New Testament passages in order to lay a firm foundation for the disciple-making process. Next, we discussed the importance of cooperating with the Holy Spirit in the task of evangelism. Finally, we outlined the role of the church in fulfilling the Great Commission.

In this section, we will focus both on the words and commands of Jesus as well as His methods. Focus is a very good thing. Without focus we would walk around with our hands out in front trying to navigate the blur. Sometimes I feel that way in ministry. However, when we focus on Jesus and on what He did and how He did it, certain things come into focus. As we examine what Jesus had to say about being and making disciples, our focus will become sharp and we can concentrate on the priorities in front of us. Those priorities will then drive the disciple-making process as the reader embraces the successive steps of obedience.

5 Obeying Everything Jesus Commanded

Dave Earley

What If Jesus Meant the Stuff He Said?

A few months ago, I had lunch with Shane Claiborne. Shane is a Christian activist who intentionally lives with the urban poor in Philadelphia. While the two of us do not agree on all things political and theological, we do agree on the most important things, and we both passionately desire to be people who live the gospel. Shane put words to a question that deeply resonated with me: "What if Jesus meant the stuff he said?"[1]

What an important question! If Jesus really meant everything He said, then we must do something about it. From that moment, I began asking myself this question: *If I really believed, read, studied, memorized, and obeyed everything Jesus commanded every day, would my life look any different?*

A few weeks after my conversation with Shane, I was having lunch with a couple of megachurch pastors. I asked them: "Would your church look any different if your people really believed, read, studied, memorized, and obeyed everything Jesus commanded every day? Would your life look any different if your people really believed, read, studied, memorized, and obeyed everything Jesus commanded every day?"

The response was immediate and somewhat emotional. One said, "I am ashamed to say, my church would look very different and so would I." Another said, "I really want to live that way. How did I get off track?"

Then they asked me how I was planning on fully living everything Jesus commanded. The next thing I knew, the vision for a multiplying church plant in a large, spiritually needy city with a large downtown university came pouring out.

As a result of the conversation, I am now planting Grace City Church in "Sin City," Las Vegas (www.gracecityvegas.com), near the notorious casino strip across from the University of Nevada at Las Vegas. The community we selected (part of an area ironically called Paradise) has 50,000 people, yet only one English-speaking Evangelical Protestant church. It has more than a dozen casinos, five strip clubs, three Mormon meeting places, three New Age meeting places, but only one English-speaking Evangelical Protestant church. It has 29,000 students driving into UNLV each day, but only one Evangelical Protestant church.

In this book, we do not know exactly how you will obey everything Jesus commanded and live out the Great Commission. We are determined to help you do it and do it well.

The Great *Omission* in the Great Commission

Consider again the Great Commission passage:

> "Go, therefore, and make disciples of all nations, baptizing them in the name of the Father and of the Son and of the Holy Spirit, *teaching them to observe everything I have commanded you.* And remember, I am with you always, to the end of the age." (Matt 28:19–20)

I have heard many sermons and read quite a few books on the Great Commission. They are great for motivating people to go and telling them how to share the gospel. Some even link the Great Commission with the local church by focusing on the word *baptizing*. Most leave out a key component. As John Piper notes, "Jesus' final command was to teach all his commandments." Actually, the final command was more precise than that. He did *not* say, "Teach them all my commandments." He said, "Teach them *to observe* all my commandments."[2] Jesus commanded all of His disciples to teach everyone in the world to obey all of His commands. Therefore, we cannot say that we are fulfilling the Great Commission until we are teaching our disciples to "observe everything Jesus commanded." The failure to teach it *all* and obey it *all* is the Great Omission in the Great Commission.

The Great *Assumption* in the Great Commission

When Jesus commanded His eleven men to make disciples by teaching them to observe everything He had commanded them, He was making a rather large and important assumption. In demanding them to make disciples, He was assuming they *were* already living as disciples. In commanding them to obey everything He had demanded, He was assuming they were already obeying everything He had commanded. Therefore, before you can make a disciple, you need to *be* a disciple.

Before you can be a disciple, you need to begin *obeying* everything Jesus commanded.

For the past three years, I have been reading the words of Jesus every day. Frankly, it is messing up my life. It is turning much of what I have thought, believed in, valued, and dreamed inside out. During this time, I have been asking myself some tough questions. I challenge you to ask yourself the same questions:

- Do you even *know* everything Jesus commanded? If someone held a gun to your head and handed you a sheet of paper and a pencil, could you write down everything Jesus commanded?
- Are you really *obeying* everything Jesus commanded? Are there some commands you avoid because they are too difficult? Have you made . excuses for why you are not doing *everything* Jesus commanded?
- Have you taught your "disciples" to obey *everything* Jesus commanded? Do they know what He commanded, and are they living it out?

Disciples *Obey* Jesus' Commands

The word *disciple* means student or learner. It describes a protégé who learns and follows his teacher's precepts and instructions. It speaks of a follower who adopts the lifestyle of his master. In the first century, a disciple-making relationship was based on intimacy and obedience. No wonder Jesus made the following statements linking the two:

If you love Me, you will *keep My commandments*. (John 14:15)

If you *keep My commands* you will remain in My love, just as I have kept
My Father's commands and remain in His love. (John 15:10)

You are My friends if you *do what I command* you. (John 15:14)

A few months ago, I had lunch with a couple of pastors and seminary
professors. I asked them the questions I was wrestling with: "Do I really
believe Jesus meant everything He said, and if I did, how would my life look
any different?" I was stunned by their response. One told us he just preached
a sermon on obedience. Another told how he had recently lectured his class
about obeying Jesus. A third said the week before he had shared a message at a
pastors' lunch about obeying Jesus. "Good," I said, "but are *you* really obeying
everything Jesus said, or are you just talking about it? My concern is that too
often we fall into the trap of *talking about* real Christianity instead of actually
living it." I continued, "I don't want to be guilty of merely talking about real
Christianity without ever having lived it."

I am not alone in my frustration. Nineteenth-century Danish philosopher
Søren Kierkegaard writes,

> The matter is quite simple. The Bible really is easy to understand. But we
> Christians are a bunch of scheming swindlers. We pretend to be unable to
> understand it because we know that the moment we understand, we are
> obligated to act accordingly. Take any words in the New Testament and
> forget everything except pledging yourself to act accordingly. My God,
> you will say, if I do that my whole life will be ruined.[3]

Kierkegaard did not stop there. He continues,

> Christian scholarship is the Church's prodigious invention to defend
> itself against the Bible, to ensure that we can become good Christians
> without the Bible coming too close. . . . Dreadful it is to fall into the
> hands of the living God. Yes, it is even more dreadful to be alone with the
> New Testament.[4]

I fear that for much of the last seven years I have had the privilege of spending
my life writing books, giving lectures, offering seminars, and preaching sermons
about Christianity. Yet, I have not lived Christianity as fully as is demanded by
the Gospels.

Speaking of those things "*demanded* by the Gospels" may cause some
discomfort. We need to be very clear about something: God *demands* absolute
obedience to His commands. Consider the following words of Jesus:

> Not everyone who says to Me, "Lord, Lord!" will enter the kingdom
> of heaven, but only the one who *does the will of My Father* in heaven.
> (Matt 7:21)

> Therefore, everyone who hears these words of Mine and *acts on them*
> will be like a sensible man who built his house on the rock. (Matt 7:24)

David Platt captures the weight of these passages: "First, from the outset you need to commit to *believe* whatever Jesus says . . . then second you need to commit to *obey* what you have heard. The gospel does not prompt you to mere reflection; the gospel requires a response . . . 'What shall I do?'"[5]

C. T. Studd is one of my heroes. He was a wealthy Cambridge graduate who also happened to be the best cricket player in the world when cricket was one of the most popular games in the world. He was the most popular athlete of the late 1900s. Yet, he gave it all up to obey a missionary call to China. In a talk he gave at a businessman's luncheon, he told how obeying the commands of Jesus changed his life:

> I once had another religion: mincing, lisping, bated breath, proper,
> hunting the Bible for hidden truths, but no obedience, no sacrifice. Then
> came a change. The real thing came before me. . . . Words became deeds.
> The commands of Christ became not mere Sunday recitations, but battle
> cries to be obeyed. . . .[6]

The Great Commission and the commands of Jesus are, indeed, "battle cries" to be obeyed. Are you obeying the battle cries of Jesus?

Is Discipleship *Radical*?

Discipleship is not merely a matter of information remembered. It is about a lifestyle that is practiced. It is a lifestyle of absolute abandonment to loving God and obeying His commands. Unfortunately, discipleship has been so smothered by the quest for the American Dream that real discipleship is often viewed as radical and unrealistic. Francis Chan declares, "Taking the words of Christ literally and seriously is rarely considered. That's for 'radicals' who are 'unbalanced' and who go 'overboard.'"[7]

He continues, "Lukewarm people are moved by stories about people who do radical things for Christ, yet they do not act. They assume such action is for 'extreme' Christians, not average ones. Lukewarm people call 'radical' what Jesus expected of all His followers."[8]

Shane Claiborne had a friend who told him, "I gave up Christianity in order to follow Jesus." In his book *The Irresistible Revolution: Living as an Ordinary Radical*, Shane writes, "I wondered what it would look like if we decided to really follow Jesus."[9] When he and a few of his friends began to try and live it out, others called them "radicals." He writes, "If by radical we mean 'root,' I think it is precisely the right word for what we are trying to do: get down to the roots of what it means to be Christian disciples. Most of the time though, I think that if what we are doing seems radical, then that says more about the apathy of Western Christianity than about the nature of our discipleship."[10] When was the last time someone accused you of being a radical follower of Jesus?

Disciples Obey *Everything* Jesus Commanded . . . Even the Hard Stuff

Some of the commands of Jesus are more disturbing and challenging than others. As a result, they are often overlooked. Consider the command for a disciple to "hate your father and mother." Luke 14:26 states, "If anyone comes to Me and does not hate his own father and mother, wife and children, brothers and sisters—yes, and even his own life—he cannot be My disciple." I do not recall ever seeing a church sign marquee with the message "Hate Your Mother," but more on this in a later chapter.

What about Mark 10:21: "Sell all you have and give to the poor." I have never seen that on a plaque at the Christian bookstore. Yet, true disciples obey *all* of Jesus' commands, even the hard ones. For a full list of the commands of Jesus, take a look at http://www.wowzone.com/commandm.htm.

Are you obeying everything Jesus commanded? Even the hard stuff?

Obeying Everything Jesus Commanded Is *Impossible* . . . Without God

Not long ago, I posted this question on Facebook: "What would happen if we began to obey everything Jesus commanded?" I received many interesting comments. One rebuke came from a former pastor and retired theology professor. He said, "Are you crazy? Obeying everything Jesus commanded is impossible." John Piper agrees but maintains that Jesus left us with hope:

> With man it is *impossible*, but not with God. For "all things are possible with God" (Mark 10:25–27). Therefore, the person who sets himself

to obey Jesus' final commission—for example, to teach a rich man to *observe* the command to "renounce all that he has" (Luke 14:33)—attempts the impossible. But Jesus said it was *not* impossible. "All things are possible with God."[11]

Are you depending upon God to give you the grace to obey fully everything Jesus commanded?

Everything Jesus Commanded

Several years ago, I started a practice of reading through the Gospels at least once a year while listing everything Jesus commanded. I found more than two hundred imperatives. I quickly noticed that some of the commands were specific to person and time, such as: "Go into the village ahead of you. At once you will find a donkey tied there, and a colt with her. Untie them and bring them to Me" (Matt 21:2). Obviously those are not the commands we all are to obey and teach others. Yet, I came up with a list of one hundred universal commands applicable to all of us who want to be followers of Jesus.

Peter Wittstock lists 125 commands given by Jesus. He combines them into 70 major themes.[12] John Piper states that by including implied commands (e.g., "Blessed are the merciful" implies "Be merciful") and counting the multiple restatements among the Gospels, he came up with a list of more than *five hundred* commands of Jesus.[13] He grouped them into categories to come up with fifty chapters.[14]

If this all sounds overwhelming to you, start by obeying the three biggies: (1) the Great Commandment: love God with everything you've got and love your neighbor as much as you love yourself (Matt 22:37–40); (2) the New Commandment: love one another (John 13:34–35); and (3) the Great Commission: make disciples who make disciples.

— Questions to Ponder —

1. Are you really *obeying* everything Jesus commanded?
2. Are there some commands you avoid because they are too difficult?
3. Have you made excuses for why you are not doing *everything* Jesus commanded?
4. Have you taught your "disciples" to obey *everything* Jesus commanded?
5. Do they know what He commanded, and are they living it out?

Notes

1. Shane Claiborne, *The Irresistible Revolution: Living as an Ordinary Radical* (Grand Rapids: Zondervan, 2006), 72.

2. John Piper, *What Jesus Demands from the World* (Wheaton, IL: Crossway, 2006), 17; italics his.

3. Søren Kierkegaard, *Provocations: Spiritual Writings of Kierkegaard*, ed. Charles Moore (Farmington, PA: Plough, 2002), 201.

4. Kierkegaard, *Provocations*, 201.

5. David Platt, *Radical: Taking Your Faith Back from the American Dream* (Colorado Springs, CO: Multnomah, 2010), 20; italics his.

6. C. T. Studd, quoted in Norman Grubb, *C. T. Studd: Cricketer and Pioneer* (Ft. Washington, PA: Christian Literature Crusade, 1933), 108.

7. Francis Chan, *Crazy Love* (Colorado Springs, CO: David C. Cook, 2008), 68.

8. Ibid., 70–71.

9. Claiborne, *Irresistible Revolution*, 71.

10. Ibid., 129–30.

11. Piper, *What Jesus Demands from the World*, 17–18.

12. Peter Wittstock, *Hear Him! The One Hundred and Twenty-Five Commands of Jesus* (Longwood, FL: Xulon Press, 2004), 221–22.

13. Piper, *What Jesus Demands of the World*, 34.

14. Ibid., 35, 7–11. Piper's listing of fifty categories of commands that Jesus demands of the world is as follows:

1) You Must Be Born Again
2) Repent
3) Come to Me
4) Believe in Me
5) Love Me
6) Listen to Me
7) Abide in Me
8) Take Up Your Cross and Follow Me
9) Love God with All Your Heart, Soul, Mind, and Strength
10) Rejoice and Leap for Joy
11) Fear Him Who Can Destroy Both Soul and Body in Hell
12) Worship God in Spirit and Truth
13) Always Pray and Do Not Lose Heart
14) Do Not Be Anxious about the Necessities of Life
15) Do Not Be Anxious about the Threats of Man
16) Humble Yourself by Making War on Pride
17) Humble Yourself in Childlikeness, Servanthood, and Brokenhearted Boldness
18) Do Not Be Angry—Trust God's Providence
19) Do Not Be Angry—Embrace Mercy and Forgiveness

20) Do the Will of My Father Who Is in Heaven—Be Justified by Trusting Jesus

21) Do the Will of My Father Who Is in Heaven—Be Transformed by Trusting Jesus

22) Strive to Enter through the Narrow Door, for All of Life Is War

23) Strive to Enter through the Narrow Door, for Jesus Fulfills the New Covenant

24) Strive to Enter through the Narrow Door, for You Are Already in the Kingdom's Power

25) Your Righteousness Must Exceed That of the Pharisees, for It Was Hypocritical and Ugly

26) Your Righteousness Must Exceed That of the Pharisees—Clean the Inside of the Cup

27) Your Righteousness Must Exceed That of the Pharisees, for Every Healthy Tree Bears Good Fruit

28) Love Your Enemies—Lead Them to the Truth

29) Love Your Enemies—Pray for Those Who Abuse You

30) Love Your Enemies—Do Good to Those Who Hate You; Give to the One Who Asks

31) Love Your Enemies to Show That You Are Children of God

32) Love Your Neighbor as Yourself, for This Is the Law and the Prophets

33) Love Your Neighbor with the Same Commitment You Have to Your Own Well-being

34) Love Your Neighbor as Yourself and as Jesus Loved Us

35) Lay Up for Yourselves Treasures in Heaven by Giving Sacrificially and Generously

36) Lay Up for Yourselves Treasures in Heaven and Increase Your Joy in Jesus

37) Lay Up for Yourselves Treasures in Heaven—"It Is Your Father's Good Pleasure to Give You the Kingdom"

38) Do Not Take an Oath—Cherish the Truth and Speak It Simply

39) Do Not Take an Oath—Let What You Say Be Simply "Yes" or "No"

40) What God Has Joined Together Let No Man Separate, for Marriage Mirrors God's Covenant with Us

41) What God Has Joined Together Let No Man Separate, for Whoever Divorces and Marries Another Commits Adultery

42) What God Has Joined Together Let No Man Separate—One Man, One Woman, by Grace, until Death

43) Render to Caesar the Things That Are Caesar's and to God the Things That Are God's

44) Render to Caesar the Things That Are Caesar's as an Act of Rendering to God What Is God's

45) Do This in Remembrance of Me, for I Will Build My Church
46) Do This in Remembrance of Me—Baptize Disciples and Eat the Lord's Supper
47) Let Your Light Shine before Others That They May Glorify Your Father Who Is in Heaven
48) Let Your Light Shine before Others—the Joyful Sacrifice of Love in Suffering
49) Make Disciples of All Nations, for All Authority Belongs to Jesus
50) Make Disciples of All Nations, for the Mission Cannot Fail

6

Understanding the First Step of Obedience

Dave Earley

Tozer

A few months ago, we got a miniature schnauzer puppy. He is named after A. W. Tozer, who happens to be one of my favorite authors. In some ways Tozer looks the same as the day we brought him home from the breeder. He has the same black hair and the same white spots on his toes, chest, and under his chin. In other ways he looks different. He weighed just over three pounds when we brought him home; he weighs thirteen pounds now. Since the moment we brought Tozer home from the breeder, he has been in *puppy discipleship training*. His training is all about obedience. Every week he has taken several steps of development:

1. "Trust us" and "don't make a mess on the floor."
2. "Don't bite" and "don't wet" in the house.
3. Obey the command to "sit" and to "come" . . . and "don't wet" in the house.
4. Master the games of "find it," "hide and seek," "fetch," and "jump through the hoop."
5. Obey the command to "sit and wait" until released. Catch cheerios "out of the air" . . . and "don't eat deer droppings in the backyard."

6. Learn to "walk on a leash." Stop "eating deer droppings in the backyard."

He has remained a puppy all along. As Tozer has gotten older, we have expected more of him, and he has been able to trust and obey us at a deeper level. He is learning that the more he trusts and obeys, the more fun he has, and the more fun we have with him. The better he learns to trust and obey, the closer we feel to him and he feels to us.

The key to Tozer realizing his potential is learning to trust us and take his next step of obedience. Like Tozer, the key to a disciple realizing their potential is trusting God and taking the next step of faith and obedience.

Taking the Next Step

As we begin surveying what it means to be a disciple of Jesus, let me frame our discussion with a few thoughts:

First, Jesus was a Jewish Rabbi, or teacher, who used a rabbinical method for disciple making. We will discuss this is more detail later.

Second, the word *disciple* means "learner" or "follower." It was often used in a technical sense in first-century Judaism to describe the student of a rabbi.

Third, the process Jesus used to make disciples was a rabbinical system built on progressive levels of commitment, trust, obedience, and learning. At each step He demanded greater commitment, which gave His followers greater impact. The process progressed over a four-year period culminating with the Great Commission (Matt 28:19) and the launching of the first church in history.

Fourth, the key for a disciple realizing their potential is trusting God and taking the next step of faith and obedience.

Fifth, the further a disciple goes in the process, the fewer number of those who will join him or her.

Sixth, the moment a disciple stops trusting and obeying, they find themselves moving back down the steps.

Three Stages of Discipleship

In the modern era, probably A. B. Bruce in his classic text on discipleship, *The Training of the Twelve,* best helped us understand the progressive nature of following Jesus. Bruce writes, "The twelve arrived at their final intimate relation to Jesus only by degrees, three stages in the history of their fellowship with Him being distinguishable."[1]

Stage One: Declaration
(Investigation Leading to Repentance and Faith in Jesus)

Bruce writes, "In the first stage they were simply believers in Him as the Christ, and His occasional companions at convenient, particularly festive seasons."[2] A chronological study of the disciple-making ministry of Jesus reveals that this process covered about a year, from the baptism of Jesus through the wedding in Cana. The Gospels say little about this stage, but it is briefly discussed in John 1:35–2:12.

We see Jesus inviting others, besides the Twelve, into this stage as He preached the message "Repent and believe in the good news" (Mark 1:15). He called Nicodemus to be "born again" (John 3:3–8) and the woman at the well to drink of living water (John 4:13–14). This stage is a call to investigate the person and work of Jesus. The goal is to arrive at a place of committed belief. At the time of His resurrection, there were more than five hundred brethren at this stage (1 Cor 15:6). I refer to this first stage as *declaration*, which is characterized by *investigation leading to repentance and faith in Jesus*.

Stage Two: Development
(Immersion, Abandonment, and Apprenticeship into Ministry)

Bruce writes, "In the second stage, fellowship with Christ assumed the form of an uninterrupted attendance upon His person, involving entire or at least habitual abandonment of secular occupations."[3] With the twelve disciples, we see that this stage covered about a year. At this point the followers of Jesus entered into the initial level of a rabbinical apprenticeship with their Rabbi. The Twelve spent extended periods of time with Him, observing Him doing miracles and listening to Him teach. I refer to this second stage as *development*, focusing on the importance of *immersion, abandonment, and apprenticeship into ministry*.

Stage Three: Deployment
(Intentional Global Commissioning)

Bruce discusses the third stage stating, "From the evangelic records it appears that Jesus began at a very early period of His ministry to gather round Him a company of disciples, with a view to the preparation of an agency for carrying on the divine kingdom."[4] This final stage lasted two years. Much of the Gospels encompass the events of these final two years. This stage climaxed at the giving of the Great Commission as Jesus declared them fit to reproduce the process in the lives of others. The Rabbi had successfully trained His disciples to be disciple makers. This they did as they launched the first church. I call the third stage *deployment*, calling disciples to *intentional global commissioning.*

Summary of the Three Stages

There are different ways to illustrate these three stages:

1. The first stage asks the question: *Will you believe in Jesus?* The second stage asks: *Will you follow Jesus?* The third stage asks: *Will you go for Jesus?*
2. The first stage results in *regeneration.* The second stage produces *transformation.* And the third stage yields *reproduction and multiplication.*
3. The first stage is about *laying aside your doubts.* The second stage is about *leaving your "nets."* The third stage is about *launching out.*
4. The first stage is a matter of being *saved.* The second stage is a matter of being *trained.* The third stage is a matter of being *sent.*
5. The first stage is *coming to* Jesus. The second stage is *being with* Jesus. The third stage is *going for* Jesus.
6. The first stage is about Jesus being your *Savior.* The second stage is about Jesus being your *Master.* The third stage is about Jesus being your *Commissioning Officer.*
7. The first stage is about becoming a *committed believer.* The second stage is about becoming a *devoted follower.* The third stage is about becoming a *multiplying leader.*
8. The focus of stage one is *committed belief.* The focus of stage two is *reckless obedience.* The focus of stage three is *radical reproduction.*

Discipleship only occurs as the disciple takes the next step of dependence upon, obedience to, and abandonment for Jesus. On the next page is a chart that provides a visual look at the discipleship requirements Jesus gave at each of the three stages of discipleship.

So What?

The Gospels reveal that discipleship is a matter of taking the next step. It is a progressive relationship based on increasing levels of faith, obedience, and commitment. As the disciples completed a stage, Jesus invited His followers into the next level of relationship with Him. At this new stage, they were exposed

THE DISCIPLESHIP REQUIREMENTS OF JESUS

BELIEVER → **DISCIPLE** → **DISCIPLE MAKER**

STAGE ONE	STAGE TWO	STAGE THREE
BELIEVER	**DISCIPLE**	**DISCIPLE MAKER**
Will you *believe* in Jesus? DECLARATION	Will you *follow* Jesus? DEVELOPMENT	Will you *go* for Jesus? DEPLOYMENT
Investigation leading to repentance and faith in Jesus	Immersion, abandonment, and apprenticeship into ministry	Intentional multiplication of leaders
REPENTANCE AND FAITH Committed belief	**LOVE AND OBEDIENCE** Reckless obedience	**MINISTRY AND MISSION** Multiplying leader
Savior	Master	Commissioning Officer
Committed believer	**Devoted follower**	**Multiplying leader**
Regeneration	Transformation	Reproduction and multiplication
Laying aside your doubts	Leaving your "nets"	Launching out
Coming to Jesus	Being with Jesus	Going for Jesus
SAVED	**TRAINED**	**SENT**
Repent and believe the gospel (Mark 1:15; Matt 4:17) You must be born again (John 3:3–8) Drink of living water (John 4:13–14) Love the Lord with all of your heart and love your neighbor as yourself (Matt 22:37–40)	Follow Jesus and fish for men (Matt 4:18–22) Be with [Me] and be sent out (Mark 3:13–14) Do the will of God (Mark 3:35) Obey the Sermon on the Mount (Matthew 5–7) Deny yourself, take up your cross, and follow Me (Luke 9:23–27) Follow Me and don't look back (Luke 9:57–62) Continue in My Word (John 8:31–32) Pray for laborers (Matt 9:37–38) Don't worry, don't fear, seek the kingdom, sell possessions, give to the poor, invest in eternity (Luke 12:24–33) Love Jesus more than anything and everything else (Luke 14:25–33) Compel the lost, pursue the lost (Luke 14:16–24; 15:1–7) Follow Jesus and lose your life (Luke 17:32–33) Sell all and give to the poor (Luke 18:18–30) Be the servant of all (Mark 10:43–45) Make Father's house a house of prayer (Mark 11:17) Watch, endure, be ready, use your talents, keep working (Matthew 24–25) Love one another (John 13:34–35)	Die to multiply (John 12:23–27) Ask in His name (John 14:14; 15:16; 16:23–24) Keep His commands (John 14:15, 21–24) Abide in Christ and bear much fruit (John 15:1–8, 16) **Fulfill the Great Commission** Live sent as Jesus lived sent (John 20:21) Feed my sheep, follow Me (John 21:15–20) Preach the gospel to all creatures (Mark 16:15) **Make disciples (Matt 28:19–20)** Be His witness in Jerusalem, Judea, Samaria, and furthest parts of the world (Acts 1:8)

to a lifestyle and philosophy that challenged them to embrace it as their own. When they did, Jesus then issued an invitation to the next level of relationship.

Each level called for greater faith, obedience, and commitment.
Each level yielded greater intimacy with Jesus.
Each level produced greater impact on others.

Understanding this process will help you as you wrestle with your own level of discipleship. Further, it will greatly aid you as you work with others to help them become disciples. Add this all up and the conclusion is that being a disciple is a matter of taking your next step of faith, obedience, and commitment.

Stage One: Declaration
(Investigation Leading to Repentance and Faith in Jesus)

The Gospels record little about this stage. Most of what we know about stage one is covered in John 1:35–51; 2:1–12. The thrust of this stage is for the potential disciple to come to a place of settled belief in Jesus as the Messiah, the Son of the Living God.

The first disciples of Jesus were already God-fearing young men who had attached themselves to John the Baptist (John 1:35). At the baptism of Jesus, John pointed Andrew and John to Jesus by stating, "Look! The Lamb of God!" (John 1:36). So, they sought Jesus out. Jesus then issued them an invitation to investigate for themselves (John 1:37–39). Spending time with Jesus was enough for Andrew to tell his brother Simon (later called Peter) that he had discovered the Messiah (John 1:40–42).

The next day, Jesus issued the invitation to Philip's friend Nathanael to "Follow Me" as a potential disciple would follow a rabbi (John 1:43–51). The day after that, Jesus and His new protégés attended the famous wedding where He did His first miracle of turning water into wine (John 2:1–10). This was the evidence they needed to believe in Him as the Messiah (John 2:11).

"Repent and Believe"

Elsewhere in the Gospels we see Jesus dealing with others at the initial stage of discipleship. In His first sermon, He read out of Isaiah and proclaimed Himself the Messiah (Luke 4:16–21). Unfortunately, the ones in the synagogue that day rejected His invitation (Luke 4:22–30).

The subject of Jesus' initial sermons to the crowds as He travelled around Galilee was "Repent, because the kingdom of heaven has come near!"

(Matt 4:12–17). Or, put another way, "The time is fulfilled, and the kingdom of God has come near. Repent and believe in the good news!" (Mark 1:15).

Later in John's Gospel, Jesus is talking with Nicodemus and issuing the invitation to be born again by believing in Him (John 3:1–21). Later we see Nicodemus defending Jesus before the Pharisees (John 7:50). Nicodemus might have been a stage one disciple considering we see him at the tomb of Jesus bringing spices to anoint His body for burial (John 19:39).

To the Samaritan woman at the well, Jesus used water as a bridge to the gospel. He presents Himself to her as the one offering living water (John 4:10) and a well springing up for eternal life (John 4:14). In their conversation, He essentially called her to repentance by pointing out her immoral lifestyle (John 4:16–18). Then He revealed to her that He was the Messiah (John 4:26). This led her to the initial stage of saving faith as she proclaimed her belief throughout the town, drawing others to faith (John 4:39–42).

The demonized man of the tombs also became a stage one disciple. After his deliverance, he became a vibrant witness for Christ (Mark 5:19–20). There were many others who reached this stage during Jesus' ministry, including those He healed or freed of demons. Jesus also commended the friends who let the paralyzed man down through the roof for their faith (Mark 2:5). He recognized the Gentile mother of the demonized girl for her faith (Matt 15:28).

The Roman centurion, whose son was healed by Jesus, was also commended for his faith (Matt 8:10). One of the thieves crucified next to Jesus was told he would be joining Jesus in paradise (Luke 23:43). We also know that Joseph of Arimathea became a stage one disciple as he publically identified with Jesus by asking to have Jesus' body buried in Joseph's own tomb (Matt 27:57–58; Mark 15:43; John 19:38). As we mentioned earlier, at the time of His resurrection there were more than five hundred brethren at stage one (1 Cor 15:6).

It Is All About Jesus

As we think through each of the above mentioned examples, note carefully that the issue in each case was the identity of Jesus:

> Is Jesus the Messiah?
> Can He be trusted?
> Does He merit an intense investigation and sincere pursuit?
> Is He someone worth giving up everything for?

The whole issue in stage one is Jesus. The first stage of discipleship is a call to investigate the person and work of Jesus. When a person gives Jesus an honest hearing, they end up turning from their previous life and following Him.

Steps within Stage One

One of my mentors is Dr. Elmer Towns. In his book *Winning the Winnable*, he discusses the process whereby most people come to salvation. He writes,

> I did not become a Christian the first time I heard the gospel. . . . I was not seeking God nor was I concerned with my eternal destiny. I went to a youth rally when I saw Christian young people who had something I did not have. I wanted to be like them. Next I went to hear Jack Wyrtzen, a youth evangelist preach the gospel. For the first time I sensed I was lost and going to hell. I did not go forward to get saved, but I was no longer satisfied in my sin. Then I went to a revival meeting where I heard the gospel. I was told to invite Jesus Christ into my heart to be saved. I did it. . . . It took several stair-steps for me to realize my need and to be saved.[5]

For Towns, as with the rest of us, the first stage of discipleship is a series of steps to Jesus leading to repentance from sin and faith in Christ.

The First Stage of Discipleship Is a Process Leading to an Event

As discussed in the book *Evangelism Is . . .* , salvation is a process leading to an event. In Scripture it is compared with the birth process (John 3:1–8) and the plowing, planting, watering, harvesting cycle in agriculture (1 Cor 3:6–9).[6] A missionary named James Engle wanted to depict a typical journey a person takes to conversion and beyond. On a scale, he identified each step a person, or even a group of persons, may take toward Christ.[7] Engle's scale was later modified to include God's role, the role of the gospel communicator, along with that of the unbeliever's response.

Engle's scale is generally true of most people. Yet, it is helpful to keep in mind that not everyone comes to Christ in exactly these steps or always in this order. The process of salvation is mysterious (see John 3:8) and not always linear, but there is definitely a process (John 3:3). This process leads to repentance and faith producing regeneration and a new creation.

Moving from Curious to Convicted to Convinced to Converted

In the sixth chapter of the Gospel of John, we find that Jesus had been busy healing the sick. To top that off, He had performed the amazing miracle of feeding 5,000 men with a boy's lunch of five small barley loaves and two small fish (John 6:1–15). The crowds were curious about the identity of this miracle man, so they followed Him in droves, wondering what He would do next and hoping He would meet more of their needs (John 6:26–28).

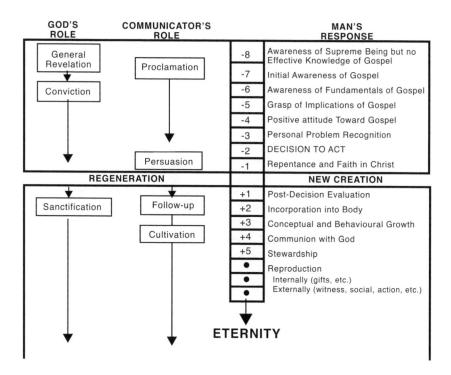

GOD'S ROLE	COMMUNICATOR'S ROLE		MAN'S RESPONSE
General Revelation	Proclamation	-8	Awareness of Supreme Being but no Effective Knowledge of Gospel
		-7	Initial Awareness of Gospel
Conviction		-6	Awareness of Fundamentals of Gospel
		-5	Grasp of Implications of Gospel
		-4	Positive attitude Toward Gospel
		-3	Personal Problem Recognition
	Persuasion	-2	DECISION TO ACT
		-1	Repentance and Faith in Christ
REGENERATION			NEW CREATION
	Follow-up	+1	Post-Decision Evaluation
Sanctification		+2	Incorporation into Body
	Cultivation	+3	Conceptual and Behavioural Growth
		+4	Communion with God
		+5	Stewardship
		●	Reproduction
		●	Internally (gifts, etc.)
		●	Externally (witness, social, action, etc.)

ETERNITY

As the chapter unfolds, Jesus discerned the shallowness of their dedication. By bringing them to a point of decision about His identity, He called them to the level of commitment to Him that would make them true followers (John 6:29–65). Sadly, at this point some who had been taking steps to Jesus turned back, but not all:

> From that moment *many of His disciples turned back* and no longer accompanied Him. Therefore Jesus said to the Twelve, "You don't want to go away too, do you?" Simon Peter answered, "Lord, who will we go to? You have the words of eternal life. We have come to believe and know that You are the Holy One of God!" (John 6:66–69)

While salvation often begins with *curiosity*, it takes more than curiosity in Jesus to experience true conversion. It takes experiencing the *conviction* of the Holy Spirit as He convinces us of our sin, our lack of true righteousness, and the resulting judgment (John 16:8). It takes being *convinced* that Jesus is indeed the Christ, the sinless Son of God, by believing the Word of God (John 16:30–31). It takes confident faith that He truly has the Words of life, and a resulting *commitment* to follow Jesus (John 6:68–69).[8]

Truly following Jesus will result in our turning *from* our old lifestyles of sin and turning *to* God in complete trust in Jesus and in determined obedience to His Word. Such a *conversion* results in a truly changed life.

1. *Curious*: Curious about who Jesus is and what Jesus can do for you.

2. *Convicted*: Convicted by the Holy Spirit of your sin and the resulting judgment.

3. *Convinced*: Convinced that Jesus is the sinless Son of God and that salvation comes only through Him.

4. *Committed and Converted*: Converted (turned around) through active faith that leads you to turn from sin and turn to God for salvation.

Jesus made disciples in three stages. Being a disciple requires taking your next step of faith and obedience. The first stage—declaration—is about becoming a *committed believer*. The second stage—development—is about becoming a *devoted follower*. The third stage—deployment— is about becoming a *multiplying leader*. All of the stages take place in the context of a local church/body of believers. Stage one is about a serious investigation of the person and work of Jesus, resulting in committed belief. Have you decided that Jesus is someone who is worth everything? Does your life reflect your response?

— Questions to Ponder —

1. What are the three stages of following Jesus?
2. What stage are you in currently?
3. How did you come to accept Jesus?
4. How have you grown since that time?
5. Who are you helping to know and grow in Christ?

Notes

1. A. B. Bruce, *The Training of the Twelve* (Grand Rapids, MI: Kregel, 1988), 11.
2. Ibid., 11.
3. Ibid.
4. Ibid., 12.
5. Elmer Towns, *Winning the Winnable* (Lynchburg, VA: Church Leadership Institute, 1986), 13.
6. Dave Earley and David Wheeler, *Evangelism Is . . .* (Nashville, TN: B&H Academic, 2010), 81–82.
7. James F. Engel and Wilbert Norton, *What's Gone Wrong with the Harvest?* (Grand Rapids, MI: Zondervan, 1975), 146.
8. Earley and Wheeler, *Evangelism Is . . .* , 72.

Realizing the Second Step of Obedience

Dave Earley

Rabbi Jesus

I have a confession to make. For most of my life, I was oblivious to the fact that Jesus was a Jewish rabbi. If pressed, I would be able to tell you that, yes, Jesus was Jewish and, yes, His followers called Him "Master" or "Teacher" or "Rabbi." But those facts rarely colored the words I read in the Gospels . . . my loss.

Jesus was Jewish. Jesus grew up in a Jewish culture, ate Jewish food, and memorized the Jewish Law. He frequently visited the Jewish temple in Jerusalem. He was raised in the Israeli province of Galilee. He frequently taught in Galilean synagogues, using them as a platform for His ministry.

Jesus was a Jewish rabbi. Jesus was called *Rabbi* by His disciples (Luke 7:40). He also was called *Rabbi* by both Pharisees and Sadducees (Luke 19:39; Matt 22:35–36; Luke 20:27–28) and ordinary people in the crowds that followed Him (Luke 12:13). As a rabbi, Jesus had *disciples.* Like the disciples of other rabbis in that day, He demanded total commitment from them because His goal was for them to become rabbis themselves, one day making their own disciples.

In the last chapter, we observed how several young men spent about a year investigating Jesus to determine whether He was a credible rabbi. . . . They discovered that He was much, much more. We call this first stage *declaration,* which is characterized by investigation leading to repentance and faith in Jesus. Those men concluded this stage of discipleship by expressing committed faith in Jesus as Messiah. The journey of discipleship did not end there. Jesus called them to the next stage: *development*.

Stage Two: Development (Immersion, Abandonment, and Apprenticeship into Ministry)

"Follow Me"

Several young men (including Andrew, Peter, and John) had been interested in Jesus' ministry and teachings (John 1:35–50). Their pursuit led them to repentance and faith in Jesus. The discipleship process did not end there. Jesus called them to the next stage of *development*:

> As He was walking along the Sea of Galilee, He saw two brothers, Simon, who was called Peter, and his brother Andrew. They were casting a net into the sea, since they were fishermen. "Follow Me," He told them, "and I will make you fish for people!" Immediately they left their nets and followed Him. Going on from there, He saw two other brothers, James the son of Zebedee, and his brother John. They were in a boat with Zebedee their father, mending their nets, and He called them. Immediately they left the boat and their father and followed Him. (Matt 4:18–22)

The decision to follow a rabbi meant total commitment. They would have to memorize His words and replicate His lifestyle. By following Him, they were choosing to be with Him, to learn from Him, and to become like Him. In order to accept this invitation, they would have to abandon everything else to follow Him.

Yet, just as they were making a significant commitment to Him, He was making a weighty commitment to them. He would spend the next three years of His life living with them and training them to become "fishers of men," or rabbis in their own right.

Being a disciple of Jesus is more than merely belief in Jesus. The second stage of discipleship requires that we embrace the cross (see chap. 9), forsake all to follow Jesus (see chap. 10), and bear fruit by abiding in Christ (see chap. 11). But it begins with immersion into a deeper relationship with Jesus, immersion into Christian community, immersion into learning the words of Jesus, and immersion into ministry.

1. Immersion into a Deeper Relationship with Jesus

When Andrew, Peter, James, and John saw Jesus that day and heard His invitation to follow Him, it did not come out of the blue. They had been following Him as stage one disciples for about a year already. Now they understood that this was a summons into a serious and significant apprenticeship of discipleship under a rabbi with the goal of becoming a rabbi. To say yes and follow Him was to immerse their lives into a new level of relationship with Him. No longer would they be spectators as Jesus taught and performed miracles. They would now literally "be with Him" (Mark 3:14).

Jesus did not say, "Follow a set of rules" or "Follow a series of rituals." He said, "Follow *Me*." To be the disciple of a rabbi was an intensely personal relationship. They would literally live with Him for months at a time for the next three years.

While not every aspect of the first-century rabbinic discipleship model applies to us today, it is universally relevant that all disciples of Jesus must immerse themselves into a relationship with Him. He needs to become their premier relationship. As God, Jesus is to be loved with all their "passion and prayer and intelligence" (Matt 22:37 MSG). As we will discuss in chapter 11, this means that ongoing and close connection with Him must be cultivated and maintained (John 15:1–17).

Pray

After Jesus ascended into heaven, the disciples sustained their deepening relationship with Him by maintaining a powerful *prayer* life. The very first thing they did was convene a seven-day *prayer* meeting (Acts 1:14, 24). When the church was born, they transcribed *prayer* into its DNA (Acts 2:42). In the face of persecution, they fell to their knees in *prayer* (Acts 4:24–31). As administrative responsibilities increased, they refused to be distracted by the "tyranny of the urgent" and, instead, reprioritized *prayer* as of prime importance (Acts 6:4). Difficult decisions were made as the result of *prayer* (Acts 1:24; 6:6). When deadly opposition grew intense, *prayer* became more intense (Acts 12:5). Above all else, the disciples were men of *prayer*.

The early Christians were Jewish and adopted the Jewish pattern of observing significant prayer times three times a day. The early church continued the practice. For example, church father Tertullian maintains:

> As regards the time, there should be no lax observation of certain hours:
> I mean of those common hours which have long marked the divisions of

the day, the third, the sixth, and the ninth, and which we may observe in Scripture to be more solemn than the rest.[1]

At the time he wrote those words, the day started at 6 a.m. Therefore, the third, sixth, and ninth hours represent 9 a.m., noon, and 3 p.m. Yet many of the early church leaders observed more than three daily prayer times. For example, Hippolytus, in the beginning of the third century, spoke of praying *six* times a day:

> If you are home, pray at the third hour [9 a.m.] and bless God. But if you are somewhere else then, pray to God in your heart. . . . Pray likewise at the sixth hour [noon]. . . . Let a great prayer and a great blessing be offered also at the ninth hour [3 p.m.]. . . . Pray as well before your body rests on its bed [9 p.m.]. But toward midnight rise up, wash your hands and pray [12 a.m.]. . . . And at the cockcrow rise up and pray once more [6 a.m.].[2]

You and I cannot hope to live the life of a disciple without a serious and significant prayer life. As you consider living the life of a disciple maker, commit yourself to living a life of prayer.

2. Immersion into Christian Community

When Jesus called the disciples to follow Him, He called them to live a life of community. They not only began to spend months at a time travelling and living with Him, they also spent months at a time living with each other. Their learning was not only influenced and enhanced by being with the Master but also by being with each other. For them, discipleship was not learning information in a classroom; it was learning Jesus with others.

All of us have a relentless yearning to attach and connect, to love and be loved. This relational hunger is, perhaps, the fiercest longing of the human soul. Our need for community with people, and the God who made us, is to the human spirit what food, air, and water are to the human body. That need never goes away. It marks us from the cradle to the grave. We need face-to-face interactions with others—to be seen, known, understood, and served, and to do the same for others.

From the first chapter of Genesis through the rest of the Bible, God speaks of our relational DNA. For example, Gen 2:18 states, "It is not good for the man to be alone." From this text we clearly see that even before the fall, God said that isolation was not the ideal state. Humanity needed to be in community with humanity. Aloneness was not an optimum, healthy, or acceptable way to go through life.

In Gen 1:26 God said, "Let *Us* make man in *Our* image." Note the use of the words "us" and "our." They remind us that God has always existed in eternal community of triunity, named elsewhere in the Scriptures as Father, Son, and Holy Spirit. All three Persons of the Trinity are separate, yet all are vitally linked as one. In other words, the "Great Three-in-One" is an eternal manifestation of intimate community and glorious *inter*dependence.

Genesis 1:27 states, "So God created man in His own image." Human beings made in the image of God beckons back to the communal essence of God Himself. As those created in the image of God, we also have a deep, unique, embedded relational identity. Yet, instead of finding the fulfillment of our communal craving in ourselves, as God does, we find it in Him *and* in one another. In other words, we not only have a "God-shaped void," we also have an "others-shaped void" etched into our hearts. *We need one another.*

Life is not meant to be lived as only "Jesus and me." It is meant to be lived as "Jesus and *we*." No human can be complete without healthy relationships with other humans. Community is what you and I were created for. This is why making disciples in the context of the local church is so important. The church is the relational context for disciple making.

The Christianity practiced by the first Christians was more than following a religion, ritual, creed, or doctrinal statement. It was a vibrant relationship with God *and* with each other. Discipleship was not a program; it was a communal relationship. From the very first day of their Christian lives, the first believers dove deep into community with each other (Acts 2:42). Biblical history tells us that "They *devoted themselves* to the apostles' teaching, and *to fellowship*, to the breaking of bread, and to the prayers. . . . Every day they devoted themselves to meeting together in the temple complex, and broke bread from house to house" (Acts 2:42, 46). They put two meetings at the top of their priority list. They attended the large celebration times of teaching and worship in the temple courts, where thousands would gather at a time, *and* they met in smaller groups several times a week for fellowship (Acts 5:42).

These first Christians faced a world where they were persecuted for their faith in the resurrected Messiah. They not only wanted to be together, they *needed* to be together. That same need still exists in our culture. Chuck Colson states, "No Christian can grow strong and stand the pressures of this life unless he is surrounded by a small group of people who minister to him and build him up in the faith."[3]

To Jesus, living in loving community with others was the distinguishing mark of discipleship. Observe His clear command: "I give you a new command: *Love one another*. Just as I have loved you, you must also *love one another*.

By this all people will know that you are My disciples, if you have *love for one another*" (John 13:34–35). We have found that the basic way to begin to establish community with others is to meet together with others at least weekly in some type of small-group environment. Whether they are called life groups, cell groups, house churches, or missional communities, the purpose is the same: following Jesus in the company of friends. When operated effectively, the group members live on mission as they experience true fellowship, or *koinonia*, and share life together.

3. Immersion into the Words of Jesus

Education centered on the practice of memorization in the first century. At age five, Jewish children would begin to memorize large portions of the Torah (the first five books of the Old Testament). By age twelve, boys would have completed memorizing the Torah and gone on to learning key chunks of the Old Testament while girls learned the Psalms. Ben Witherington observes:

> Among the Jews, rabbis were encouraged to memorize entire books of the OT, indeed the whole OT. All of Jewish education consisted of rote memory. . . . Disciples in early Jewish settings were learners, and, yes, also reciters and memorizers. This was the way Jewish educational processes worked. In fact it was the staple of all ancient education, including Greco-Roman education.[4]

At age twelve, boys would begin to apprentice to learn a trade. Girls would learn homemaking skills in preparation for marriage. Between the age of twelve and eighteen, a boy might begin an apprenticeship to become a rabbi. He would finish memorizing the Torah, along with much of the Old Testament, *and* the teachings of his mentor.

When the twelve disciples submitted to Jesus' tutelage as their rabbi, they were committing themselves to memorize and live not only the Words of the Old Testament, but also His teachings.

> Come to Me, all of you who are weary and burdened, and I will give you rest. All of you, take up My yoke and learn from Me, because I am gentle and humble in heart, and you will find rest for yourselves. For My yoke is easy and My burden is light. (Matt 11:28–30)

"Yokes" were commonplace in Jesus' day. Oxen would be yoked together with a carefully crafted piece of wood in order to pull a load. Likewise, the term was adapted to apply to a disciple placing himself under the yoke of his rabbi's instruction. In Jewish culture, the students of a rabbi had to memorize his words. Hence, Mishna, Aboth, ii, 8 reads: "A good pupil was like a plastered cistern that loses not a drop." In the verses quoted above, Jesus said, "Take up My yoke and learn from Me." The word translated "learn" there is basically the root word from which we get the word translated in the New Testament as "disciple."

The present-day Uppsala school of Harald Riesenfeld and Birger Gerhardsson analyzed Jesus' relationship with His disciples in the context of Jewish rabbinical practices of c. AD 200. They discovered that Jesus, in the role of the authoritative teacher or rabbi, trained His disciples to believe in, *and remember*, His teachings. Because their culture was so strongly oriented towards oral transmission of knowledge, they could memorize amazing amounts of material by today's standards. "The culture's values emphasized the need of disciples to remember their teacher's teachings and deeds accurately, then to pass this on."[5] For the Twelve, the call to discipleship was a call to immerse their lives in the words of Jesus.

For a time I served as the director of discipleship for a large Christian university and prided myself on having read every book on discipleship and disciple making available at the time. Some time back, my wife, Cathy, asked, "What do you think is the best discipleship curriculum on the market?" "Matthew, Mark, Luke, and John, with the book of Acts added in," I said, "with a special emphasis on the words written in red ink."

"Is that it?" she said, rather unimpressed. "Why?"

"Because," I said, "if I can get a person living the Gospels and applying the commands of Jesus like the disciples applied them in Acts, I believe I will have made a disciple. And I believe that type of disciple will change the world."

4. Immersion into Ministry

The call into discipleship occurred at the Sea of Galilee. Matthew 4:19 states, "'Follow Me,' He told them, 'and I will make you *fish for people!*'" The Sea of Galilee is still known for the vast number of fish that live in its clear, clean waters. As a gifted teacher, Jesus tied what they knew (fishing) with what they were to learn: catching men with the gospel. As followers of Jesus, the disciples' task was to become "fishermen" for the kingdom. Their call to discipleship was a call to immerse their lives in ministry. For Jesus and the Twelve, discipleship *was* apprenticeship.

In a technical sense, apprenticeship is a system of training a new generation of practitioners in a skill. Most of the training is done while working for an employer who helps the apprentice learn the trade in exchange for their continued labor for an agreed period after they become skilled. In a society where apprenticeship was the primary method of developing a new generation of practitioners, Jesus called the Twelve into an apprenticeship with Him. Under His supervision, they could develop the skills needed to carry on His ministry after His departure. Anthony Gittins writes,

> The purpose of discipleship is mission. . . . Discipleship requires the recruitment and formation of believers who will continue the work of Jesus wherever they may be and wherever they are led. . . . The fruits of authentic discipleship will be manifest in the continuing commitment of those who have first encountered Jesus and then been sent by him on mission.[6]

Later, Jesus re-emphasized the call to discipleship by calling them not to only be with Him, but to be sent out by Him into ministry. Mark 3:13–15 states,

> Then He went up the mountain and *summoned* those He wanted, and they came to Him. He also appointed 12—He also named them apostles—to be with Him, to *send* them out to preach, and to have authority to drive out demons.

In a very real sense, a disciple is a person who has been "summoned to be sent." Any discipleship scheme that leaves out ministry is ineffective. Jesus trained them to *do* something: fish for men and be sent out to preach.

In time, Jesus would send the Twelve out on at least one extended ministry tour without Him (Matthew 10). There is no discipleship without ministry training. It was not enough for them to be with Jesus, and it was insufficient merely to learn the words of His teachings. It would take more than living in loving community with others to be a disciple. They would have to learn ministry. Ministry was the reason they were being discipled in the first place.

Ultimately, the point of being a disciple is to become a disciple maker. I will talk more about this in the next chapter but, before moving on, one final observation about Jewish rabbinic practices:

> When the teacher believed that his *talmidim [disciples]* were prepared to be like him, he would commission them to become disciple makers. He was saying, "As far as is possible you are like me. Now go and seek others who will imitate you. Because you are like me, when they imitate you they will be like me." This practice certainly lies behind Jesus'

great commission (Matt. 28:18–20). . . . As the rabbi lived and taught his understanding of the Scripture, his students (*talmidim*) listened and watched and imitated so as to become like him. Eventually they would become teachers passing on a lifestyle to their *talmidim*.[7]

– Questions to Ponder –

1. Are you currently living a life of immersion into Jesus?
2. Are you devoted to Him? Is it being evidenced by your prayer life?
3. Are you living in Christian community with other disciples? How close are you replicating the example of first-century Christians?
4. Are you in the Word? First-century disciples memorized much of the Old Testament and the teachings of their teacher. How much of the Bible (and not merely books about the Bible) are you reading, studying, memorizing, and meditating upon?
5. What is your ministry? Are you evangelizing the lost? Who are you pouring the life of Jesus into?

Notes

1. Tertullian, *De Oratione*, xxiii, xxv, in P.L., I, 1191–3.
2. Hippolytus, *Apostolic Tradition*, quoted in Boniface Ramsey, *Beginning to Read the Fathers* (Mahwah, NJ: Paulist, 1985), 165–66.
3. Charles Colson, *Kingdoms in Conflict* (Grand Rapids, MI: Zondervan, 1987), 47.
4. Ben Witherington, *The Jesus Quest* (Downers Grove: IVP, 1995), 48.
5. *Is the Bible the Word of God? A Rational Defense of the Judeo-Christian Scriptures*, chap. 2, http://www.biblestudy.org/maturart/is-bible-the-word-of-god/chapter2.html (accessed December 12, 2012).
6. Anthony Gittins, *Called to Be Sent* (Liguori, MO: Liguori Press, 2008), 1, 15.
7. Ray Vander Laan, "Rabbi and Talmidim," http://www.followtherabbi.com/guide/detail/rabbi-and-talmidim (accessed December 12, 2012).

8

Accepting the Third Step of Obedience

Dave Earley

Be a Missionary Every Day

I remember several songs I learned at church as a child. One song I found quite catchy also had a strong spiritual message. We learned it at vacation Bible school one summer. Maybe you know it:

Be a missionary every day!

Tell the world that Jesus is the way!
Be it in the town or country
or the busy avenue!
Africa or Asia, the task is up to YOU!

So be a missionary
God's own emissary
Be a missionary today!
Let's GO!!!

What if everyone in my church had taken that song seriously and lived as missionaries? We might have reached our city with the gospel. I agree with Charles Spurgeon, who said, "Every Christian is either a missionary or an imposter."[1] Disciples do not live as mere church members. They are also not content with just holding down a weekly ministry at their church. No.

Disciples live as missionaries. If you are going to be a disciple of Jesus Christ, you will be a missionary. Living on mission is not the career of a select few. It is the calling of *all* disciples, commission to *all* disciples, and command for *all* disciples. We are all called as missionaries. The question is: Will we be obedient or disobedient? In this chapter we will discuss the third and final stage of discipleship—*deployment*.

Stage Three: *Deployment*
(Intentional Global Commissioning)

As we noted in chapter 6, the disciple-making ministry of Jesus moved through three distinct phases. The first stage asks the question, *Will you believe in Jesus?* (DECLARATION). The second stage asks, *Will you follow Jesus?* (DEVELOPMENT). The third stage asks, *Will you go for Jesus?* (DEPLOYMENT). This final stage of Jesus' disciple-making strategy climaxed at the giving of the Great Commission as Jesus declared His disciples ready to reproduce the process in the lives of others (Matt 28:18–20). The rabbi had successfully trained His disciples to be disciple makers. This they did as they launched the first church (Acts 2). I call the third stage *deployment*, calling disciples to *intentional global commissioning*.

Missio Dei

Missio Dei is a Latin phrase reminding the church that its mission is not the invention, responsibility, or program of human origin. It flows from the character and purposes of God.[2] Historically, the term *mission* was used to describe the *acts of God*, rather than the activities of churches. Mission is not something the church does for God. It is, rather, the church getting in sync with the heart of God and cooperating with the activity of God.

According to Tom Jones,

God's nature is at the root of mission. The living God portrayed in the Bible is a sending God. He sends because of His love for the world (John 3:16). He sent Abraham from his home into the unknown, promising to bless the world through him if he obeyed (Gen 12:1–3). God sent Joseph into Egypt to help preserve God's people during a time of famine (Gen 45:4–8). When the time had fully come, God sent His son. Later, the Father and the Son sent the Spirit on Pentecost (Gal 4:4–6; John 14:26; 15:26; 16:7; Acts 2:33). Finally, Christ sends His church (Matt 28:19–20).[3]

The late Swiss theologian Emil Brunner has memorably stated, "The Church exists by mission, just as fire exists by burning."[4] The same could be said of a disciple. David Borsh concurs, stating, "It is impossible to talk about church without at the same time talking about mission. Because God is a missionary God, God's people are missionary people. The church's mission is not secondary to its being: the church exists in being sent and building up itself for its mission."[5] The same could be said of a disciple.

Jesus Christ: Missionary

The greatest missionary in history was Jesus Christ.[6] In His very first sermon, Jesus quoted the prophecy of Isaiah regarding the fact that the Messiah would be *sent* to preach the gospel (Isa 61:1–2; Luke 4:18). In applying that promise to Himself, He showed that He was indeed a missionary. Later, Jesus stressed that He was *sent* by His Father (John 17:21–25; Matt 10:40).

As a missionary, Jesus willingly *left* His Father, home, possessions, position, culture, comfort, convenience, safety, and security *in order to come* to earth and carry out His assignment. Compared to His prior existence in heaven, Jesus experienced unimaginable limitation, deprivation, oppression, and persecution as a missionary on earth. As a missionary, He lived among those He hoped to reach. He ate our food, wore our clothes, and spoke our language. He suffered our sorrows and shared our joys. He identified completely with us and died for us.

According to the dictionary, a missionary is "one sent on a mission."[7] Our word *mission* comes from the word "sent" or "to send." Consider Jesus' debrief with His disciples after His evangelistic interaction with the Samaritan woman at the well. Notice that He mentions His mission and then uses it as the basis of pointing out *their* mission.

> "My food is to do the will of Him who *sent Me* and to finish His work," Jesus told them. "Don't you say, 'There are still four more months, then comes the harvest'? Listen to what I'm telling you: Open your eyes and look at the fields, for they are ready for harvest. The reaper is already receiving pay and gathering fruit for eternal life, so the sower and reaper can rejoice together. For in this case the saying is true: 'One sows and another reaps.' *I sent you* to reap what you didn't labor for; others have labored, and you have benefited from their labor." (John 4:34–38)

Jesus was *sent* as a missionary to the world to make disciples. He has *sent* His disciples into the world to make disciples. To follow Jesus fully means that you and I must follow His example and be missionaries. Let me explain.

All Disciples Are *Sent*

The disciples were selected with one primary goal in mind: to be missionaries. When we go back to their calling, we see that they were *called to be sent*. Consider Mark 3:14:

> He also appointed 12—He also named them apostles—to be with Him, *to send them* out to preach.

Later, when they approached Jerusalem, Jesus re-emphasized the commission to be sent into the harvest. Matthew 9:37–38 records Jesus saying:

> The harvest is abundant, but the workers are few. Therefore, pray to the Lord of the harvest to *send out* workers into His harvest.

Jesus intended that they be the first answer to their prayers. So He sent them out:

> Summoning the Twelve, He gave them power and authority over all the demons, and power to heal diseases. Then He *sent them* to proclaim the kingdom of God and to heal the sick. (Luke 9:1–2; see Matt 10:1–5)

Later, Jesus was in the garden of Gethsemane wrestling in prayer. In this high priestly prayer, Jesus prayed for His disciples, reminding His Father that just as He had been sent, He had sent His disciples out into the world. John 17:18 states,

> As You sent Me into the world, I also have *sent* them into the world.

After Jesus' crucifixion, the disciples were huddled in secret out of fear. The Sunday night of His resurrection, Jesus appeared to them and assured them of His peace. Then He reminded them of His crucifixion and resurrection by showing them His nail-pierced hands. Then He reminded them of their mission:

> As the Father has *sent Me*, I also *send you*. (John 20:21)

Regarding this sentence, Stetzer and Putnam write, "With that one command Jesus announced two thousand years of direction for the church, still in effect for churches today." They continue, "The church is, and you are individually, God's missionary to the world. . . . We are *sent on mission* by God."[8] Maybe you are thinking, "Yes, of course the twelve apostles were missionaries. All of these commands were only given to them. I am just a normal disciple. I do not see how you can imply that I am to be a missionary." Not long after sending out the Twelve on mission, Jesus sent out seventy *others* on mission. Clearly, living on mission was not merely for the Twelve. It is for all of Jesus' followers. Luke 10:1–3, 9 records this event:

> After this, the Lord appointed *70 others*, and He *sent* them ahead of Him in pairs to every town and place where He Himself was about to go. He told them: "The harvest is abundant, but the workers are few. Therefore, pray to the Lord of the harvest to *send out workers* into His harvest. Now *go*; I'm *sending you out* like lambs among wolves. . . . Heal the sick who are there, and tell them, 'The kingdom of God has come near you.'"

It was not just twelve special men who were *sent* out as missionaries. All of us are sent. It is not only extra-special people who have been *sent* on mission for God. All disciples have been *sent*.

All Disciples Must *Go*

Since all disciples are sent, then all disciples must *go*. For example, Luke 14:16–23 records one occasion when Jesus told a parable of a great banquet in which many were invited:

> Then He told him: "A man was giving a large banquet and invited many. At the time of the banquet, he *sent* his slave to tell those who were invited, 'Come, because everything is now ready.'" (vv. 16–17)

Yet, one by one the invited guests began to make excuses. Notice how the master replied to the slave:

> "So the slave came back and reported these things to his master. Then in anger, the master of the house told his slave, '*Go* out quickly into the streets and alleys of the city, and bring in here the poor, maimed, blind, and lame!' 'Master,' the slave said, 'what you ordered has been done, and there's still room.' Then the master told the slave, '*Go* out into the highways and lanes and make them come in, so that my house may be filled.'" (vv. 21–23)

Later, when His propensity for eating with "sinners" caught the attention of the Pharisees, Jesus told another parable explaining His heart and mission for pursuing the lost. Luke 15:1–7 records:

> All the tax collectors and sinners were approaching to listen to Him. And the Pharisees and scribes were complaining, "This man welcomes sinners and eats with them!" So He told them this parable: "What man among you, who has 100 sheep and loses one of them, does not *leave the 99* in the open field and *go after the lost one* until he finds it? When he

has found it, he joyfully puts it on his shoulders, and coming home, he
calls his friends and neighbors together, saying to them, 'Rejoice with me,
because I have found my lost sheep!' I tell you, in the same way, there
will be more joy in heaven over one sinner who repents than over 99
righteous people who don't need repentance."

After His crucifixion, Jesus gave His disciples their final marching orders
in the form of the Great Commission. They had already received the mission of
inviting people to the Father's banquet and pursuing lost sheep. Now that He
was about to leave, He told them that it was time for them to *go*:

> Then He said to them, "*Go* into all the world and preach the gospel to
> the whole creation." (Mark 16:15)

> *Go*, therefore, and make disciples of all nations, baptizing them in the
> name of the Father and of the Son and of the Holy Spirit, teaching them
> to observe everything I have commanded you. And remember, I am with
> you always, *to the end of the age*. (Matt 28:19–20)

Notice that in order to fulfill the Great Commission, the disciples had to *go*.
Notice also that Jesus said the gospel was to cover *all He had commanded*, and
was to be preached to *all peoples*.

Yet, there is more. Note the last six words of the Great Commission: "to
the end of the age." By including this phrase in the Great Commission, Jesus
was commanding the perpetuity of the Great Commission. Going and making
disciples was not just an activity for the first century. It is to extend *to the end
of the age*. Of this text John Piper writes,

> The demand is not given only to the first generation of disciples. The
> mission lasts as long as the mission-sustaining promise lasts. And that
> promise is this: The all-authoritative Jesus will be with us to "the end
> of the age." As long as there is time, and as long as there are nations to
> reach, Jesus' demand to go and make disciples is valid.[9]

Therefore, the Great Commission does not merely cover all He commanded, or
extend to all nations, it also includes all generations of those who follow Jesus.

The Mission Starts Here and Now

A person's last words can be the most significant words they ever speak.
Often they are a summary of their life, mission, values, and passion. That
certainly was the case with Jesus. In His last words, He not only told His

disciples that they were to be *witnesses*, but also the extent of that witness — *to the ends of the earth*. Acts 1:8 states,

> But you will receive power when the Holy Spirit has come on you, and you will be My witnesses *in Jerusalem, in all Judea and Samaria, and to the ends of the earth.*

Remember that the disciples were *from Galilee*. To obey the Great Commission, they would have to go to Jerusalem. Starting their lives as missionaries *in* Jerusalem would be a strategic change of location for them. Yet that starting point was still within their own culture. Being a missionary does not start when you arrive in a cross-cultural context thousands of miles from home. Being a missionary starts here and now. David Platt writes, "Wherever you and I live, we are commanded to go and make disciples there. In light of Jesus' example, our primary impact on the nations will occur in the disciple-making we do right around us."[10] Jason Dukes adds, "The Sender has sent you and me to be His letter of love unto humanity. May we live sent daily. And may we begin now."[11]

Sally the Missionary

Sally, one of our small-group leaders, viewed herself as a missionary to her neighborhood. Every day she would walk through her neighborhood, interceding for the salvation of each family. She also served her neighbors and took an interest in their children. She would be the person at the door with soup and sandwiches when they moved in or when someone was sick. She was the mom with fresh baked cookies all the kids visited on their way home from school.

One Sunday, after our last worship service, Sally came up to me to ask: "Pastor Dave, would it be alright if we used one of the large classrooms in the church for a party for our neighbors next Sunday?"

"What sort of party is it?" I asked.

"Nearly a dozen of my neighbors and their children have been saved recently and are being baptized here next week," she replied. "We wanted to throw a party in their honor."

The third stage of discipleship is *deployment*, which calls all disciples to *intentional global commissioning*. Don't wait. Like Sally, start living on mission with God today. Approach each new day as a missionary would. Serve people, invest in people, love people, pray for them consistently, live the gospel, share the gospel, be the church, and make disciples.

~ Questions to Ponder ~

1. What is the "Missio Dei"?
2. How was Jesus a missionary?
3. What are some passages that reveal that we are "sent ones"?
4. What is the David Platt quote?
5. What are some ways you can live as a "sent one"?

Notes

1. Charles Spurgeon, *The Soul Winner: Or, How to Lead Sinners to the Saviour* (Grand Rapids, MI: Eerdmans, 1965), 127.

2. Stewart Murray, *Church Planting* (Scottsdale, PA: Herald, 2001), 39.

3. Tom Jones, *Church Planting from the Ground Up* (Joplin, MO: College, 2004), 10.

4. Emil Brunner, quoted by Wilbert R. Shenk, *Write the Vision* (Harrisburg, PA: Trinity, 1995), 87.

5. David J. Borsch, *Believing in the Future* (Harrisburg, PA: Trinity, 1995), 32.

6. Robert Garrett, "The Gospels and Acts: Jesus the Missionary and His Missionary Followers," in *Missiology* (Nashville, TN: B&H, 1998), 63.

7. *Webster's Ninth New Collegiate Dictionary* (Springfield, MA: Merriam-Webster, 1986), s.v. "mission."

8. Ed Stezer and David Putnam, *Breaking the Missional Code: Your Church Can Become a Missionary in Your Community* (Nashville, TN: B&H, 2006), 31, italics in original.

9. John Piper, *What Jesus Demands of the World* (Wheaton, IL: Crossway, 2006), 366.

10. David Platt, *Radical* (Nashville, TN: Thomas Nelson, 2010), 198.

11. Jason Dukes, *Live Sent: You Are a Letter* (Birmingham, AL: New Hope, 2011), 16.

9

Embracing the Cross: Declaration

Dave Earley

Would You Be Willing to Die for Jesus Christ?

On Tuesday April 20, 1999, Cassie Bernal was in the Columbine Colorado high school library reading her Bible when the two students burst in carrying guns. According to one of the witnesses, her friend Josh, one of the killers pointed his gun at Cassie and asked, "Do you believe in God?"

"She paused," Josh stated later, "like she didn't know what she was going to answer, and then she said 'yes.' She must have been scared, but her voice didn't sound shaky. It was strong. Then they asked her why, though they didn't give her a chance to respond. They just blew her away."[1]

Cassie's martyrdom was even more remarkable when you consider that just a few years ago she had dabbled in the occult, including witchcraft. She had embraced the same darkness that drove her killers to such despicable acts. But two years earlier, Cassie dedicated her life to Christ and turned her life around.

According to the *Boston Globe*, on the night of her death, Cassie's brother Chris found a Scripture she had written out just two days prior to her death. It read:

> Now I have given up on everything else—I have found it to be the only
> way to really know Christ and to experience the mighty power that
> brought him back to life again, and to find out what it means to suffer and

85

to die with him. So, whatever it takes I will be one who lives in the fresh newness of life of those who are alive from the dead. (Phil 3:10–11 TLB)

Would you die for Jesus?

Forsake to Follow

As we have seen, for the twelve young followers of Jesus, the discipleship process began with the serious investigation of Jesus that they might fully believe in Him. This led to radical immersion into the life of Jesus as potential disciple makers. In order for this consuming involvement with Jesus to occur, the disciples had to forsake safety, security, careers, comfort, families, friends, possessions, and even their own lives to follow Him.

Peter and Andrew left their nets to follow Him (Matt 4:19–20). James and John left their boat, their family business, and their father to follow Him (Matt 4:21–22). Matthew, or as he is also called, Levi, the tax collector, left his lucrative tax business to follow Jesus (Mark 2:13–14).

Any disciple-making strategy that merely adds Jesus to already busy lives is doomed for failure. Potential disciples must be called to forsake all to follow Jesus. Oswald Chambers writes, "The great word to Jesus' disciples is Abandon."[2]

Following Jesus Leads to the Cross

After following Jesus awhile, Jesus began to hammer the need for abandoning all to follow Him. He used Himself and the cross as the background to paint the picture of the high cost of discipleship:

> But He strictly warned and instructed them to tell this to no one, saying, "The Son of Man must suffer many things and be rejected by the elders, chief priests, and scribes, be killed, and be raised the third day." (Luke 9:21–22)

The way of Jesus led Him to suffering, rejection, and ultimately execution on a cross. We can certainly rejoice in a risen Savior, but we must also never forget that before He rose from the dead, Jesus suffered, was rejected, and executed. Jesus gave it all for us, and He calls us to do the same for Him. As Dietrich Bonhoeffer stated, "When Christ calls a man, he bids him come and die."[3] Make no mistake about it, following Jesus always ultimately leads to the cross. In Luke 9:23, Jesus states, "Then He said to them all, 'If anyone wants to come with Me, he must deny himself, take up his cross daily, and follow

Me.'" In his translation of this passage, Greek scholar Kenneth Wuest makes this abundantly clear:

> Assuming that anyone desires to come after me as a follower of mine, let him disregard his own interests, and let him at once and once for all pick up and carry his cross day after day, and *let him take the same road with me that I take* as a habit of life. (Luke 9:23 Wuest)[4]

The road that Jesus took led Him to the cross. If we take the same road, it will lead us to the same place. Following Jesus will always ultimately lead us to the cross. This chapter will go deeper into stage one of the discipleship process — *declaration* — exploring what it means to embrace the cross.

Embrace the Cross

1. Embracing the Cross Means Saying "No" to Self

Consider again Luke 9:23, "And He said to all, If any person wills to come after Me, let him deny himself [disown himself, forget, lose sight of himself and his own interests, refuse and give up himself] . . ." (AMP). In the first century, a man being executed on a cross had no rights. He had no future. He had no possessions. He had no friends. He had nothing. Embracing a cross is being willing to have nothing but Jesus. David Platt in his book *Radical* writes:

> . . . somewhere along the way we had missed what is radical about our faith and replaced it with what is comfortable. We were settling for a Christianity that revolves around catering to ourselves when the central message of Christianity is actually about abandoning ourselves.[5]

This denying yourself speech was something Jesus gave many times in many ways. For example, later in his Gospel, Luke recorded this statement from Jesus:

> Anyone who comes to me but refuses to let go of father, mother, spouse, children, brothers, sisters — yes, even one's own self! — can't be my disciple. Anyone who won't shoulder his own cross and follow behind me can't be my disciple. (Luke 14:25–27 MSG)

John Piper notes that embracing the cross leads to "ruptures in our relationships with people, our relationships with possessions, and our relationships with our vocations."[6] Embracing the cross demands loving Jesus more than anything or anyone else, including ourselves.

Would you die for Jesus? Maybe a better way to ask this question is: "Are you willing to let go of your vocation for Jesus? Will you say good-bye to your possessions if need be? Will you let go of your relationships with people in order to fully embrace Jesus?"

2. Embracing the Cross Means Surrendering the Direction of Your Life to Jesus

To deny yourself means to disregard your own interests. The *Message* paraphrases Luke 9:23 this way: "Anyone who intends to come with me has to let me lead. *You're not in the driver's seat*—I am." Ralph Wilson writes, "It is a matter of surrendering the throne of your heart to God. Getting off, scooting over, bowing down and letting him call the shots."[7]

Car keys are a symbol of freedom in our culture. Take your car keys out of your pocket. Would you really give the keys of your car to Jesus? On a more important note, let me ask, "Have you fully given the keys of your life to Jesus? Will you at least scoot over and let Him sit in the driver's seat of your life?"

3. Embracing the Cross Means Choosing God's Will When My Will and God's Will Cross

Take your fingers and form a cross. The finger pointing up is symbolic of God's will. The finger pointing across is your will. Following Jesus is choosing God's will when your will and His will cross. Being a disciple is not adding Jesus to our already full, self-directed way of life. Discipleship means deliberately choosing to follow *God's* way rather than our own way. This is what it means to deny yourself and take up your cross habitually, every day, as your way of life. Obviously, you would never really die for Jesus unless you are allowing Him to choose your future.

4. Embracing the Cross Means Enduring Any Sacrifice for the Joy of Obeying Jesus

When Jesus spoke of taking up the cross, He was not referring merely to a burden, load, or misfortune. The cross in Jesus' day was an instrument of torture and execution. First-century people did not recognize a figurative use of "cross" as a "burden" or "trial." Death on the cross was shameful, brutal, offensive, vulgar, excruciating, severe, intense, and protracted. This is made evident by this ancient Greek poem about crucifixion.

> Punished with limbs outstretched, they see the stake as their fate; they are fastened (and) nailed to it in the most bitter torment, evil food for birds of prey and grim pickings for dogs.[8]

In Greek, the operative verb in Luke 9:23 is *airo*, translated "lift up, take up, pick up, carry." Jesus is saying that just as a condemned man is forced to carry the crossbeam of his own cross, we are to "take up our cross" (Mark 15:21; John 19:17). In other words, let the disciple take up the position of a man already condemned to death.

The men who originally heard these words were willing to endure any sacrifice for Jesus. As mentioned previously, Philip was scourged, thrown into prison, and crucified. Matthew suffered martyrdom by the sword. Matthias was stoned at Jerusalem and then beheaded. Andrew was arrested and crucified on a cross, two ends of which were fixed transversely in the ground (thus the term, *St. Andrew's Cross*). Peter was crucified upside down, at his own request, because he said he was unworthy to be crucified in the same manner as his Lord. Luke was hanged on an olive tree in Greece.[9]

When you realize that only one of the apostles died a natural death, it becomes apparent that Jesus is not only speaking figuratively about taking up your cross and losing your life. He is talking about literal death, if need be. A disciple is willing to make sacrifices for Jesus.

5. Embracing the Cross Means Following Jesus Wherever He Leads

I appreciate the fact that in Luke 9:23 Jesus said, "Follow *Me*"—not "Follow the *rules*," or "*Believe the creed*," but "Follow me. Let's walk together." Christianity is a relationship, not a religion. *It is exciting to follow Jesus.* Think about it. He did miracles! He healed sick people, fed hungry people, and even raised dead people. He befuddled Pharisees. He chased greedy money changers out of the temple with a whip. He walked on the water. Life with Jesus was never boring. If your Christian life is boring, you should ask: "Am I really following Jesus?"

It also became uncomfortable to follow Jesus. Following Jesus meant that the disciples were considered the students of a crazy man. They were hated by the religious leaders. Following Jesus meant that they would soon be considered associates with a convicted and condemned criminal.

Following Jesus leads us into uncomfortable places. He goes to the hurting, the hopeless, and the homeless. He goes to hard places and deals with dirty people. Jesus is always calling us out of our comfort zones.

You will never fully experience Jesus by staying in your comfort zone. That could mean following Him out of your comfort zone and into teaching four-year-olds on Sunday mornings. It could mean giving the first 15 percent of your income to God. Or it might mean sharing your faith with the people at work. Or maybe it is going to China as a missionary.

You will never fully experience Jesus while staying in your comfort zone. You will only experience Him when you go where He goes. Following Jesus means following Him wherever He leads, even if it is uncomfortable. Would you be willing to die for Jesus Christ? Obviously you would never really die for Jesus unless you are fully following Him right now.

6. Embracing the Cross Means Boldly Witnessing for Jesus

Embracing the cross and embracing Jesus are inseparable realties. A few verses later in Luke, Jesus comments on this connection:

> For whoever is *ashamed of me and of my words*, of him the Son of Man will be ashamed when He comes in His own glory, and in his Father's, and of the holy angels. (Luke 9:26 NKJV)

I came across the following declaration several years ago and am always challenged when I read it. Read it slowly and see how your life compares:

The Fellowship of the Unashamed

I'm part of the fellowship of the unashamed, I have the Holy Spirit power, the die has been cast, I have stepped over the line, the decision has been made: I'm a disciple of Jesus Christ. I won't look back, let up, slow down, back away, or be still.

My past is redeemed, my present makes sense, my future is secure. I'm finished and done with low living, sight walking, smooth knees, colorless dreams, tamed visions, worldly talking, cheap giving, and dwarfed goals.

I no longer need preeminence, prosperity, position, promotions, plaudits, or popularity. I do not have to be right, first, tops, recognized, praised, regarded, or rewarded. I now live by faith, lean in His presence, walk by patience, am uplifted by prayer, and I labor with power.

My face is set, my gait is fast, my goal is heaven, my road is narrow, my way is rough, my companions are few, my guide is reliable, my mission is clear. I won't give up, shut up, let up until I have stayed up, stored up, prayed up for the cause of Jesus Christ.

I must go till He comes, give till I drop, preach till everyone knows, work till He stops me, and when He comes for His own, He will have no trouble recognizing me because my banner will have been clear.

These words were found in the possession of a young African after he was martyred for his faith in Zimbabwe.[10] He denied himself, took up his cross and fully followed Jesus.

Would you be willing to die for Jesus Christ? Obviously, you would never really die for Jesus unless you are unashamedly speaking up for Jesus right now.

7. Embracing the Cross Is the Only Way to Discover Real Life

Jesus gives a great paradox—lose your life to find it. Luke 9:24–25 describes this truth: "For whoever would save [keep safe, preserve] his life will lose it [destroy it], but whoever loses his life for my sake will save [find] it. For what does it profit a man if he gains the whole world and loses or forfeits himself." Self-sacrifice is the only way to self-discovery. Dying is the doorway to living. Giving is the key to receiving. In Mark 10:29–30, Jesus states,

> I assure you . . . there is no one who has left house, brothers or sisters, mother or father, children, or fields because of Me and the gospel, who will not receive 100 times more, now at this time—houses, brothers and sisters, mothers and children, and fields, with persecutions—and eternal life in the age to come.

John Piper adds:

> The path of God—exalting joy will cost you your life. Jesus said, "Whoever loses his life for my sake and the gospel's will save it." In other words, it is better to lose your life than to waste it. If you live gladly to make others glad in God, your life will be hard, your risks will be high, and your joy will be full. This is not . . . about how to avoid a wounded life, but how to avoid a wasted life. Some of you will die in the service of Christ. That will not be a tragedy. Treasuring life above Christ is a tragedy.[11]

"What else is better in this life? I have heard of nothing better." Jim Elliot was a promising student at Wheaton College in Illinois. He was a champion wrestler, honor student, amateur poet, and was warmly admired by students at Wheaton. He dated and married the prettiest girl at the school. He was truly the "big man" on campus.

In his studies, he read the words of Luke 9 and took them seriously. During his senior year, he wrote in his journal these now famous words: "He is no fool who gives up what he cannot keep to gain what he cannot lose."[12]

God called him to take the gospel to an unreached tribe, the Waodomi people, called the Auca or Savage Indians in Ecuador. Elliot wrote, "Glad to get the opportunity to preach the gospel of the matchless grace of our God to stoical, pagan Indians. I only hope that He will let me preach to those who have never heard that name Jesus. *What else is better in this life? I have heard of nothing better. 'Lord, send me!'*"[13]

Unfortunately, he and his four associates were killed by the warriors before they could share with them. Jim gave up what he could not keep. He gave up his earthly life to gain what he could not lose: eternal life.

Due to the publicity generated by the martyrdom of the missionaries, thousands of other young men and women committed to missions to take their place. Beyond that, the widows of the martyred missionaries went back to that tribe and led those warriors to Christ.

"Jim Elliot did not die in Ecuador." Years later, a young man traveling in Ecuador flew in a small plane over the country. The pilot knew of Jim Elliot's ministry.

"When we fly over the place where Jim Elliot and the others died, show me," the man said to the pilot.

"I can't take you there," replied the pilot.

"Why not?"

"Because Jim Elliot did not die in Ecuador."

Perplexed, the young man remarked, "Yes, I know Jim Elliot died here in Ecuador."

"Jim Elliot's body died in South America," the pilot said, "but Jim Elliot died while a college student at Wheaton College several years before when he yielded his life to God no matter the consequences."[14]

Being a disciple requires that we follow Jesus to the cross. Would you be willing to die for Jesus Christ? Not unless you are living for Jesus right now.

— Questions to Ponder —

1. What did Jesus have to say about the cross and following Him?
2. What do you think it means to "take up your cross and follow Him"?
3. Have you ever "declared" that you will follow Jesus no matter the cost?
4. If so, when and what were the circumstances?
5. If not . . . do you think you need to declare the important step?

Notes

1. Misty Bernal, *She Said Yes: The Unlikely Martyrdom of Cassie Bernall* (Nashville, TN: Thomas Nelson, 2002), 11.

2. Oswald Chambers, quoted in David McCasland, *Oswald Chambers: Abandoned to God* (Grand Rapids, MI: Discovery House, 1996), 137.

3. Deitrich Bonhoeffer, *The Cost of Discipleship,* trans. R. H. Fuller (New York: Touchstone, 1997), 44.

4. Kenneth Wuest, *Wuest's Expanded Translation of the Greek New Testament* (Grand Rapids: Eerdmans, 1961), 156, emphasis added.

5. David Platt, *Radical: Taking Back Your Faith from the American Dream* (Portland, OR: Multnomah, 2010), 7.

6. John Piper, *What Jesus Demands of the World* (Wheaton, IL: Crossway, 2006), 72.

7. Ralph Wilson, *Jesus Walk: Discipleship Training in Luke's Gospel* (Pasadena, CA: JesusWalk, 2010), 235.

8. Ibid., 236.

9. Andrew Nugent Dugger and Clarence Orville Dodd, *A History of True Religion: Traced from 33 AD to Date* (Salem, WV: The Andrew Dugger Republishing Project, 1936), 15–22.

10. From veteran missionary Louise Chapman Robinson (African missionary: 1920–1940). Quoted in Brennan Manning, *The Signature of Jesus* (Portland, OR: Multnomah, 2004), 156.

11. John Piper, *Don't Waste Your Life* (Wheaton, IL: Crossway, 2003), 10.

12. Jim and Elizabeth Elliot, *The Journals of Jim Elliot* (Grand Rapids: Fleming Revel, 2002), 123.

13. Ibid., 176 (emphasis added).

14. Quoted by Alvin Reid, "Willing to Die, Ready to Live," Sept 2, 2005, Crossmap.com (accessed August 1, 2006).

10

Disciple Making Is . . .

Forsaking All to Follow Jesus: Development

Dave Earley

Follow Me

The call to discipleship is an invitation into an amazing adventure. It is anything but boring, stuffy, routine, or dull. It is an adrenaline-laced, breathless attempt to keep up with a reckless Messiah. Following Jesus means that in addition to surrendering to Him, you must also develop your walk with Him.

When the disciples followed Jesus, they followed a man who walked on water, fed thousands with a boy's lunch, and raised the dead. They followed a man who defied the religious structures of their day and rescued captives from the demonic dungeons.

Jesus said, "Follow *Me*." Jesus did not say, "Follow a set of rules" or "Follow a series of rituals." He said, "Follow *Me*." Discipleship is an intensely personal pursuit. Make no mistake about it. Being a disciple of Jesus is more than adding a new set of activities to your already busy life. Being a disciple of Jesus is first and foremost a response to His call to pursue *Him* passionately.

The call "Follow Me" is the essence, heartbeat, challenge, and adventure of discipleship. It is a formal challenge to live with, learn from, and study under Rabbi Jesus. It is a call to be close to Him, obey His teachings, take the same path He takes, and walk the same road He walked. It involves daily growth and development at the expense of personal comfort. It demands absolute abandonment of all else in order to pursue Jesus fully. This chapter will go deeper into stage two of the discipleship process (development), exploring what it means to follow Jesus.

Forsake All Else to Follow Me

The common command in Jesus' initial encounter with His disciples was "Follow Me." In chapter 6, we discussed how Jesus opened His relationship with His future disciples with the challenge "Follow Me" (John 1:43). In chapter 7, when Jesus formally invited Simon, Andrew, James, and John into a rabbi/disciple relationship, He did so with the words *"Follow Me, . . . and I will make you fish for people!"* (Matt 4:19). Jesus issued the same call again, tying it with the proclamation that the Father was leading Him to the cross. He said, "If anyone wants to come with Me, he must deny himself, take up his cross daily, and *follow Me"* (Luke 9:23).

As Jesus neared His crucifixion, He again issued the call to pursue Him and again linked it to His impending death. This time He added the promise that just as His crucifixion would lead to a great, God-honoring harvest, so could theirs:

> Jesus replied to them, "The hour has come for the Son of Man to be glorified. I assure you: Unless a grain of wheat falls to the ground and dies, it remains by itself. But if it dies, it produces a large crop. The one who loves his life will lose it, and the one who hates his life in this world will keep it for eternal life. If anyone serves Me, he must *follow Me.* Where I am, there My servant also will be. If anyone serves Me, the Father will honor him." (John 12:23–26)

After His resurrection, Jesus appeared to a handful of His disciples on a beach at the Sea of Galilee. His primary goal in that encounter was to recommission Peter to a life of disciple making. After denying Jesus three times, Peter felt unworthy. Yet Jesus issued him a second chance and a renewed calling (John 21:15–17). This time, Jesus specifically told Peter that following Him would lead to a cross:

> He asked him the third time, "Simon, son of John, do you love Me?" Peter was grieved that He asked him the third time, "Do you love Me?" He said, "Lord, You know everything! You know that I love You." "Feed My sheep," Jesus said. "I assure you: When you were young, you would tie your belt and walk wherever you wanted. But when you grow old, you will stretch out your hands and someone else will tie you and

carry you where you don't want to go." He said this to signify by what kind of death he would glorify God. After saying this, He told him, "*Follow Me!*" (John 21:17–19)

Jesus' statement, "You will stretch out your hands and someone else will tie you and carry you where you don't want to go," was understood as a description of crucifixion. Peter's reply is somewhat expected:

So Peter turned around and saw the disciple Jesus loved following them. [That disciple] was the one who had leaned back against Jesus at the supper and asked, "Lord, who is the one that's going to betray You?" When Peter saw him, he said to Jesus, "Lord—what about him?" "If I want him to remain until I come," Jesus answered, "what is that to you? As for you, *follow Me.*" (John 21:20–22)

Jesus told Peter that every disciple had his own path to take. Every disciple had his own price to pay. The point is not to compare your cost with someone else's. The point is to be certain that you follow Jesus, no matter the cost. I agree with Oswald Chambers, who said, "Be reckless for Jesus!"[1]

The Cost of Following

Inherent in the decision to follow Jesus is the choice to forsake other things to do so. There is a cost to following Jesus. Any disciple-making strategy that merely adds Jesus to already busy lives is doomed for failure. Potential disciples must be called to forsake all to follow Jesus. Oswald Chambers writes, "The great word to Jesus' disciples is Abandon."[2]

When we follow Jesus we must realize that we abandon everything to Him and develop for Him. Not everyone wants to pay the price to follow Jesus. For example, Luke briefly recorded three incidents when those Jesus called made excuses and refused to follow:

As they were traveling on the road someone said to Him, "I will follow You wherever You go!" Jesus told him, "Foxes have dens, and birds of the sky have nests, but the Son of Man has no place to lay His head." Then He said to another, "*Follow Me.*" "Lord," he said, "first let me go bury my father." But He told him, "Let the dead bury their own dead, but you go and spread the news of the kingdom of God." Another also said, "I will follow You, Lord, but first let me go and say good-bye to those at my house." But Jesus said to him, "No one who puts his hand to the plow and looks back is fit for the kingdom of God." (Luke 9:57–62)

The Rich Young Ruler

One day, Jesus was walking from Jericho up the hill to Jerusalem when He was approached by a wealthy young man who had ascended to the highly esteemed place of leadership in the synagogue. Even though the young man had climbed the ladder of religious success, he sensed that it was not enough. Something was lacking (Matt 19:20). So he sought out the most popular rabbi in the region: Jesus. Mark 10:17 records the encounter: "As He was setting out on a journey, a man ran up, knelt down before Him, and asked Him, 'Good Teacher, what must I do to inherit eternal life?'"

It is important for you to understand that this was an actual encounter. It is not a parable or a story, but involved a real young man who was boldly confronted with the cost of following Jesus. There is a cost to following Jesus. The young man felt a hole in his life and wanted to know what else he needed to do in order to experience eternal life. Instead of telling him to believe and be saved, Jesus hit him with an unexpected question and comment: "'Why do you call Me good?' Jesus asked him. 'No one is good but One—God'" (Mark 10:18).

What was Jesus doing? I think He was striking at the core of this young man's pride. As a synagogue leader, the young man would certainly have known Psalm 14:3: "There is no one who does good, not even one" (see Pss 12:1; 53:3). Yet Jesus wanted him to see that moral goodness is not relative or casual. True goodness is an absolute that is possessed only by God. To make this clear, Jesus pointed him to the second level of the Ten Commandments (see Exod 20:12–16):

> You know the commandments: Do not murder; do not commit adultery; do not steal; do not bear false witness; do not defraud; honor your father and mother. (Mark 10:19)

The purpose of the law is to serve as a means of crushing our pride and pointing us to the need for a Savior. The young man totally missed it. He tipped his hand, revealing his pride and his self-righteousness: "He said to Him, 'Teacher, I have kept all these from my youth'" (Mark 10:20). Then, like a detective unveiling a murderer, Jesus showed that this outwardly good young man was actually an idolater who ardently loved another god:

> Then, looking at him, Jesus loved him and said to him, "You lack one thing: Go, sell all you have and give to the poor, and you will have treasure in heaven. Then come, *follow Me*." But he was stunned at this demand, and he went away grieving, because he had many possessions. (Mark 10:21–22)

This young man had originally approached Jesus asking what he needed to do to inherit eternal life. He wanted to know what else he lacked on his resume. Jesus gave him an answer that burst his pride and exposed his heart: "You lack one thing: Go, sell all you have and give to the poor, and you will have treasure in heaven. Then come, follow Me."

When Jesus exposed him to the cost of discipleship, the young man balked. He was unwilling to love God with all of his heart, soul, mind, and strength because he loved something else more: possessions—"He went away grieving, because he had many possessions."

Maybe this makes you uncomfortable. True discipleship is following the *real* Jesus, not one we have conjured up in our minds and with whom we are more comfortable. The Jesus described in the Bible made a whip and chased people out of the temple because they were not using it as a house of prayer for all nations. The Jesus the disciples preached on the day of Pentecost publically damned the Pharisees to hell. The Jesus whom we serve was beaten beyond recognition and hung as a cursed criminal on an ugly cross. Real discipleship demands that we follow the real Jesus, and He demands that we forsake all to follow Him.

Maybe your defense is that Jesus' command to sell everything and give it to the poor was an isolated incident. I have had a few people tell me they did not have to obey this command because Jesus only said it to one guy, the rich young ruler. But Jesus only told one guy that he needed to be born again (John 3:1–7), yet we view that as binding on us all, as we should. Moreover, this episode with the wealthy synagogue leader is *not* the only time Jesus told someone to sell everything and give it to the poor. For example, in Luke 12 Jesus told His disciples the same thing, linking it with seeking first His kingdom:

> Then He said to His disciples . . . "But seek His kingdom, and these
> things will be provided for you. Don't be afraid, little flock, because
> your Father delights to give you the kingdom. *Sell your possessions and
> give to the poor.* Make money-bags for yourselves that won't grow old,
> an inexhaustible treasure in heaven, where no thief comes near and no
> moth destroys. For where your treasure is, there your heart will be also."
> (Luke 12:22, 31–34)

Maybe you don't like this passage of Scripture. It seems too much, too steep, too costly. Let's think about it. If Jesus really is worth more than everything else, then it only makes sense to forsake everything else to follow Him.

Hate Your Family

We live in an American church culture that seemingly values doing and saying anything necessary to gather and keep as large a crowd as possible. The underlying notion is that the bigger the crowd, the better the church. The more popular the speaker, then the more godly and blessed he or she must be. Yet, Jesus was set on making disciples, not merely getting a crowd. In fact, He often seemed set on thinning the crowd. For example, read this challenge in Luke 14:25–26:

> Now great crowds were traveling with Him. So He turned and said to them: "If anyone comes to Me and does not hate his own father and mother, wife and children, brothers and sisters—yes, and even his own life—he cannot be My disciple."

Did He really say that? Hate your father and mother? Hate your wife and kids? Hate your siblings? Hate yourself? Yes, He did. Certainly He didn't mean "hate," did He?

J. D. Pentecost has a rather lengthy discussion of this passage in his book, *Design for Discipleship*. He argues that in this passage Jesus "is not dealing with affections, he rather is dealing with the area of authority in a man's life."[3] He observes that "our Lord is dealing here with a question of authority. He is dealing with the question of the right to rule, the question of whom and with whom we are yoked."[4] Pentecost paraphrases Luke 14:26 as follows:

> Jesus says, If a man hears my invitation and comes to me and is not willing to set aside every authority which would seek to exercise its authority over him and submit absolutely and finally to my authority, he cannot be my disciple.[5]

So the question is this: who really is the authority in your life: you, your family, your possessions, or Jesus?

Jesus is Lord. That is a fact. Disciples are simply people who recognize that fact and live it out when tough choices must be made. They are continually involved in a life of developing and maturing in Christ.

Pentecost uses the discussion of Jacob and Esau from Mal 1:1–2 to show that the biblical contrast between "love" and "hate" is a matter of choice. God *loved* (chose) Jacob and *hated* (did not choose) Esau. Pentecost also mentions that a Jewish father, when adopting a child, was said to *love* the one he chose and *hate* those he did not choose. It was not a matter of affection or emotion, but of purpose and will.[6]

Sometimes the best way to interpret Scripture is by comparing it with other Scriptures. Consider this: after His discussion with the rich, young ruler, Jesus had a debriefing time with His disciples. He mentioned the cost of discipleship as it impacted family relationships, but this time He included a promise:

> Peter began to tell Him, "Look, we have left everything and *followed* You." "I assure you," Jesus said, "there is no one who has left house, brothers or sisters, mother or father, children, or fields because of Me and the gospel, who will not receive 100 times more, now at this time—houses, brothers and sisters, mothers and children, and fields, with persecutions—and eternal life in the age to come. But many who are first will be last, and the last first." (Mark 10:28–31)

Disciples choose to forsake all in order to follow Jesus. Jesus promises that the Father rewards such a choice one hundred times over. So when it comes right down to it, will you choose Jesus above your family? When push comes to shove, will you choose Jesus above yourself? If God calls you to overseas missions, will you leave your family and go? If God calls you to leave your career to follow Him into a fulltime life of disciple making, will you do it?

Count the Cost

In Luke 14:28–33, Jesus continued His commentary on the price of discipleship by challenging His hearers to count the cost:

> For which of you, wanting to build a tower, doesn't first sit down and calculate the cost to see if he has enough to complete it? . . . "Or what king, going to war against another king, will not first sit down and decide if he is able with 10,000 to oppose the one who comes against him with 20,000? . . . In the same way, therefore, every one of you who does not say good-bye to all his possessions cannot be My disciple.

Sell Out! Give All!

I mentioned earlier how C. T. Studd was the most outstanding cricket player in England at the end of the nineteenth century. By 1882, he was considered one of the best cricket players in the world and, probably, the best known athlete of his day in England. However, in 1884, after his brother George became seriously ill, Studd was confronted by the question: "What is all the fame and flattery worth when a man must face eternity?"[7]

His brother's illness had a profound impact on him. Consequently, and against the wishes of his family, he decided to forsake fame to serve the Lord through missionary work in China. Along with six other students from Cambridge (together they became known as "the Cambridge Seven"), Studd served as a pioneer missionary under Hudson Taylor with the China Inland Mission.

On his twenty-fifth birthday, Studd inherited $145,000, a vast fortune in that day. He had already determined it would all go into the work of the Lord. He sent out huge checks to several ministries and gave the rest to his new wife, Priscilla.

Priscilla, who also viewed herself as a disciple of Jesus, refused. She said, "Charlie, what did the Lord tell the rich young man to do?" "Sell all." "Well then, we will start clear with the Lord at our wedding."[8] They proceeded to give all of the rest of the money away for the Lord's work.

After ten years in China, Studd and his family began a ministry in India, hoping the climate would be better for his asthma. The Lord used them greatly as people were converted to Jesus every single week. After nearly a decade in India, they returned to England because of his wife's health. There, Studd heard about the urgent need for missionaries in the wild, unexplored interior of Africa. He was fifty years old and had become something of a Christian celebrity in England. Yet, after discussing it with his now nearly invalid wife, Priscilla, they agreed that he should go to Africa without her. She would stay home and recruit others to join him.

Studd left his family in England, compelled to go where no Christian had ever been before. He went into the fiercest place on earth in order to take the gospel to those who needed to hear. One of the last messages he gave in England was on counting the cost:

> What are the conditions? They are the same, "Sell out!"
>
> God's price is one. There is no discount. He gives all to such as give all.
>
> "All! All! Death to ALL the world, ALL the flesh, to the devil, and perhaps to the worst enemy of all: YOURSELF!" . . . I don't care what happens to me, life or death, aye, or hell, so long as my Lord Jesus is glorified![9]

⟶ Questions to Ponder ⟵

1. When it comes to your life . . . who is your authority?
2. What does the phrase "hate your father and mother" really mean?
3. How can you show that Christ is your authority?
4. Are you developing in your walk with Christ?
5. What does your development involve?

Notes

1. Oswald Chambers, quoted in David McCasland, *Oswald Chambers: Abandoned to God* (Grand Rapids, MI: Discovery House, 1993), 160.

2. Oswald Chambers, *Studies in the Sermon on the Mount* (Fort Washington, PA: The Christian Literature Crusade, 1960), 137.

3. J. D. Pentecost, *Design for Discipleship* (Grand Rapids, MI: Zondervan, 1971), 67.

4. Ibid.

5. Ibid., 68.

6. Ibid.

7. C. T. Studd, quoted in Norman P. Grubb, *C. T. Studd: Cricketeer and Pioneer* (Fort Washington, PA: Christian Literature Crusade, 1985), 34.

8. Pricilla Studd, quoted in Norman P. Grubb, *C. T. Studd*, 66–67.

9. C. T. Studd, "The Chocolate Soldier or Heroism—The Lost Chord of Christianity" on Wholesome Words, http://www.wholesomewords.org/missions/msctserm.html (accessed February 12, 2012).

11

Disciple Making Is . . .

Abiding in Jesus and
Bearing Fruit: Deployment

Dave Earley

The Unfruitful

We have all met them. They are nice, clean, friendly people who have been to numerous Christian seminars, completed dozens of Christian courses, and filled out a vast variety of workbooks. They attend church services faithfully. They do not drink, smoke, cuss, or gamble. Many even have diplomas from Christian schools of higher learning. Yet, they have never led a person to Christ. Jesus is not living evidently *through* them. They would have no idea how to start and lead a missional home group focused on reaching their neighborhood with the gospel. They are not making disciples. Are they disciples?

According to the Gospels, discipleship is about much more than the accumulation of information. True discipleship always results in spiritual *transformation* and *reproduction*. It must lead to loving, community penetration. It ultimately ends up catalyzing spiritual multiplication and church planting. This chapter will go deeper into stage three of the discipleship process (*deployment*), exploring the importance of abiding in Jesus and bearing fruit.

No Fruit, No Discipleship: The Proof of Disciple Making Is Continual Fruit Bearing

It was His final address to His disciples before His crucifixion. Jesus and His disciples are in the garden of Gethsemane. Fresh on His mind was the departure of Judas, who would betray Him. Jesus used the analogy of a vine and branches to teach about the nature of true discipleship (John 15:1–16). In the image, He is the vine and we are the branches. In this address, He made two major points. First, the proof of discipleship is fruit bearing (John 15:8). Second, the power to bear fruit flows from Jesus as the disciple stays vitally connected to Him (John 15:4–5).

Let's start with the first point. John 15:8 summarizes, "My Father is glorified by this: that you produce much *fruit* and *prove to be My disciples.*" Our ultimate goal in life is, of course, to glorify God (chap. 1). But how is this done? Jesus said that God is glorified as we are producing fruit, *and* it is in producing fruit that we prove to be His disciples. According to Jesus, the measure of discipleship is not the number of seminars attended, workbooks finished, certificates earned, or courses completed. The measure of discipleship is fruit. No fruit, no discipleship.

Repeatedly in this teaching, Jesus mentioned the importance of fruit bearing in the life of the disciple (eight times in this passage). In fact, in His mind, the notion of a sterile branch was unacceptable. For the disciple, fruit bearing is so significant that Jesus states, hyperbolically, that the branch that failed to produce fruit is removed and cast into the fire. His point is clear: No fruit, no discipleship:

> Every branch in Me that does not produce fruit He removes, and He prunes every branch that produces fruit so that it will produce more fruit. . . . If anyone does not remain in Me, he is thrown aside like a branch and he withers. They gather them, throw them into the fire, and they are burned. (John 15:2, 6)

The *measuring mark* of discipleship is fruit bearing. No fruit, no discipleship. Jesus also made it clear that the *purpose* of discipleship is fruit bearing. John 15:16 states, "I appointed you that you should *go out and produce fruit* and that your fruit should remain." He appointed disciples *with the express purpose* that they would bear fruit.

Jesus said His disciples were chosen that they may "go and produce fruit." Of course, later He would make this commission even more explicit when He said, "Go, therefore, and make disciples of all nations" (Matt 28:19–20). Fruit bearing is the purpose of discipleship. The difference between effective and ineffective disciple making is the issue of what you are training this person to *be* and what you are equipping this person to *do*. Disciples are made to *be* something (fruit bearers) and *do* something (bear fruit). Therefore, if you are not bearing fruit, you are not a disciple.

The use of present tense verbs throughout the passage implies that fruit bearing is a continual, ongoing, unceasing reality in the life of the disciple. The evidence of discipleship is not merely bearing fruit once upon a time, way back in the day. The expectation for disciples is that they will *continuously* bear fruit.

Therefore, if you are not continuously bearing fruit, you are not a disciple.

What Is Fruit Bearing?

Since the mark of discipleship is continuous fruit bearing, the question becomes: What is fruit bearing? "Fruit" in this chapter is a broad term that embraces at least four aspects. First, from the context, there is *the spiritual fruit of Christlike love*. John Piper writes:

> Since the fruit is simply the out-forming of what has passed through the branch from the vine, we should ask, What is it that we receive from the vine? Jesus' answer is *love*. Abiding in Jesus means abiding in his love . . . according to verse 9—"As the Father has loved me, so have I loved you. Abide in my love." "Abide in me" is replaced by "Abide in my love," and this shows more specifically what we receive when we are united to the vine, namely, the sap of divine love. And it stands to reason, then, that what we receive from the vine flows through the branch and crops out in the fruit of love, for the nourishment and refreshment of other people.[1]

Second, there is *the fruit of the Spirit: love, joy, peace, patience, kindness, goodness, faith, gentleness, self-control* (Gal 5:22–23). Obviously, as the life of Jesus streams through the disciple (Gal 2:20; Col 1:27), the character of Jesus will be formed in the disciple.

Third, there is the *fruit of spiritual gifts*. The purpose of spiritual gifts is that the body of Christ will be edified (see Eph 4:12 NKJV). When a disciple discovers, develops, and uses his or her gift, the body of Christ grows stronger. The fruit of a healthy, mature body, then, is the ability to reproduce new churches!

Fourth, and most importantly, there is *the fruit of new disciples*. Just as the fruit of a healthy apple tree is apples, and the fruit of a healthy orange tree is oranges, the fruit of a healthy disciple is more disciples. In the immediate context of John 15:16, Jesus links fruit bearing with disciple making:

You did not choose Me, but I chose you. I appointed you that you
should *go out and produce fruit* and that your *fruit* should remain, so
that whatever you ask the Father in My name, He will give you.

Earlier, after His evangelistic episode with the Samaritan woman, Jesus
gave His disciples a challenge that clearly links fruit bearing with evangelism
and disciple making. John 4:35–36 records Jesus saying:

"Don't you say, 'There are still four more months, then comes the
harvest'? Listen to what I'm telling you: Open your eyes and look at the
fields, for they are ready for harvest. The reaper is already receiving pay
and gathering *fruit* for eternal life, so the sower and reaper can rejoice
together."

In this incident, Jesus links fruit bearing with evangelism. He had just finished
introducing the woman to the truth of His identity, the result of which was her
testimony to others who also believed in Him (John 4:39).

So, Jesus told us that an evidence of discipleship is continual fruit bearing.
Disciples bear spiritual fruit and do so continuously. The fruit comes in the
form of Christlike love, Christian character, and most importantly, other
Christians. Yet, such fruit is supernatural. It is the outflow of Jesus Himself in
the disciple's life. How does a human produce supernatural fruit?

No Abiding, No Fruit: The Key to Bearing Fruit Continually Is Staying Constantly Connected to Jesus

The proof of discipleship is continuous fruit bearing (John 15:8). The
power to bear fruit continually flows from Jesus as the disciple stays vitally
connected to Him. Jesus states in John 15:4–5:

Remain in Me, and I in you. Just as a branch is unable to produce fruit by
itself unless it *remains* on the vine, so neither can you unless you *remain* in
Me. I am the vine; you are the branches. The one who *remains* in Me and I
in him produces much fruit, because you can do nothing without Me.

As the branch stays closely connected to the vine, the life-giving, fruit-produc-
ing sap flows into it and surges out of it in the form of fruit. Jesus is the vine.
As a disciple stays attached to Him, His life pours into them and explodes out
of them as spiritual fruit. That fruit takes the form of compassion, character,
and converts.

Jesus made His point clear. Just as a branch is merely a dead and useless
piece of wood without its connection to the vine, so also a disciple is destined

to barrenness apart from a close connection to Him. Without actively pursuing intimacy with Him, the disciple has no hope of bearing spiritual fruit. The vital communion between the disciple and Jesus is of such importance that Jesus mentioned it ten times in John 15:4–10. There is no discipleship without fruit bearing, and there is no fruit bearing without abiding in Christ.

On the one hand, Jesus maintains it is impossible to live the fruitful life without abiding in Him. He stated, "Just as a branch is unable to produce fruit by itself unless it remains on the vine, so neither can you unless you remain in Me" (John 15:4). He also said, "You can do nothing without Me" (John 15:5). On the other hand, Jesus promised, "The one who remains in Me and I in him produces much fruit" (John 15:5). The key to producing fruit is abiding in Christ.

"He Was in God All the Time"

As founder and director of the China Inland Mission, Hudson Taylor endured incredible stress. He had the continual pressure of raising money and recruiting workers from England while living in China. He saw his missionaries deal with severe deprivation and persecution, many to the point of martyrdom. Shortly after sending his children back to England to be cared for because the conditions in China were too dangerous, he saw his young wife and newborn son die. Yet somehow he remained calm, peaceful, and full of faith. His passion to reach "every creature" continued contagiously, engulfing others and bearing fruit.

How did he do it? His biographer records the words of a friend who wrote:

> Dwelling in Christ, he drew upon His very being and resources . . . and this he did by an attitude of faith as simple as it was continuous. . . . He was in God all the time and God in him. It was the true "abiding" of John fifteen.[2]

For Hudson Taylor, this disciple life of abiding in the vine produced a great harvest. At his death, his mission agency included 205 mission stations with more than 800 missionaries and 125,000 Chinese Christians. So, if an ongoing connection to Jesus is so absolutely essential for the disciple, the question is how to do it? Jesus gives three requirements:

1. Abiding in the Word of Jesus

John 15:2–3 states, "He prunes every branch that produces fruit so that it will produce more fruit. You are already clean because of the word I have spoken to you."

The wise vinedresser knows that pruning back the vine produces more fruit. He or she will cut off the superficial, sap-draining branches in order for all of the life-giving sap to flow to those branches that have the greatest potential to bear fruit. Jesus promised that the Father (the vinedresser) will prune us in order that we may bear more fruit. He also told us the tool He uses to prune us is His words.

As we read, study, memorize, and meditate on the words of Jesus, the Holy Spirit will use them to cut us with conviction (Heb 4:12). As we agree with God about our sins and repent of them, He is faithful to cleanse, or prune, all unrighteousness (1 John 1:9). (The word translated "cleanse" in 1 John 1:9 and "prune" in John 15:2–3 is the same in the Greek: *kathairo*.) This cleansing allows us to experience more of Jesus flowing through our lives and, as a result, see more fruit produced.

Also in John 15:7, Jesus spoke of the disciple remaining in Him and His words remaining in them. According to John Piper, this command means: "Keep on trusting my word. Keep on trusting what I have revealed to you about myself and my Father and my work."[3]

Jesus also spoke of the essential element of *obeying* His words: "If you keep My commands you will remain in My love, just as I have kept My Father's commands and remain in His love" (John 15:10). Earlier, Jesus had also linked discipleship with abiding in, trusting, obeying, and experiencing His words.

> As He was saying these things, many believed in Him. So Jesus said to
> the Jews who had believed Him, "If you *continue in My word*, you really
> are My disciples. You will know the truth, and the truth will set you
> free." (John 8:30–32)

When Jesus commanded the disciples to "continue" in His word, He used the same word He mentioned ten times in John 15. It means to "abide" or "remain." Here in John 8, the condition for discipleship is continuing in Jesus' word, thereby intimately experiencing the truth and freedom it produces.

It is worth noting that in each of these verses (John 8:31; 15:2–3, 7, 10) Jesus speaks of *His* words. Of course all of Scripture is His word because He is God. Could it be that a forgotten element of discipleship is that, while not ignoring the rest of Scripture, the fruit-bearing disciple focuses especially on the words of Jesus?

Fruitful disciples abide in Christ by investing time meeting God daily in the Word and prayer. Joel Comiskey researched the largest, fastest growing cell churches in the world. He surveyed the cell-group leaders of these churches looking for common denominators of those who were fruitful and those who were not. Interestingly, he found that spiritual gifts, personality types, education, and income levels had no impact on fruitfulness.

His survey revealed an interesting correlation between time spent in prayer and the multiplication of small groups. It revealed that those who spent ninety minutes or more in daily devotions multiplied their groups twice as much as those who spent less than half an hour.[4]

According to his biographer, Hudson Taylor's life was "full of joy and power." Taylor discovered the secret of fruitfulness "in daily, hourly fellowship with God, and this he found could only be maintained by secret prayer and feeding upon the Word."[5] The biographer continued, "From two to four AM was the time he usually gave to prayer, the time he could be most sure of being undisturbed to wait upon God."[6] Taylor himself counseled:

> Take time. Give God time to reveal Himself to you. Give yourself time to be silent and quiet before Him, waiting to receive through the Spirit, the assurance of the His presence with you, His power working through you. Take time to read His Word as in His presence, that from it you may know what He asks of you and what He promises you. Let the Word create around you, create within you a holy atmosphere, a holy heavenly light, in which your soul will be refreshed and strengthened for the work of daily life.[7]

2. Living in Absolute Dependency on Christ

As we have discussed earlier, the disciple cannot bear fruit apart from Jesus. In John 15:4–5 Jesus states:

> Remain in Me, and I in you. Just as a branch is unable to produce fruit by itself unless it remains on the vine, so neither can you unless you remain in Me. I am the vine; you are the branches. The one who remains in Me and I in him produces much fruit, because you can do nothing without Me.

Self-sufficiency and independence will not produce spiritual fruit. Only the life of Jesus produces spiritual fruit. On their own, no disciple can fabricate or replicate the life of Jesus. The only way to produce fruit is to be so closely connected to Jesus, the Vine, that His life flows though you. Everything we try to do without Jesus ultimately comes to nothing unless it is done as a result of a conscious, abiding, dependence upon Him (John 15:5). Experiencing His power to produce fruit is always a result of ongoing faith and prayer.

3. Dying to Everything Other Than Jesus

The goal of a disciple is to glorify God by multiplying disciples. This is a high and lofty goal not easily achieved. In fact, multiplication is only accomplished one way—death. Previously, Jesus had stated in John 12:24–26:

> I assure you: Unless a grain of wheat falls to the ground and dies, it
> remains by itself. But if *it dies, it produces a large crop.* The one who
> loves his life will lose it, and the one who hates his life in this world will
> keep it for eternal life. If anyone serves Me, he must follow Me.

Hudson Taylor saw the life of Christ in him powerfully multiplied to the point of producing hundreds of missionaries, hundreds of Chinese church leaders, and thousands of new disciples. He lived keenly aware of the price:

> An easy, non-self-denying life will never be one of power. Fruit-bearing
> involves cross-bearing. There are not two Christs; an easy-going one
> for easy-going Christians and a suffering one toiling for exceptional
> believers. There is only one Christ. Are you willing to abide in *Him*, and
> thus bear much fruit?[8]

Being a disciple requires abiding in Jesus and bearing spiritual fruit. Fruit-bearing is the purpose and evidence of discipleship. The power for fruit bearing comes only from continuously abiding in Christ. Abiding includes living in His Word, depending upon Him in prayer, and dying to everything that is not Jesus.

Is there an evident increase in love, joy, and peace in your life?

Are you using your spiritual gift in the body of Christ?

Are you currently bearing spiritual fruit?

Who is following Jesus today as a spiritual fruit of your life?

Is successful evangelism something that used to be true in your life, or is it true in your life today?

– Questions to Ponder –

1. Finish this phrase: "No fruit, no . . ."
2. What are the four different types of fruit mentioned in this chapter?
3. What is your strongest area of "fruit" production?
4. What is your weakest area of "fruit" production?
5. What can you do to improve your weak area?

Notes

1. John Piper, from sermon given October 11, 1981 at Bethlehem Baptist Church, http://www.desiringgod.org/resource-library/sermons/i-chose-you-to-bear-fruit (accessed October 22, 2011).

2. Hudson Taylor, quoted by Howard Taylor, *Hudson Taylor's Spiritual Secret* (Chicago: Moody, 1989), 231–32.

3. John Piper, *What Jesus Demands* (Wheaton, IL: Crossway, 2006), 65.

4. Joel Comiskey, *Leadership Explosion* (Houston, TX: TOUCH, 2000), 38.

5. Hudson Taylor, quoted in Howard Taylor, *Hudson Taylor's Spiritual Secret*, 238.

6. Ibid.

7. Ibid., 239.

8. Ibid., 239–40.

Part 3

Disciple-Making Methods: Making a Disciple

So far we have looked at the biblical and theological foundations of what it means to be a disciple of, and make disciples for, Jesus (part 1). We have also examined what Jesus Himself had to say to those who would follow Him (part 2). The basics of the disciple-making process progress through a series of stages from declaration, to development, to deployment. In this section, we will take time to explore some disciple-making methods.

This section will build on the biblical, theological, and philosophical foundations of disciple making. It will also explain and illustrate how to apply the teachings of Jesus and explore the disciple-making methods of Jesus. The focus is on demonstrating that Jesus was extremely intentional in His approach to developing His followers.

12

Disciple Making Is . . .

Discerning the Power of Multiplication

Dave Earley

An Unstoppable Force

The first church in history was an unstoppable force. From the birth of the church in Jerusalem in AD 30 until the end of the first century, the Great Commission was being fulfilled. From the 500 brethren who witnessed the resurrected Christ (1 Corinthians 15) and the 120 men and women meeting in the upper room to pray at Pentecost (Acts 1:13–15), the church multiplied to more than *one million* followers of Jesus in seventy years.[1] The church spread from Jerusalem, through Judea, to Samaria, across the Roman Empire, and into Asia and Africa. Eventually, the Roman Empire, the most dominant world power in history, yielded to the power of the church.

All of this growth was facilitated without mass media, without advertising, without church buildings, and without seminaries. The primitive church expanded at a rate never equaled in the nineteen centuries since.[2]

How did this happen? Jesus made disciples who made disciples. In other words, He multiplied.

Never Underestimate the Power of Multiplication

Addition is good, but multiplication is better. If you win someone to Jesus, you have added someone to the kingdom. You have not multiplied *until* that person is winning people to Jesus who are winning people to Jesus. Addition produces incremental growth, but multiplication produces exponential growth.

Never underestimate the power of multiplication to fulfill the Great Commission. When you totally commit yourself to a life of radical discipleship, and making disciples, you can unleash an unstoppable force. Walter Henrichsen writes:

> Some time ago there was a display at the Museum of Science and Industry in Chicago. It featured a checkerboard with 1 grain of wheat on the first, 2 on the second, 4 on the third, then 8, 16, 32, 64, 128, etc. Somewhere down the board, there were so many grains of wheat on the square that some were spilling over into neighboring squares.
>
> Above the checkerboard display was a question: At this rate of doubling every square, how much grain would be on the checkerboards by the 64th square? To find the answer to this riddle, you punched a button on the console in front of you, and the answer flashed on a little screen above the board: Enough to cover the entire subcontinent of India 50 feet deep.[3]

If you want to make a huge impact, implement the power of multiplication.

The *slow* process of raising multiplying leaders is the *fastest* way to fulfill the Great Commission. Walter Henrichsen noted, "Multiplication may be costly, and in the initial stages, much slower than addition, but in the long run, it is the most effective way of accomplishing Christ's Great Commission . . . and the only way."[4] The world is growing by multiplication, and yet, too often the church is trying to grow through addition. In order to catch up with, and keep pace with, the multiplying population of the world, we must multiply multipliers.

For example, in an addition model, you reach a person this year and another next year and another one the year after that. The number of believers has added from one to two after year one, from two to three after year two, from three to four after year three, and is poised to go to five the fourth year. In a multiplication model, you reach a person this year and train them to reach others. You both reach people in year two and train them to reach others. In the third year, all of you reach another and train them to reach others. The number of Christ followers goes from one to two after year two, then multiplies to four after year three, and then multiplies to eight after year four.

Reaching that fourth generation by addition leaves you with *four believers.* Reaching the fourth generation by multiplication leaves you with *eight disciple makers.* Which is better, four believers or eight disciple makers with that number going to sixteen in the next year? The Great Commission does not say, "Go make *believers.*" It says, "Go make *disciples.*" It does not call us to add. It challenges us to multiply.

Neil Cole claims that by lowering the bar of how and where church was done, and by raising the bar on what it means to be a disciple, within five years his little house church of twelve disciples in Long Beach, California, grew to sixty-eight organic churches reaching five generations of churches. The mother church had daughter churches, granddaughter churches, great-granddaughter churches, and great-great-granddaughter churches.[5]

Multiplying disciple makers is a seemingly small, slow, unappreciated process. Waylon Moore notes, "Disciple making has no prestige rating, no denominational category; but the results are consistently better than anything I have experienced in thirty years of working with people."[6] By using this small process of multiplication, we can have a big impact. By using the slow process of multiplying leaders, we can reach the most people in the least amount of time. We must remember that "we need never fear beginning something quietly and on a small scale. God will cause what is his to grow."[7]

Be Like Jesus

Jesus changed the world. How did a poor carpenter from a forsaken, enslaved nation change the history of the world? He used the power of multiplication. Robert Coleman observes:

> Jesus came to save the world, and to that end He died, but on His way to the cross He concentrated His life on making a few disciples. These men were taught to do the same until through the process of reproduction the gospel of the kingdom would reach to the ends of the earth.[8]

The core of Jesus' ministry was training a handful of Jewish men so He could reach an entire world of Greeks, Romans, Asians, Germans, Indians, Arabs, Latinos, Russians, and Americans. The training of the Twelve was the primary global ministry strategy of Jesus Christ. He knew He would have to leave. He also knew one of His disciples would fail, but He never wavered from His plan. His plan hinged on eleven trained disciple makers. His plan to reach the whole world, over and over, generation after generation, was that simple.

Jesus left His disciples when He ascended into heaven. Yet, His ministry has grown and multiplied many times over because He left behind *multiplying* leaders. Within days after Jesus left, His eleven disciple makers and the seventy other disciples were ready to handle a harvest of three thousand new converts in a citywide network of house churches (Acts 2:41–47). Later, when the Jerusalem church was persecuted and the church scattered, their disciples went everywhere preaching the gospel (Acts 8:1, 4), and churches like the one in Antioch were born (Acts 11:19–20).

What is world-changing ministry? It is anchored in mentoring and multiplying disciples. You can begin spiritually multiplying yourself today and start a dynamic process that could reach beyond you to touch your city. It could stretch past your generation and into the next century. It could reach beyond a handful and eventually touch the world.

One Becomes Eighty Thousand

In 1971, Jerry Falwell hoped to reach the world by starting a Christian university. Forty years later, Liberty University numbers more than eighty thousand students and has graduates serving the Lord on every continent and in almost every nation.

"Produce Reproducers!"

Ten years before World War II touched America, Dawson Trotman rose two hours early every morning and took his Bible and a map to the Sierra Nevada Mountains. For the next forty days, he asked God to multiply his life by multiplying Christian leaders in every state in the United States and every continent. After the forty days of prayer, he began to turn his dream into reality by "training trainers of men."[9]

His commitment to multiplication of leaders was highly effective and strategically designed. Ten years later, by the beginning of World War II, Dawson Trotman and his organization, the Navigators, had trained "key men" for every ship in the United States Navy. He stated, "It thrills me to touch the life of a man who will touch a great host of men. Our best investment is with faithful men who shall be able to teach others also."[10] He believed that the multiplication of leaders was the key to "reaching the greatest number of people in the most effective way in the shortest possible time."[11] His method and his message were simple: produce reproducers.[12]

Multiplying by Twelve in Your Lifetime

In 1983, Cesar Castellanos and his wife, Claudia, launched a church in Bogata, Columbia, with a small group of eight people. Twenty-five years later, the church has more than 250,000 members. How did it happen? Not by addition.

Cesar got a vision for multiplying his life into twelve disciples. Believing that every Christian can mentor and lead twelve people in the Christian faith, he began to meet weekly with twelve young men. He prayed for them and poured his life into them with the primary focus on training each of them to lead twelve others in a small group. The goal of each of their twelve was to find their own twelve and so on. Over the years, the number of leaders in the church continued to multiply by twelve, going from 12 to 144 to 1728 to 32,288.[13]

In order for this model to work, the members must be radically devoted disciples. They must sell out to Jesus and to the vision of multiplying their lives. They must be willing to sacrifice their time. They must spend a great deal of time praying. The members of a group of twelve must meet with their leader every week *and* meet with the twelve they are training every week. The model sustains itself because leaders not only pour into others every week but are also poured into every week. The vision to multiply stays on the forefront as it is reinforced in the weekly meetings.

Multiply by Two

Maybe multiplying by twelve seems a bit staggering to you. The point is not what number you multiply by as much as it is that you do multiply. Over time, the church that Rod Dempsey and I planted multiplied several times over. We began as a church with twelve people meeting as a small group, and in just a few years it grew to 1,400 adults and teens meeting weekly in more than a hundred small groups. We also had the privilege of leading some of our leaders through the discipleship process to the point where they planted new churches. Two of our converts started a daughter church at Ohio State University. That church recently multiplied by planting a daughter church at the University of Pittsburg. One couple planted a church in a nearby suburb and a few years later moved to China to take the gospel there.

We multiplied disciples by asking every small-group leader to multiply by two. This means we asked them to pray-in one potential small-group leader apprentice each year whom they could spend a year training to launch a new group. In this way, one group became two, two groups became four, four groups became eight, and so on. Of course not every group multiplied every year, but even if only half of them did, we still saw our small-group disciple-making ministry grow at a rapid rate. More importantly, we saw the number of disciples in our church multiply.

Be Like Paul

Paul had been a rabbinic disciple of Gamaliel, one of the most prominent rabbis of his day (Acts 22:3). As a young man, Paul had become a leading young Jewish rabbi in his own right (Acts 7:58; 8:1–3). After his conversion, Paul immediately began making disciples. The Scriptures mention more than thirty men and women by name who served as Paul's fellow laborers. Many are described as having lived and travelled with Paul during his thirty years of ministry. These disciples would have also worked alongside of Paul as he did pioneer evangelism and church planting. Some of them no doubt also went out and started churches of their own.

Second Timothy 2:2 illustrates Paul's philosophy of ministry and the necessity of mentoring multipliers. Notice the four generations of spiritual multiplication in this passage: "And what *you* have heard from *me* in the presence of many witnesses, commit to *faithful men* who will be able to teach *others* also."

Even as Paul was busy fulfilling his calling as an apostle to the Gentiles, he also fulfilled the Great Commission by making disciples. He took what the Lord had deposited into him and committed it to faithful men who in turn taught others also. There may have been as many as thirty little "Pauls," or more, doing ministry even after he was imprisoned in Rome.

Disciple making is multiplying your life by investing in "faithful men." God's plan for your life may not be to pastor a megachurch. It may not be for you to become a bestselling author. Without a shadow of a doubt, God's plan is for you to invest everything He has given you into a few "faithful men" (or women) who will then invest in others.

Be a Multiplier

Rod and I want to be up-front with you. Our goal in writing this book is so that you would not only live the radically devoted life of a biblical disciple but also that you would settle for nothing less than a life of intentional disciple making resulting in the multiplication of lives, groups, and churches.

You only have one life. Lost people matter to God. Time is short. Christianity is waning in North America. Do not be content with anything but a life of missional living, disciple making, and multiplication. You can launch an unstoppable force through the power of multiplication. You can start now. Ask God to show you who you can begin to disciple. Build your relationship with them. Then intentionally begin regularly meeting with them, training them to train others.

— Questions to Ponder —

1. Look over this chapter and give one illustration of the power of multiplication.
2. How did Jesus use multiplication?
3. How did the church model multiplication?
4. Are you involved in multiplying disciples?
5. What can you do to multiply new disciples?

Notes

1. David Barrett, ed., *World Christian Encyclopedia: A Comparative Study of Churches and Religions in the Modern World A.D. 1900–2000* (Oxford: Oxford University Press, 1982), 3.

2. Dennis McCallum and Jessica Lowery, *Organic Disciplemaking* (Houston, TX: Touch, 2006), 28.

3. Walter A. Henrichsen, *Disciples Are Made—Not Born* (Wheaton, IL: Victor Books, 1979), 143.

4. Ibid.

5. Neil Cole, *Organic Church* (Grand Rapids: Baker, 2005), 28–29.

6. Waylon B. Moore, *Multiplying Disciples* (Colorado Springs, CO: NavPress, 1981), 5.

7. Ibid., 112.

8. Robert Coleman, quoted by Leroy Eims, *The Lost Art of Disciple Making* (Grand Rapids, MI: Zondervan, 1980), 9.

9. Dawson Trotman, quoted by Betty Skinner, *Daws: the Story of Dawson Trotman, Founder of the Navigators* (Grand Rapids, MI: Zondervan, 1977), 158.

10. Ibid., 250.

11. Ibid., 303.

12. Ibid., 265.

13. For more on this model, see Joel Comiskey, *Groups of 12* (Houston, TX: TOUCH Publications, 1999).

13 Helping Others Go to the Next Level

Dave Earley

Lessons Learned

I have been attempting to follow the Lord's commission to "make disciples" for my entire adult life. It began at age seventeen when I began to follow Jesus and "fish for men" at my large public high school. It continued as I launched discipleship groups in my dorm at college. I spent summers evangelizing and disciple making in markets and coffee shops in England, apartment buildings in Manhattan, and youth groups across the US.

I learned many ways not to do it during my time as an associate and interim pastor at a rural church. Yet, I learned several things that did work during the few years I spent training three hundred small-group leaders for a Christian college and as I started a church that attempted to be based on multiplying small groups through disciple making.

As I look back over a lifetime of disciple making, I have a deeper respect for *the power of the Word of God* to transform people's lives. It is the best curriculum.

I also have a profound esteem for *the power of prayer* in the disciple-making process. The Holy Spirit works mightily in the lives of my disciples as I pray for them and as they pray for others.

I have learned *the power of community* in disciple making. Solo disciple-making efforts are not nearly as effective as the work God does as disciples live in community with one another.

Never underestimate *the power of obedience* to transform a life. I have seen every discipleship effort fail that emphasizes information over obedience.

I have witnessed *the power of ministry involvement* to revolutionize the life of a disciple. On the other hand, I also have seen disciple making fall flat when the disciple is not forced into an environment where they must minister to others.

Beyond all of that, I have learned the hard way *that disciples must be continually pushed to go to the next level*: from believing to immersing, abandoning, and serving; from obeying to multiplying. Letting them stop at level one (belief) will inevitably result in decline in their spiritual lives. Allowing them to stop at level two (immersion) will also never accomplish multiplication and, therefore, will never reach the world.

In many ways the role of the disciple maker is to be a human voice in the ear of the disciple, providing continual encouragement to go to the next level. Disciple makers are sergeants exhorting their troops to take the next hill. They are coaches challenging their best players to keep getting better.

After Jesus' followers believed in Him as Messiah, He did not allow them to rest there. He called them to forsake all, follow Him, and fish for men. As time went on, He kept going back to those themes, adding to them the need to abide in Him so they would have the strength to bear spiritual fruit. He kept showing them the needs of the lost world. He kept calling them to take the gospel to the world. Yet, His task was not finished until they were ready to obey by launching a disciple-making movement of their own—the church.

What If Jesus Had Stopped at Level One?

As we saw in chapter 6, being a fully developed follower of Jesus is a matter of taking the next step. The disciple-making process employed by Jesus was built on three progressive levels of commitment, trust, obedience, and learning. At each step, He demanded greater commitment and gave His followers greater impact. It took the twelve disciples about four years to complete the process.

Jesus led His protégés through three distinct stages: (1) investigation leading to repentance and faith in Jesus (*declaration*); (2) immersion, abandonment, and apprenticeship into ministry (*development*); and (3) intentional global commissioning (*deployment*). We can say that the person who has completed stage one is a *believer*. The product of level two is a *disciple*, and the person who is living at level three is a *disciple maker*.

Stage one—Declaration. After His resurrection, Jesus appeared to five hundred *brethren* at once who believed in Him (1 Cor 15:6). The Gospels record how many of the people whom Jesus encountered believed in Him (John 4:39–41; 10:38; 11:45; Mark 5:18–20; Matt 8:10).

Stage two—Development. Jesus also had seventy disciples who were developed to the point where they could be sent out to evangelize (Luke 10:1–5). We can assume that the people who prayed down Pentecost from the upper room included these men, plus the apostles, plus many of the women who followed Jesus (Acts 1:12–15).

Stage three—Deployment. Jesus poured His life into twelve disciples, also called apostles. He commissioned eleven of them as disciple makers (Matt 28:18–20).

What if Jesus had stopped at level one? What would have happened to Christianity after He ascended into heaven? Christianity would definitely not have spread throughout the world. It probably would have disappeared soon after that first generation of believers passed away.

Why is Christianity on a steep decline in North America? Could it be that, in part, we have failed to take people all the way through the process. We have stopped too soon, failing to lead people past level one?

Our goal in writing this book is not merely to challenge you to go beyond being a believer in Jesus to becoming a disciple. Our goal is to call you to a life of disciple making. It is not enough for you to *believe* in Jesus. It is not enough for you to add new believers to God's kingdom. You must go on and *make disciples* and reproduce disciple makers.

If being a fully developed follower of Jesus is a matter of taking the next step, then being a disciple maker is a matter of *helping others take the next step*. If Jesus led His followers through a three-stage process that resulted in multiplication, why shouldn't we? Below is the chart we introduced earlier that shows the three stages of discipleship requirements that Jesus expected of His followers.

Possibly the most important aspect of this chart is the arrow indicating that a person is to progress from one stage to the next until he or she is eventually going off the chart and into the world. Jesus did not stop at stage one and neither should you or I.

Remember that each time a person takes a step across the chart to the next level there is an increase in commitment. The person moves from leaving

THE DISCIPLESHIP REQUIREMENTS OF JESUS

STAGE ONE	STAGE TWO	STAGE THREE
BELIEVER	DISCIPLE	DISCIPLE MAKER
Will you believe in Jesus? DECLARATION	*Will you follow Jesus?* DEVELOPMENT	*Will you go for Jesus?* DEPLOYMENT
Investigation leading to repentance and faith in Jesus	Immersion, abandonment, and apprenticeship into ministry	Intentional multiplication of leaders
REPENTANCE AND FAITH Committed belief	LOVE AND OBEDIENCE Reckless obedience	MINISTRY AND MISSION Multiplying leader
Savior	Master	Commissioning Officer
Committed believer	Devoted follower	Multiplying leader
Regeneration	Transformation	Reproduction and multiplication
Laying aside your doubts	Leaving your "nets"	Launching out
Coming to Jesus	Being with Jesus	Going for Jesus
SAVED	TRAINED	SENT
Repent and believe the gospel (Mark 1:15; Matt 4:17) You must be born again (John 3:3–8) Drink of living water (John 4:13–14) Love the Lord with all of your heart and love your neighbor as yourself (Matt 22:37–40)	**Follow Jesus and fish for men (Matt 4:18–22)** Be with [Me] and be sent out (Mark 3:13–14) Do the will of God (Mark 3:35) Obey the Sermon on the Mount (Matthew 5–7) Deny yourself, take up your cross, and follow Me (Luke 9:23–27) Follow Me and don't look back (Luke 9:57–62) Continue in My Word (John 8:31–32) Pray for laborers (Matt 9:37–38) Don't worry, don't fear, seek the kingdom, sell possessions, give to the poor, invest in eternity (Luke 12:24–33) Love Jesus more than anything and everything else (Luke 14:25–33) Compel the lost, pursue the lost (Luke 14:16–24; 15:1–7) Follow Jesus and lose your life (Luke 17:32–33) Sell all and give to the poor (Luke 18:18–30) Be the servant of all (Mark 10:43–45) Make Father's house a house of prayer (Mark 11:17) Watch, endure, be ready, use your talents, keep working (Matthew 24–25) Love one another (John 13:34–35)	**Die to multiply (John 12:23–27)** Ask in His name (John 14:14; 15: 16:23–24) Keep His commands (John 14:15, 21–24) Abide in Christ and bear much fruit (John 15:1–8, 16) **Fulfill the Great Commission** Live sent as Jesus lived sent (John 20:21) Feed my sheep, follow Me (John 21:15–20) Preach the gospel to all creatures (Mark 16:15) **Make disciples (Matt 28:19–20)** Be His witness in Jerusalem, Judea, Samaria, and furthest parts of the world (Acts 1:8)

their doubts, to leaving their "nets," to being willing to die as they launch out to take the gospel to the world. Yet, along with this increased commitment comes enhanced impact. In the chart given below, we have the same levels of discipleship, but this time they are viewed through the lens of the disciple maker.

THE DISCIPLE-MAKING STRATEGY OF JESUS

STAGE ONE	STAGE TWO	STAGE THREE
HELP SEEKERS BECOME BELIEVERS Declaring Christ	HELP BELIEVERS BECOME DISCIPLES Developing Everyone	HELP DISCIPLES BECOME DISCIPLE MAKERS Deploying Disciples
Evangelize	*Disciple*	*Train*
1. Intercede—pray for the lost 2. Invest—build a relationship with them 3. Inquire—ask questions and listen 4. Invite—ask for appropriate next step commitments 5. Instruct—proclaim the Gospel 6. Involve—connect them to others on the journey 7. Inspire—encourage them to take their next step, such as repent, believe, and be baptized	1. Intercede—pray for the growing disciple 2. Invest—deepen your relationship with them 3. Inquire—ask questions and listen 4. Invite—ask for appropriate next step commitments 5. Instruct—discuss the commands of Jesus 6. Involve—connect them to others on the journey through a small group 7. Inspire—encourage them to take their next step, such as deeper immersion, greater abandonment, or more active ministry	1. Invest—build relationships with potential disciples 2. Intercede—ask God for disciples 3. Invite & involve—ask the disciple to become involved in your disciple group 4. Involve—give them opportunities for on-the-job training 5. Intercede for them and their disciples daily

Therefore, the goal of the *disciple maker* is threefold:

1. *Win the lost* by cooperating with the Holy Spirit in seeing every person within your sphere of influence become a repentant believer in Jesus who has experienced believer's baptism and is active in the body of Christ.

2. *Disciple the saved* by helping every believer become a devoted disciple of Jesus who has abandoned all for the gospel and is prayerfully winning others to Christ.

3. *Multiply disciples* to be disciple makers.

The sad reality is that as you move across the chart and deeper into discipleship, fewer people will go with you. The cost is considered too high. The sacrifice is viewed as too great. At the time of His resurrection, Jesus would have counted approximately 500 believers, 120 disciples, and 11 soon-to-be disciple makers. Yet, that was enough to change history. The first goal is to *win the lost* to Christ. I will briefly introduce this goal here and cover it in greater detail in the next chapter.

Goal 1: Win the Lost

Evangelism Is Sharing Good News

The "gospel" means "good news." The word *gospel* or *good news* is used 130 times in the Bible, and 109 times in the New Testament. The word *evangelism* literally means "to communicate good news." According to Paul, the content of the gospel is that Jesus died on the cross to pay for our sins and open the way for us to get to God (1 Cor 15:3–4). This is very good news. In fact, it's the best news. Having such information does others no good unless, or until, we share it. We have to proclaim the good news.

Evangelism Is Harvesting a Crop

Although most of us are not farmers, we do understand that there is a process involved in harvesting a crop. For example, if a farmer wants to harvest a crop of corn, he does not merely hop on his tractor, ride out into the fields, and start collecting corn. A lengthy process must be followed. First he has to plow the ground. Then he must plant the seed. The young plant must be fertilized, watered, and weeded. It also must be given time to grow. This entire process must be followed before the harvest can occur.

The apostle Paul likened the process of the evangelization of the Corinthians to farming. He said that their conversion was the result of spiritual planting and watering prior to the reaping (1 Cor 3:6–9).

In one sense, everyone we meet is a spiritual field. Our responsibility is to cooperate with God and others to plow the soil of their heart, plant the seed of the Gospel, water the seed, and wait for God to bring the harvest. Salvation is a process leading to an event.

Jesus Christ: Disciple-Making Evangelist

Jesus' disciple-making ministry opened with His evangelizing others by preaching the good news of the kingdom of God: "The time is fulfilled, and the kingdom of God has come near. Repent and believe in the good news!" (Mark 1:15). He told Nicodemus that he needed to be born again (John 3:1–17). He told the Jews: "Anyone who hears My word and believes Him who sent Me has eternal life and will not come under judgment but has passed from death to life" (John 5:24). He later preached, "Unless you repent, you will all perish" (Luke 13:3, 5). He told His disciples that the reason He had come was to proclaim the gospel (Mark 1:38). He later said that His purpose in coming to earth was "to seek and to save the lost" (Luke 19:10).

Paul: Disciple-Making Evangelist

The last half of the book of Acts is essentially an account of Paul's evangelism efforts. For Paul, life was Christ and seeing Christ preached (Phil 1:18–21). He lived under a solemn obligation to preach the gospel because it is "the power of God for salvation" (Rom 1:15–17 NASB). He told the Romans, "My aim is to evangelize where Christ has not been named" (Rom 15:20). He said that evangelism was his priestly duty and driving compulsion (Rom 15:16; 1 Cor 9:16).

As those who want to follow Jesus, we must follow Him into a lifestyle of evangelism. As those who want to make disciples, we must motivate, instruct, and train our disciples to evangelize.

William Booth: Disciple-Making Evangelist

In the late 1800s in the squalor of the ghettoes of London, William Booth literally raised an army, a "salvation army," of spiritual soldiers. They ministered to the material needs of the poor masses of London and made disciples. His main converts were alcoholics, morphine addicts, prostitutes, and other "undesirables" unwelcomed into polite Christian society. Faced with intense persecution, he developed a militant edge to his mercy ministry. Within twenty-five years, his movement spread to nineteen countries, including the United States, Argentina, Germany, Jamaica, Australia, and Norway. His movement eventually spread all over the world.

What fueled this mighty mercy movement of justice, evangelism, and discipleship? It was a flaming passion for winning the lost. In a campaign to see 100,000 souls won to Christ, Booth pleaded with his troops, "Go for souls. Go straight for souls, and go for the worst."[1]

Often criticized for his unorthodox methods, his critics failed to see the wisdom in his "madness." He said, "If I thought I could win one more soul to the Lord by walking on my head and playing the tambourine with my toes, I'd learn how!"[2]

I love his fiery passion and militant mindset to cooperate with Jesus in building a church that would kick in the gates of hell. He said,

> We are not sent to minister to a congregation and be content if we keep things going. We are sent to make war and to stop short of nothing but the subjugation of the world to the sway of the Lord Jesus.[3]

Booth maintained that every believer is "called" to be a soul winner:

> "Not called!" did you say? "Not heard the call," I think you should say. Put your ear down to the Bible, and hear Him bid you go and pull sinners out of the fire of sin. Put your ear down to the burdened, agonized heart of humanity, and listen to its pitiful wail for help. Go stand by the gates of hell, and hear the damned entreat you to go to their father's house and bid their brothers and sisters and servants and masters not to come there. Then look Christ in the face—whose mercy you have professed to obey—and tell Him whether you will join heart and soul and body and circumstances in the march to publish His mercy to the world.[4]

⌐ Questions to Ponder ⌐

1. Who are you seeking to win to Christ?
2. Who are you developing for Christ?
3. Who are you equipping to be deployed for Christ?

4. List the names of five people you are praying for to come to know Christ?

5. List the names of five people you are helping to be developed and deployed for Christ?

Notes

1. William Booth to Rudyard Kipling, quoted on website "The Booths: Quotes from the Founders," http://www.ourchurch.com/view/?pageID=12281 (accessed November 2, 2011).

2. Ibid.

3. Ibid.

4. Ibid.

14

Winning the Lost—
A Passionate Pursuit

Dave Earley

John Wesley: Disciple-Making Evangelist

John Wesley, his brother Charles, and George Whitefield were used of God to bring about a Great Awakening in the British Isles by preaching Christ to the masses. In doing so, John risked his life to go outside into the fields and preach the gospel to the poor. Regarding this practice he said:

> It is no marvel that the devil does not love field preaching! Neither do I; I love a commodious room, a soft cushion, a handsome pulpit. But where is my zeal if I do not trample all these underfoot in order to save one more soul?[1]

At Wesley's death, the Methodist movement numbered 100,000 disciples meeting in 10,000 small groups. What fueled such incredible growth and disciple-making multiplication? It was the burning passion for winning souls that Wesley passed on to his disciples:

> You have nothing to do but to save souls. Therefore spend and be spent in this work. And go not only to those that need you, but to those that need you most. It is not your business to preach so many times, and to take care of this or that society; but to save as many souls as you can; to bring as many sinners as you possibly can to repentance.[2]

In the previous chapter we discussed the three-fold goal of the disciple maker and briefly introduced the first goal: win the lost. This chapter will explore this first goal more deeply, looking at key principles from the ministries of Jesus and Paul.

How to Make Disciples, Goal 1: Win the Lost

Whether we are talking of seekers needing to be won as believers, believers needing to be trained as disciples, or disciples needing to be developed into disciple makers, I have found that the elements needed at each step are essentially the same. I see seven of them in the ministry of Jesus and Paul: (1) intercede, (2) invest, (3) inquire, (4) invite, (5) instruct, (6) involve, and (7) inspire.

1. Pray for Lost People (Intercede)

Although it seems obvious, we must not overlook the necessity of prayer in effective evangelism. Jesus was, and is, an evangelistic intercessor (John 17:20; Rom 8:34; Heb 7:25). He lamented, "Jerusalem, Jerusalem. . . . How often I have wanted to gather your children together, as a hen gathers her chicks under her wings, but you were not willing!" (Luke 13:34). His heart was broken, and He wept in prayer for the lost:

> As He approached [Jerusalem] and saw the city, He wept over it. (Luke 19:41)

> When he looked out over the crowds, his heart broke. So confused and aimless they were, like sheep with no shepherd. (Matt 9:36 MSG)

Paul, too, was an evangelistic intercessor who stated "my heart's desire and prayer to God for Israel is that they may be saved" (Rom 10:1 NKJV). High-impact disciple makers are prayer warriors and evangelistic intercessors. They pray for those they are winning, training, and sending. They pray for themselves to have opportunities to minister and strategically leverage those opportunities to their fullest.

"NO GREATER JOY"

Neil Cole is an organic church planter, author, and the founder and executive director of Church Multiplication Associates. In his book, *Search and Rescue*, Cole tells of training a group of new disciple makers. He writes, "I remember a holy moment in my life when the potent power of simply praying daily for people's souls struck me in a new way."[3]

He continues by telling of getting goose bumps all over as he realized that these new Christians, who were now making disciples of their own, were people whose names were checked off a praying-for-the-lost card he carried in his Bible. He said, "I was struck . . . with how powerful the simple idea of prayer is." He concludes,

> Of course, we are not praying for souls so that we can check off names on our list and feel good about ourselves. But there is no greater joy than to watch a life born again into the kingdom of God. To that end we pray, God answers, and we rejoice.[4]

PRAYER EVANGELISM

John Edmiston is an Australian missionary who has been in full-time Christian ministry for more than thirty years. He has served in Australia; Papua, New Guinea; and the Philippines. In an article titled "Prayer Evangelism," he gives this testimony:

> In 1993, I led a Bible Study series with a group of twenty or so rather boisterous university students who asked to be taught about prayer. In the process we had a book for the prayer points with three columns: Request, Date Entered, and Date Answered.
>
> They started praying for their friends' salvation, and within a couple of weeks the converts started rolling in, two or three a week, and often ending up at the Bible study. Every person "put in the book" for prayer came to Christ and, naturally enough, the prayer journal became known as the "book of life."
>
> If memory serves me correctly about 25 people came to Christ, through prayer alone, that semester. Prayer worked, even with inexperienced believers, who hated witnessing, and people were saved.[5]

HOW TO PRAY FOR THE LOST

- Pray for individual people by name (Exod 33:17; Isa 43:1).
- Pray with others in agreement (Matt 18:19–20).
- Ask in faith (Matt 21:22; Mark 11:24).
- Pray persistently (Luke 18:1–8).
- Pray with a willingness to be part of the answer (Matt 9:37–10:1).

When you meet those you are discipling, be sure to spend time praying for the lost. While it is good to pray for the lost in general, focus specific prayers on a few specific people that God has brought into your lives. Together, two or three of you should pray by name for those people until they come to Christ.

WHAT TO PRAY FOR THE LOST

1. Thank You that You desire _____ to be saved and to come
   to a personal knowledge of the truth (1 Tim 2:5–6; 2 Pet 3:9).
2. Lord, please draw _____ to Yourself (John 6:44).
3. Lord, please convict _____ of sin, righteousness, and
   judgment (John 16:8–11).
4. Bind Satan from blinding _____ from the truth (2 Cor
   4:4; 2 Tim 2:25–26).
5. Cause _____ to experience their spiritual emptiness and
   hunger for more (Luke 15:15–16).
6. Please soften the soil of _____ heart (Mark 4:3–20).
7. Give me the opportunity to share the gospel with _____
   (Matt 9:37–38; Col 4:3–6).
8. Bind Satan from stealing the seed from their hearts (Mark 4:15).
9. Cause _____ to admit their spiritual poverty, and desire
   what only the Father can provide (Luke 15:17–18).
10. That they would come to the Father to repent of their sin (Luke
    15:19–21), believe the gospel (Mark 1:15), and declare Jesus as Lord
    (Rom 10:9, 13).
11. May the gospel seed produce a multiplied harvest of spiritual fruit
    (Mark 4:9, 20).

2. Build a Relationship (Invest)

Thom Rainer interviewed a dozen people who made the surprising trek
from non-Christian beliefs to faith in Jesus Christ. In his book *Unexpected
Journey*, Rainer shared the conversations with those who journeyed to
Christ from Mormonism, Judaism, Hinduism, Atheism, Jehovah's Witness,
Agnosticism, Wiccan Paganism, Buddhism, Unitarianism, Astrology, Islam,
and Satanism. He discovered that their conversion stories all had one thing in
common: they had been actively loved to Jesus.

All of them said the same thing: they were not argued into faith in Jesus
Christ. They were loved into it. They were not reached through a program or
an event. They were reached through a relationship. In each case, acceptance,
nonjudgmental behavior, active love, and real listening is what reached these
people who had been on paths leading them far from God.[6]

Effective evangelistic disciple makers understand that real ministry runs
on the track of relationships. Jesus moved into the neighborhood of those He

wanted to win (John 1:14). He invited the men who eventually became His disciples to follow Him home for the day (John 1:35–39), and He was notorious for eating with sinners (Luke 15:1–2).

3. Ask Questions and Really Listen (Inquire)

Jesus was a master at using questions to build bridges for the gospel. He asked the woman at the well to give Him a drink (John 4:7). He asked the woman caught in adultery what had happened to her accusers (John 8:10). Later, when He began to raise the level of commitment needed to follow Him, some left. So, He asked those who remained, "You don't want to go away too, do you?" (John 6:67). Later, He asked His disciples, "Who do people say that I ... am?" (Matt 16:13 NKJV).

I have found that people's favorite subject of conversations is ... themselves. So, by honestly inquiring about their opinions and beliefs, I have found that I can engage almost anyone in conversation. Learn to ask people for help. When I go shopping, I play dumb (it is not all that big a stretch), asking people where such and such is found, or which item they would recommend.

People love to give their opinions. I have found success asking, "What do you think is the best restaurant in this area?" What is the best movie you have seen this year? "Who do you think will win the game this weekend?" or "Who will win the election?"

People with tattoos are easy to engage in conversation because every tattoo has a story. So ask them, "Do you mind telling me the story behind your tattoo?" "If you could do it all over again, would you?"

Once a relationship has been established and a conversation is started, a good leading question is simply, "Will you tell me your story?" I have also had success with these questions: "If you could be doing anything as a job five years from now, what would you being doing?" "What would it take to make your life complete?" "If you could ask God any question, what would you ask Him?" "What was the worst day of your life and why?"

The key to using questions is actively *listening* to the other person's responses. A bridge is built from their heart to yours when they feel like they have been heard. People are starving to have someone truly listen to them. I currently have a Jewish veterinarian pursuing me to talk about Jesus. How did this happen? The first times we met I asked him questions and listened to him tell his story.

Rainer writes, "Listening means we are willing to learn from others. Listening means we are not threatened in our own Christian beliefs by hearing what someone else believes. Listening means we really care for the person."[7]

4. Ask for Appropriate Commitments (Invite)

If you study the ministry of Jesus, you will see a master at inviting people to make the appropriate commitment at exactly the right time. For example, He did not call His disciples to take up the cross and die for Him *until* they had known Him for nearly three years. Initially, He simply invited them to hang out with Him and make up their own minds (John 1:35–39). There were dozens of other smaller commitments He asked them to make first, each one requiring a bit more faith and commitment on their part.

It is the same way for us. My goal for everyone I meet is that they would be willing to die for Jesus as they make disciples and take the gospel to the uttermost parts of the earth. I do not start by asking someone to make that commitment. I invite them to say yes to a commitment when they are ready to say yes. Gradually, I help them establish a pattern of saying yes to Jesus, until they have said yes to repenting of their sin and calling Him Lord.

For example, when we moved into a new neighborhood, we discovered that our next door neighbors, Shawn and Karen, were a young couple who were living together. My wife, Cathy, went out of her way to connect with Karen and listen to her challenges as a young woman in her first serious relationship. I prayed for them, spent time with them, and tried to serve them.

After a good conversation with Shawn, I asked him to say yes to a simple commitment, "Would it be ok if I prayed for you and Kathy right now?" He said yes. Then he remarked that no one had every prayed for him before. After our next good conversation, we invited Shawn and Kathy over to share a new dessert my wife Cathy had made. They both said yes.

They invited us to attend their wedding. Even though it was out of the way and very inconvenient, we went and tried to connect positively with as many of their friends and family members as possible.

After a few weeks, we invited them to visit the new church we had started in order to tell us what they thought. They said yes and came the next day. Afterward, I asked them what they thought, and they said they liked it. So, I invited them to come back the next week. They said yes.

After a few weeks of coming to church, we asked if we could drop by and talk with them about what they thought God had been doing in their lives. They said yes.

After sharing the gospel with them, we invited them to get on their knees and repent of their sin, calling upon Jesus as Lord. They said yes, and both got on their knees and surrendered their lives to Jesus. As we left, we invited them to tell several other people about their new faith in Christ within the next week. They said yes.

A few weeks later, they accepted the invitation to be baptized. Then they accepted the invitation to take the membership class and get actively involved in the ministry of the church.

Remember this about commitments: *the larger the commitment, the more time someone needs to count the cost.* We met Shawn and Karen in January, and they were not saved until about six months later. They were not ready to be saved when we first met them, but after six months of praying, investing, listening, and strategically inviting, they crossed the bridge of faith and began the path of being disciples.

5. Tell Them the Gospel (Instruct)

There comes a point in every evangelistic relationship where the disciple maker needs to evangelize (literally "tell good news") by proclaiming the gospel. Consider Paul's words in Romans:

> If you confess with your mouth, "Jesus is Lord," and believe in your
> heart that God raised Him from the dead, you will be saved. One
> believes with the heart, resulting in righteousness, and one confesses with
> the mouth, resulting in salvation. . . . For everyone who calls on the name
> of the Lord will be saved. But how can they call on Him they have not
> believed in? And how can they believe without hearing about Him? And
> how can they hear without a preacher? (Rom 10:9–10, 13–14)

In this passage, Paul outlines the process by which a person trades their inadequate self-righteousness for the required righteousness that is only available through faith in Jesus Christ. The steps are given below, from the last step to the first:

> 5. The lost person *confesses* that Jesus is Lord (10:9–10) . . . but only
> after . . .
> 4. They *call* upon the name of the Lord to save them (10:12–13) . . . but
> only after . . .
> 3. They *believe* in Jesus (10:14) . . . but only after . . .
> 2. They *hear* about Jesus (10:14) . . . but only after . . .
> 1. Someone *preaches or proclaims* to them the truth about Jesus (10:14).

Notice that this process begins with someone *preaching* or proclaiming the gospel to the lost. People need enough information about Jesus in order to believe in Jesus and commit their lives to Him.

Salvation is the result of believing certain truths. These truths include: (1) there is a God; (2) I am responsible to God; (3) I have erred in my responsibility—I have sinned; (4) sin has some negative consequences—death/ separation from God; (5) Jesus never sinned; (6) Jesus died to pay for my sin; (7) His righteousness is good enough; and (8) I can have His gift of eternal life by receiving it. Romans 10:14 is clear: people will not believe these truths until they hear them. They will not hear them unless we tell them.

6. Connect Them with Others on the Journey (Involve)

After years of trying to do evangelism and make disciples one-on-one with limited success, I noticed that both Jesus and Paul made disciples *in groups*. For example, Jesus had a whole group of young men who hung out with Him for nearly a year before they became believers (John 1:35–2:12). Evangelism will become more effective when lost people are allowed to belong *before* they are expected to believe.

I have found that every time I can help a seeker to get personally involved in reading God's Word with others on the journey, they have gotten saved. Cathy and I experienced this when we started a Bible study group for four couples, all of whom were unbelievers. We met in our house weekly for twelve weeks while their children participated in a children's club at our church.

As they got involved each week in reading the Bible with others on the same journey, God worked in their hearts. Week after week, one by one, they began to submit to Jesus as Lord until all eight were saved and baptized.

The small group for seekers idea worked so well that Cathy and I began leading one every fall and every spring. Time after time, by the end of the term, the lost people in the group had gotten saved and baptized.

7. Encourage Them to Take the Next Step (Inspire)

The difference between effectiveness and ineffectiveness as a disciple maker is often as simple as encouraging the other person to take their next step. After Peter proclaimed the gospel on the day of Pentecost, the audience was cut to the heart and ready to respond. He pointed them to their next step—repentance and baptism:

> When they heard this, they came under deep conviction and said to Peter and the rest of the apostles: "Brothers, what must we do?" "Repent," Peter said to them, "and be baptized, each of you, in the name of Jesus Christ for the forgiveness of your sins, and you will receive the gift of the Holy Spirit." (Acts 2:37–38)

Once a person is saved, their journey has not ended; it has just begun. After you have helped someone across the bridge of repentance and faith in Jesus, the next step is to encourage them to confess Him as Lord publically through water baptism.

The task does not end when they are baptized. After 3,000 were baptized on the day of Pentecost, they were immediately assimilated into the life of the missional community. Acts 2:41–42 records:

> So those who accepted his message were baptized, and that day about 3,000 people were added to them. And they devoted themselves to the apostles' teaching, to fellowship, to the breaking of bread, and to the prayers.

Disciple makers win the lost and train their disciples to do the same. They intercede for the lost, invest time into relationships with the lost, ask them important questions, invite them to move closer to Jesus, share the gospel, involve them with others on the journey, and inspire them to take their next step.

— Questions to Ponder —

1. Is evangelism part of your lifestyle?
2. How often do you pray for the lost?
3. When during an average week do you share the gospel?
4. When was the last time you shared the gospel?
5. When was the last time you led someone to Christ?

Notes

1. John Wesley, "John Wesley on Evangelism," http://christian-quotes.ochristian.com/christian-quotes_ochristian.cgi?find=Christian-quotes-by-John+Wesley-on-Evangelism (accessed October 22, 2011).

2. Ibid.

3. Neil Cole, *Search and Rescue: Becoming a Disciple Who Makes a Difference* (Grand Rapids: Baker, 2008), 174.

4. Ibid.

5. John Edmiston, "Practical Prayer Evangelism," http://www.holytrinity newrochelle.org/yourti82508.html (accessed November 2, 2011).

6. See Thom S. Rainer, *The Unexpected Journey* (Grand Rapids: Zondervan, 2005).

7. Ibid., 200.

15

Disciple Making Is . . .

Growing Disciples Like Jesus

Dave Earley

It All Started in the Bathroom

I began intentionally and consistently making disciples as a nineteen-year-old college student. It all started in the bathroom.[1] I had just returned from Christmas break during which time I had read a book about the need for disciple making, and I was eager to get started. I recalled that Jesus had prayed for the Father to direct Him to disciples (Luke 6:12–13). I also remembered that He had told His disciples to pray in their own disciples (Matt 9:37–38). So I began to pray for someone to disciple.

I prayed for two weeks. One evening, a guy in my dorm named Darrell stopped me in the hall and said, "I heard that you are really good at spending time with God every day. I have always struggled to do it. Between working full time and taking classes, I can't seem to make time for God," he confessed. "Would you show me what you do?" Darrell was the answer to my prayer for someone to disciple. "Yes," I said. "When are you free to meet?"

We compared schedules only to discover that the only time we both had available was at 11:15 p.m. That could be a challenge since our Christian college had a very strict lights out policy. The only place in our dorm where a student could talk and have a light on after 11:15 p.m. was the large dorm bathroom. That was how the Bathroom Baptist Temple was born.

145

The Bathroom Baptist Temple

The next night at 11:15 p.m. in the bathroom of dorm eight, Darrell and I sat down on the floor and opened our Bibles. After a short time of prayer and sharing about our day, we went back and forth memorizing a Bible verse together. Then we read a passage of Scripture and shared about the big truth in it. We prayed for each other and then prayed through a short list of prayer requests. We decided to meet every night. Laughing, we joked that we had launched a new church—the "Bathroom Baptist Temple."

That night in bed, I thanked the Lord. I was excited as I realized that we had launched the beginning of what could be a mini-multiplication movement. Since prayer had worked before, I asked the Lord to give me another guy to disciple.

Darrell and I met faithfully every night as the "Bathroom Baptist Temple." I prayed every night for another guy to join us. One evening, exactly two weeks after we began to meet, we had just sat down and opened our Bibles when a tall young man came over to us carrying a Bible. He sat down and introduced himself. "Hey, my name is Tim," he said. "I live at the other end of the hall. I want to join the Bathroom Baptist Temple."

We were shocked. Neither of us could remember seeing him before, and we had no idea how he had even heard of the Bathroom Baptist Temple. "Every night I brush my teeth down at the other end of the bathroom," Tim explained, "For the last two weeks I have been listening to you guys. I need what you are doing. So I thought I'd ask." We were astounded and excited. The Bathroom Baptist Temple had grown 50 percent in two weeks. That would make us the fastest growing church in America.

I was becoming addicted to the thrill of taking what the Lord gave me and pouring it into others. I was excited as I realized that the often slow process of multiplying my life was beginning. As I lay in bed that night thanking the Lord for what had taken place, I felt led to ask for another guy. So I did.

Tim, Darrell, and I met faithfully every night as the Bathroom Baptist Temple. I prayed every night for another guy to join us. One evening, exactly two weeks after Tim had joined the Bathroom Baptist Temple, we had just sat down and opened our Bibles. Tim opened in prayer. Then, a short, curly-headed young man burst into the bathroom. He looked around and rushed over to us.

"I'm not too late, am I?" He asked.

"Too late for what?" I asked. I had never seen him before.

"Too late to join the Bathroom Baptist Temple," he said.

Skeptical, I asked, "How do you know about the Bathroom Baptist Temple?"

"Tim is my roommate," he said. "All he talks about anymore is the Bathroom Baptist Temple. He has changed so much in the last two weeks. Whatever you guys are doing, I want in on it." So Tim's roommate Jim became a member of the Bathroom Baptist Temple that night. We had grown another 33 percent, making us the fastest growing church in Virginia.

I continued to pray and God continued to answer. Soon there were so many of us cramming into the Bathroom Baptist Temple every night that the resident assistant gave us our own room. It would be packed out several nights a week for the rest of the semester.

Seeing the Bathroom Baptist Temple grow so quickly was thrilling, but what was even more exciting was that the Bathroom Baptist Temple multiplied. The next year, Darrell, Jim, and Tim each led their own groups. In the previous chapter we discussed the first of the three goals for disciple making: win the lost. This story illustrates the second goal, namely, to *disciple the saved* by helping every believer become a devoted disciple of Jesus who has abandoned all for the gospel and is prayerfully winning others to Christ.

How to Make Disciples, Goal 2: Growing Disciples Like Jesus

Once you have helped a person cross the bridge to repentance and faith in Jesus and they have taken the next step by confessing Jesus as Lord through water baptism, the task is not finished. This new believer needs to be established in the faith and taught to obey everything Jesus commanded. They need to be discipled.

There is no single method to mentor multiplying disciple makers, but the ministry of Jesus remains a helpful paradigm. In what follows are five principles for growing disciples like Jesus.[2]

1. Ask God for Disciples

Jesus had quite a group of young men (at least eighty) with whom He had built relationships. Just as I did with the Bathroom Baptist Temple, Jesus "prayed in" His potential disciples. Jesus prayerfully selected twelve young men in whom He would strategically and intentionally pour His life. Consider Luke 6:12–13:

> During those days He went out to the mountain to pray and spent
> all night in prayer to God. When daylight came, He summoned His
> disciples, and He chose 12 of them—He also named them apostles.

Jesus also commanded them (and us) to pray that the Lord of the harvest would send laborers into the harvest (Matt 9:37–38). Never underestimate the power of prayer to find potential disciples. As I mentioned at the beginning of this chapter, it works.

One way that I find potential disciples is to get them together, share the vision of the harvest, and have them join me in praying about the harvest. Several great things happen. First, the harvest gets prayed for. Second, I get to see which ones have a heart for the harvest. Third, God speaks to them about the harvest. Fourth, the Lord directs me as to which ones I am to invite into an intentional disciple-making relationship.

2. Build Relationships in Potential Disciple Makers

At His baptism, John the Baptizer pointed to Jesus and said, "Look! The Lamb of God!" (John 1:36). A few hungry young men heard it and became curious about Jesus. He invited them to spend the rest of the day with Him (John 1:37–39). The next thing we know, He had a small posse of young men with whom He was spending time (John 2:1–2). They followed Him as He launched His ministry. Eventually, they reached a place of believing faith in Him (John 2:11).

At that point they continued to follow Him around as He did ministry. They witnessed Him share the gospel with Nicodemus (John 3) and with the Samaritan woman (John 4). It was only after at least a year of relationship building that He invited them into a formal discipleship relationship (Matt 4:18–22).

HE CHANGED OUR LIVES

When I was a wayward teenager, our church hired a new youth pastor. Lee Simmons was an ordinary young man with an extraordinary passion to serve God. He poured his life into several of us who eventually became pastors, including me.

Simmons had a dream of helping us mature in Christ and in ministry. He demonstrated to us a life of effective ministry. He selected a few of us whom he believed had ministry potential. (I think a few of us selected him more than he selected us.) He built a relationship with us. He played softball with us, taught us to water ski, and wrestled with us. We were at his house so much that it sometimes annoyed his wife. He influenced us because he built a relationship with us.

Disciple making is not running a program; it is investing in people. It is all about people. Without people, there is no one to disciple. Goals, plans, and projects are all very important, but only to the extent that they help people.

I am more of a project person than a people person. I learned early on that discipleship effectiveness is closely tied with my ability to get along with people and to influence them. As the Chinese proverb states, "He who thinks he is leading and no one is following, is only taking a walk."

Disciple-making effectiveness is contingent on effectiveness with people. Simply put, if people do not like you, they will not come to your discipleship group. Beyond that, if you do not effectively love people, you will not be able to positively influence them.

RELATIONAL BANKING

Relationships can be understood as bank accounts. Realize it or not, you have a relational account with every person within your sphere of influence. Every positive interaction makes a deposit in that account while every negative encounter results in a withdrawal. We influence people most easily when there is a positive balance in the relational account. We struggle to influence people when there is little or no equity in the relationship account.

Disciple makers who practice good people skills continually make deposits in the relational accounts of others. Then, when they need to call them to make a change or go to a new level of commitment, that person is much more willing to follow.

Effective disciple makers determine to master relational banking. They constantly think of ways to make deposits in the lives of those they hope to disciple. They are not only well liked, but they are also easily followed. They understand that effective discipleship ministry runs on the train track of healthy relationships and thrives in the atmosphere of positive relational bank accounts.

3. Invite the Potential Disciple into a Discipleship Group

God ultimately is the disciple maker. The Holy Spirit will use His Word to sanctify potential disciples (John 17:17). My job as a disciple maker is to get the new believer into an environment of mutual accountability and learning under the Word of God.

Jim Putnam started Real Life Church in Post Falls, Idaho. Real Life was started in 1998 and in the first twelve years had grown to eight thousand members with 90 percent of the fellowship involved in small groups. Regarding the importance of relationships in disciple making, Putnam writes, "When it comes to discipleship, relationships are the pipe. They are the conduits that deliver the precious ingredients of discipleship."[3]

John Wesley preached outdoors in fields to massive crowds numbering as many as twenty thousand people. Hundreds would be spiritually awakened by the power of the gospel. Yet, the field preaching was simply a door to gather the spiritually hungry into small groups that he called "class meetings." In his mind, the class meetings were essential. He coached his disciple makers, "Preach in as many places as you can. Start as many classes as you can. Do not preach without starting new classes."[4]

Once someone has become a believer and has shown an interest in investigating Christ, I invite them to join me in a weekly small-group Bible study. The group becomes their greenhouse for growth as they engage the Word, prayer, love, and accountability.

NEVER UNDERESTIMATE THE POWER OF THE GROUP

When Jesus called out potential disciples, He called them into a group of twelve (Mark 3:13–14). When He trained them, He did so in groups no smaller than three others plus Himself.

After years of spotty success trying to make disciples one-on-one, and after noticing that both Jesus and Paul made disciples in groups, I switched my tactics. I began to do most of my disciple making in groups. Of course, my success rate dramatically increased. When done well, the best tool for disciple making is the small group. That is so significant it bears repeating: *When done well, the best tool for disciple making is the small group.*

THE FIVE COMPONENTS OF THE DISCIPLESHIP GROUP

In the discipleship groups I lead, I like to strive for a balance of several components: welcome, worship, Word, works, and witness.

Welcome is the focus on each other. It involves informally greeting as they arrive. It involves having some snacks for them to enjoy as they mingle with each other. Welcome also involves ice breakers that, when done well, draw the group closer to each other as they get to know each other.

Worship is the focus on God. It involves nonmusical worship through prayer or thanksgiving to God for what He has done, and praise to God for who He is. This type of worship may include words of confession of sin, or surrender to God, or declarations of His greatness, or our desire to follow Him. It also can include musical worship as we sing our praise and thanks to God.

Word is the focus on the Bible. Usually this is a discussion-oriented Bible study where the emphasis is more on application than information.

Works is where God works in our lives through accountability. This can involve simply asking individuals how they intend to apply the Word in their lives in the coming week. It can also involve more focused accountability in gender-specific smaller groups of two or three. This time can involve focused response to a series of accountability questions.[5] It should always include praying for one another.

Witness is taking time each week to pray for the lost by name using the type of prayers discussed in the last chapter. It can also involve developing strategic plans for evangelism. The goal is to have everyone praying for specific lost persons every day and asking God to give them opportunities to witness. As two or three pray over the same lost people each week, God not only works in the lives of the people being witnessed to, but especially in the lives of those doing the witnessing.

Sample Weekly Group Agenda

WELCOME: 6:50–7:20 p.m.*
    Informal greeting: 6:50–7:05
    Icebreakers: 7:05–7:20
WORSHIP: 7:20–7:30 p.m.
WORD: 7:30–8:00 p.m.
WORKS: 8:00–8:20 p.m.**
WITNESS: 8:20–8:30 p.m.

*You should start at 6:00 p.m. with a shared meal at least once a month
**Gender-specific accountability groups of two or three

4. Give Them On-the-Job Training

Jesus turned the goal of world evangelization over to His disciples before He ascended (Acts 1:8). This did not occur in a vacuum, nor was it a shock to His followers. He spent considerable time, and took significant opportunities, breaking them in slowly prior to His departure.

First, He allowed them be alongside Him as He did ministry. Second, before letting them get their feet wet, He gave them a thorough briefing regarding what to expect (Matt 10:5–42; Luke 9:1–5; 10:1–12). Third, He let them try it without Him, but with a partner (Matt 10:5; Luke 9:2). Fourth, He had a time of debriefing (Luke 9:10; 10:17–20).

When I am training an apprentice to lead a group, I intentionally have to give more and more of the ministry away. In that way they get the on-the-job training they need to have the confidence necessary to launch and lead their own group eventually.

5. Pray for Them and for Their Disciples Every Day

Jesus did not stop praying for His disciples once they joined His group. Several times in the Gospels we see Him wrestling with God in prayer. He specifically told Peter that He prayed for Him (Luke 22:32). In the garden of Gethsemane, we observe Jesus praying for His disciples (John 17:9). I like to pray for my disciples the same prayer Jesus prayed for His. It includes several petitions:

- Glorify Your Son through them (John 17:1).
- Unite them (John 17:11, 21–22).
- Fill them with complete joy (John 17:13).
- Protect them from the evil one (John 17:11, 15).
- Sanctify them through the Word of truth (John 17:17).
- Send them out (John 17:18).

One thing to note about this prayer of Jesus for His disciples is that He extends it to *their* disciples. He had discipled them to be disciple makers: "I pray not only for these, but also for those who believe in Me through their message" (John 17:20).

It is not enough to pray people *into* your discipleship group. We must also pray them *through* it and out the other side until they are leading their own groups. Recall the results of Joel Comiskey's research. He found that those disciple makers who "spent 90 minutes or more in daily devotions multiplied their groups twice as much as those who spent less than half an hour."[6] More specifically, he also found that those disciple makers who pray daily for those in their disciple groups "are far more likely to multiply" their disciples into disciple-making leaders than those who only pray for them once in a while.[7]

– Questions to Ponder –

1. Who are you investing in for the future?
2. What can you do to develop disciples for King Jesus?
3. If not you, who?
4. If not here, where?
5. If not now, when?

Notes

1. This story is adapted from Dave Earley and Ben Gutierrez, *Ministry Is . . .* (Nashville TN: B&H Academic, 2010), 271–72.

2. I first published these principles in Dave Earley, *Pastoral Leadership Is . . .* (Nashville TN: B&H Academic, 2010), chap. 22.

3. Jim Putnam, *Real-Life Discipleship* (Colorado Springs, CO: NavPress, 2010), 47.

4. John Wesley, quoted in George Hunter, *To Spread the Power: Church Growth in the Wesleyan Spirit* (Nashville, TN: Abingdon, 1987), 56.

5. Neil Cole uses a series of eleven accountability questions he calls "Character Conversation Questions." See Neil Cole, *Search and Rescue: Becoming a Disciple Who Makes a Difference* (Grand Rapids, MI: Baker Books, 2008), 168–69.

1. Have you been a testimony this week to the greatness of Jesus Christ with both your words and actions?
2. Have you been exposed to sexually alluring material or dishonored another with sexual thoughts this week?
3. Has the desire for money, material possessions, or status at any time controlled your thoughts, conversations, or behavior?
4. Have you damaged another person by words, either behind their back or face to face?
5. Have you been honoring, understanding, and generous in important relationships this week?
6. Have you given in to an addictive behavior this past week?
7. Have you continued to remain angry toward another?
8. Have you secretly wished for another's misfortune so that you might excel?
9. Did you finish the Scripture reading and hear from God? What are you going to do about it?
10. Have you been completely honest with me?
11. _____ (Your personalized accountability question)

6. Joel Comiskey, *Home Cell Group Explosion* (Houston, TX: TOUCH Publications, 1998), 34.

7. Ibid., 38.

16

Multiplying Disciple Makers Like Paul

Dave Earley

Paul: Disciple

We mentioned earlier that the man we know as the apostle Paul studied as a disciple of Gamaliel, one of the most prominent rabbis of his day (Acts 22:3). Before his conversion, Paul was a member of one of the strictest Jewish sects, the Pharisees (Acts 23:6–8; 26:4–5; Phil 3:5). Just like other rabbis-in-training, he would have memorized most, if not all, of the Old Testament. He also learned the interpretations of the great rabbis, as well as those of his teacher Gamaliel.

As a young man of about the age of thirty, he quickly became a well-known rabbi in his own right. According to the book of Acts, he used this position to persecute the church (Acts 7:58; 8:1–3). Yet, he did not become a believer in Jesus as Messiah, Savior, and Lord until Jesus confronted him on a trip to Damascus as a voice and a blinding light (Acts 9:1–9). Then the Lord sent a believer named Ananias to confirm Paul's calling as an apostle to the Gentiles, to restore his sight, to bring to him the gift of the Holy Spirit, and to baptize him (Acts 9:10–18). From that point, Paul spent about three years learning the words of Jesus from Jesus Himself (Gal 1:11–12, 15–18).

As a young believer, Paul became the disciple of a church leader named Barnabas. Barnabas defended Paul before the church leaders in Jerusalem (Acts

9:27). Later, he took Paul under his wing as they spent several years helping establish the fledgling church at Antioch (Acts 11:25–26). Later, the two of them were sent out by the church in Antioch to make disciples and plant churches among the Gentiles (Acts 13:1–3). On their journey, Barnabas turned over more and more leadership to Paul until he assumed the lead role in their evangelistic church-planting venture (Acts 13:4–13).

Paul: Disciple Maker

As a rabbi, Paul would have had his own disciples. It would appear that after his conversion, they followed him into a relationship with Jesus. When Paul needed to escape persecution in Damascus, it was his disciples who lowered him over the city wall in a basket (Acts 9:25).

Over the next thirty years, dozens of others were discipled by Paul. The Scriptures mention more than thirty men and women by name as Paul's fellow laborers. Numerous ones are described as having lived or travelled with Paul during his ministry. These disciples include Luke, Silas, Timothy, Titus, Aquila, and Priscilla. Also mentioned were Erastus, Sopater, Aristarchus, Secundus, Gaius, Tychicus, and Trophimus.

During their ministry travels, Paul would have imparted his extensive knowledge of the Old Testament and the personal revelations he had received from the Lord. They also worked alongside of Paul as he did pioneer evangelism, church planting, disciple making, and leadership training. These thirty or more people became the leaders of the many churches Paul started. So Paul fulfilled the Great Commission by making and multiplying disciples.

Paul: Multiplier

One of Paul's closest disciples was a young man named Timothy. Paul later entrusted Timothy with the leadership of the strategic church of Ephesus. From this strategic city they evangelized all of Asia Minor (Acts 19:10; Revelation 2–3). It was to this young pastor that Paul wrote the important letters of 1 and 2 Timothy. In them Paul reminded Timothy of the necessity of mentoring multipliers:

> And what *you* have heard from *me* in the presence of many witnesses,
> commit to *faithful men* who will be able to teach *others* also. (2 Tim 2:2)

Note the four generations of spiritual multiplication. The first generation was Paul ("me"). He mentored the young man to whom he wrote this letter—Timothy ("you"). As the second generation, Timothy was to pass it on to a third generation ("faithful men"). They were then to pass it on to, yet, a fourth generation ("others"). Paul reminded Timothy, in the midst of all of his many responsibilities as the lead pastor of a significant church, not to forget the main thing: invest in making and multiplying disciple makers.

The life and ministry of Paul serves as a paradigm for the third, and final, goal of the disciple maker: to *multiply disciples* to be disciple makers. In the previous two chapters we discussed the first two goals for disciple making: *win the lost* and *disciple the saved*. In this chapter, we suggest six principles for multiplying disciples like Paul.

How to Make Disciples, Goal 3: Multiply Disciples Like Paul[1]

1. Get a Firm Grasp on the Things God Has Taught You

EVERYTHING JESUS COMMANDED

While in the isolation of Arabia, Paul received three years of revelations from the Lord. This was the basis of what he passed on to others. We have the privilege of reading four books of the Bible dedicated to the life and teachings of Jesus (Matthew, Mark, Luke, and John). As we have discussed, disciples obey everything Jesus commanded, which implies that they *know* everything Jesus commanded.

I have a simple reading plan that keeps me learning and obeying everything Jesus commanded. I read one chapter of the Gospels every day in correspondence with the day of the month. For example, this month I am reading Matthew. Today is the eighth day of the month, so I read Matthew 8. Tomorrow, the ninth, I will read Matthew 9. During the course of that day, I try to read that same chapter three times in concert with the three prayer times I observe each day.

Each time I finish reading through the Gospels, I start again using a different translation, study Bible, or commentary. In doing this, I have found that there is enough information in the Gospels alone to spend years passing on to others.

THE THINGS YOU HAVE LEARNED FROM PAUL

Paul told Timothy to take the things he had learned from him and pass them on to others (2 Tim 2:2). We have the privilege of having Paul's letters preserved for us in the New Testament. Along with reading the words of Jesus every day, you can also read one chapter from the letters of Paul each day. Or, after you finish a five-month cycle through the Gospels and Acts, you can start a cycle through the letters of Paul beginning with Romans chapter 1 on the first day of the month.

THE LIFE LESSONS GOD HAS TAUGHT YOU IN THE WILDERNESS

While in the deserted wildness of Arabia, Paul received teachings from the Lord. All of us have had wilderness times. We have all endured seasons of suffering and sorrow. Allow God to redeem these painful periods by recording the tough lessons you learned and passing them on to others. Consider some of the hardest things you have ever gone through. List a few of those experiences and what God taught you through them in the space below:

OTHER LESSONS GOD HAS TAUGHT YOU

You also have other valuable lessons to share with your disciples. I was just a nineteen-year-old college sophomore when I began intentionally making disciples. I did not know much or have much to give, but I had enough to get started with a few guys who were just a step or two behind me. I did know the basics of quiet time, prayer, memorizing Scripture, and of leading someone to Jesus. So that is what I passed on to them.

List five things you have learned that help you better live a life of following God.

List the top five things you wish someone had taught you when you first became a Christian.

Write down the top ten Scripture verses that have positively marked your life.

List the five Christian books that have most positively marked your walk with God.

2. Identify a Few Potential "Faithful Men"

Paul told Timothy to focus his disciple-making efforts on *faithful* men (or "women"). Effective discipleship, mentoring, and discipleship training will take a significant commitment from you. You want your efforts to be as fruitful as possible. *Optimal fruitfulness calls for wise selectivity.* You want to invest in the people who will go the furthest the fastest.

It was out of a substantial number of young men that Jesus selected twelve to be His closest disciples, and He called them apostles (Mark 3:13–14; Luke 10:1–3). When looking for disciples to mentor, I start by looking for people with three primary characteristics:

Faithful: Paul told Timothy to entrust truth to "faithful" men. When possible, I look for indications of reliability, dependability, and consistency.

Available: Discipleship takes time. Many believe that when Jesus launched His ministry, He selected some very young men, maybe even as young as twelve years old. Think about it: what if you focused on a handful of middle school students and poured your life into them? Think of the impact they may be able to have in high school and college. Focus on people who are available for you to meet with and to do ministry alongside of. I have shifted my focus to young adults who are single because they have the discretionary time necessary to be thoroughly discipled.

Teachable: You cannot teach someone who already knows it all. Look for spiritually hungry people.

WHERE TO LOOK FOR POTENTIAL MULTIPLIERS

I have found solid disciple makers in a variety of places. These include:

Discipleship group members: This is the most obvious place to look since these people are already in a discipleship relationship with you.

Those in your group who show initiative in serving others: I routinely test to see who has disciple-maker potential. One of my tests is to ask, "Who will contact the people who were absent tonight?" The person who takes the initiative to volunteer, who follows through, generally has good potential to be an effective multiplier.

Those who are willing and able to faithfully commit to meeting with you: Training a multiplier takes time. You must meet together consistently. Look for those who both have the time and the desire to meet with you for training.

Past group members: These are people you had a relationship with in the past. They were part of a church or a group in which you participated. They were, perhaps, not ready in the past, but they are showing signs of growth that indicate they are now ready to be trained to multiply.

Unconnected church attenders: There are many people who attend worship services faithfully but, for whatever reason, have failed to get plugged into a place of service. Invite them to your training group and see where it goes from there.

Family members: The New Testament leaders James and Jude were both half-brothers of Jesus Christ. Jesus' discipleship tree included many who were brothers, cousins, aunts, and nephews of one another. God is sovereign in how He puts families together. Sometimes our best ministry is in our own family. Currently, some of my top trainees are my sons.

Friends: Look at your friends and your friends' friends. Also look at the friends of your children and their parents. These individuals have been some of our most fruitful relationships.

New converts: New Christians often make great apprentices. They have more contacts with non-Christians and are often more evangelistic minded. They are enthusiastic, teachable, and spiritually contagious.

Broken, desperate people: Neil Cole strongly believes that the best target group for future disciples is broken, desperate people. He writes, "We must start with desperate people who will cling to the Good News as if they are about to go down for the third count."[2] He also states, "Bad people make good soil. There is a lot of fertilizer in their lives."[3]

3. Plan a Regular Meeting Time for Your "Faithful Men"

Paul told Timothy to take what he had learned from Paul and to commit it to faithful disciples (2 Tim 2:2). God has already made a priceless deposit of truth into your life. You have a sacred obligation of investing that truth into the lives of others. This entrustment does not happen in one short meeting. It happens over months and years as you regularly invest in others. Paul invested in his potential disciple makers all day, nearly every day, for months and even years at a time as he completed his missionary journeys. Imagine how many hours he must have spent talking with his disciples as they walked from city to city sharing the gospel.

How many times a week does it take to make the necessary deposit into the life of the faithful man? The answer is: the more often you meet the better. This is especially true in the early stages. I met with my first few disciples almost every night of the week for months before they began to disciple others. On another occasion, I met with a young man once or twice a week for lunch over a period of three years. He and his wife also came to our house for dinner and Bible study weekly for about a year. Today, he is a dynamic disciple-making pastor. I am currently meeting with some young men once a week for dinner and Bible study, and four times a week for prayer. I also try to get together with them once a month for one-on-one conversation over lunch or dinner.

We are all so busy doing what we think of as "ministry" that we often miss the real ministry that occurs when we simply "waste" time together with our potential disciple makers.

4. Do Ministry Together

Paul invited Timothy to join him on his second missionary journey (Acts 16:3). Timothy had the opportunity to see Paul in action for a three-year period as he did evangelism and discipleship. He witnessed Paul and Silas as they planted churches in Philippi (Acts 16:12–13), Thessalonica (Acts 17:1–10), and Corinth (Acts 18:1–18), among others. Timothy learned to do ministry by watching Paul do ministry and doing it with him. He learned in the laboratory of real life. Young disciple makers need to see you in action. They often learn much more from your model than your message.

All of our sons worked alongside Cathy and me as we led a Bible study group for nonchurched high school students. Our group had more than fifty kids showing up every week, with several coming to Christ every month. We also trained new leaders and sent them off with new groups every year. At the time, I really did not see the whole thing as much more than just something I did on Wednesday nights.

I was wrong.

When my boys went to college, they all became dynamic group leaders and trainers of group leaders. Andrew had as many as a hundred kids showing up to a group he led on Friday night. Daniel had sixty showing up regularly for an intense prayer group. When Luke was only eighteen, he began training small-group leaders who were several years older than himself.

One day they were all at home for lunch. I asked them how they learned to become such effective leaders and disciple makers. "We just watched you guys and did what we saw you do," they said.

5. Let Them Do Ministry without You

During his second missionary trip, Paul was chased out of Thessalonica by a mob of Jews seeking to kill him. He fled to Berea, where he started a church. But the Thessalonian Jews found him and chased him out of Berea. Yet the new church in Berea did not suffer for lack of leadership. When Paul left for Athens, he appointed Silas and Timothy to run the ministry there in his absence (Acts 17:14).

The best and most basic means of developing a potential leader into an effective leader is on-the-job training. The process is very simple (we will discuss this process in more detail in the next chapter).

1. You do ministry as they watch and learn.
2. They do ministry as you watch and coach.
3. They do ministry without you.

You will never multiply your ministry if you hang onto your ministry. You need to start turning parts of it over to your disciples so they can get a taste for it and learn what questions to ask. If they remain under your leadership without serving, their growth will often plateau. But once they begin to minister on their own, you will likely see greater progress.

6. Keep Them Focused on the Big Picture

Remember, 2 Timothy contains the last recorded words of the apostle Paul. They are his final legacy to his protégé, Timothy, and to us. Paul powerfully reminded Timothy that he was to take what he had learned from him and invest it into faithful disciples, who would be able "to teach others also" (2 Tim 2:2). Paul's deposit into the life of Timothy was for one primary purpose: so he would pass it on by investing in others. Paul was telling Timothy to multiply!

Do not lose sight of the goal. The goal is multiplication.

In speaking of the big picture of multiplying disciple-making cell groups, Joel Comiskey writes, "Cell reproduction is so central to a cell ministry that the goal of cell leadership is not fulfilled until the new groups are also reproducing. . . . The theme of reproduction must guide cell ministry. The desired end is that each cell grows and multiplies."[4] He also states, "The principle job of the cell leader is to train the next cell leader; not just fill the house with guests."[5]

I find that if you fail to consistently remind your faithful disciples of the big picture of multiplying their lives into faithful disciples, they will lose focus and get sidetracked. It is not enough to get them to minister effectively. The task is not completed until they are multiplying by making disciples who are making disciples.

Disciple making is a matter of multiplying disciples. From the life of the apostle Paul, we get six principles necessary in the process of disciple making: (1) get a firm grasp on the things that God has taught you; (2) identify a few potential "faithful men"; (3) plan a regular meeting time for your "faithful men"; (4) do ministry together; (5) let them do ministry without you; and (6) keep them focused on the big picture: multiplication.

— Questions to Ponder —

1. How did the apostle Paul multiply disciples?
2. How were his methods like the methods of Jesus?
3. What were some of the apostle Paul's multiplication steps?
4. Which of these steps are you working on with your disciples?
5. What is your next step?

Notes

1. Much of the material in this chapter is adapted from Dave Earley, *Pastoral Leadership Is . . .* (Nashville, TN: B&H Academic, 2012), chap. 23.

2. Neil Cole, *Search and Rescue: Becoming a Disciple Who Makes a Difference* (Grand Rapids, MI: Baker Books, 2008), 175.

3. Ibid., 58.

4. Joel Comiskey, *Leadership Explosion* (Houston, TX: TOUCH Publications, 2000), 39.

5. Ibid., 40.

17

Discerning the Overall Goal and Process

Dave Earley

When I was in high school, I committed my life to Christ. As a young disciple, I led a lunchtime Bible study group. The best part was leading others to Christ. For example, I was overwhelmed with the explosion of joy that filled my soul when my good friend Scott gave his heart to the Lord. I danced and shouted all the way home. I thought nothing could compare with that feeling.

But I was wrong.

Six months later Scott led someone to Christ. It was one of the happiest days of my life. My "disciple" had begun to multiply. Disciple makers derive greater joy from their disciple's progress than they do from their own. Disciple makers obtain greater joy when their apprentices lead well and multiply their lives than from their own ministry.

One of the primary goals of ministry is to reproduce additional ministers. The challenge is not to develop more followers, or even more helpers, but more multiplying leaders. The task of a multiplying disciple group leader is not complete until their potential leaders are leading their own groups and sending out their own leaders. In the previous chapter, we discussed goal three of the disciple maker: sending out disciples like Paul. In this chapter, we will expand on what we learned about multiplying disciples from the life and ministry of the apostle Paul.

The Goal of Disciple Making

Let's be very clear on this point. The goal of developing a disciple is to develop them to *do* something. The objective of disciple making is to cooperate with God in *creating more disciple makers*. The purpose is *multiplication*. All of the energy, sacrifice, prayer, and accountability involved in developing a disciple is done for the purpose of *multiplying disciples who multiply disciples*. If your paradigm is using small groups as your primary disciple-making vehicle, the goal is to multiply more small-group leaders. If it is cell church, the goal is not merely to build your cell group. It is to build up multiplying cell-group leaders. If your orientation is house church, the goal of disciple making is multiplying house-church planters. Disciple makers constantly develop and deploy new disciple makers.

Developing Multiplying Disciple Makers

A Descriptive Definition

When we speak of developing *disciple makers,* we are talking about the process of cooperating with God by using every available resource to help another person become a multiplying *disciple maker.*[1] Notice the various pieces of this definition. First, developing disciples is a process, not an event. That means it takes time. It involves steps. It is taking someone from one level to another.

Second, developing disciples is *cooperating with God.* God is deeply invested in making disciples. He is already at work in their lives. He works in ways that are deeper, more powerful, and more effective than we could ever work on our own. He will use circumstances and events. He will use all the elements of His body. The job of the multiplying disciples is simply cooperating with what God is already doing. This makes prayer and sensitivity to the Holy Spirit key components of the disciple maker's tool kit.

Third, developing disciples is *using every available resource.* There are several essential resources the wise disciple maker must employ:

1. *The Word of God.* I have found that the best curriculum for making disciples is the Word of God. It is living, powerful, and able to discern the thought and intents of the heart (Heb 4:12).
2. *Relationships.* The rising disciple needs a close personal relationship with a disciple maker where they can see what it looks like to follow Christ. They also need close relationships with others who are at a similar place in the journey.

3. *A Small Group.* Small groups provide disciples with a weekly centering place. The group session must include discussion and application of the Word, accountability, confession of sin, and prayer for one another.
4. *Missional Living.* All of the other things are practically pointless without a consistent challenge to live on mission. Leading your disciples to pray persistently and passionately for and witness to lost friends and family members is essential for true discipleship.
5. *Other Aids.* Secondary resources available to the multiplying leader include classes, books, podcasts, seminars, workbooks, and websites.

Fourth, developing disciples is *helping another person become a multiplying small-group leader.* How do you know if you have done the job? The answer is obvious: The other person is effectively leading a group that is making disciples and multiplying leaders.

The Steps of Developing Disciple Makers

Once a person has been attempting to live out the requirements of discipleship, they should be trained to help others do the same. We have discovered the best system to be an apprenticeship system. Apprenticeship is a system of training a new generation of practitioners in a certain skill. In disciple making, the goal is training apprentices to make more disciple makers by using the resources mentioned above. We have found the best environment for doing this is a discipleship group. With the disciple group as the laboratory, the disciple maker walks the apprentice through a simple process.

1. The Disciple Maker Does It; the Apprentice Watches

The multiplying disciple maker leads the group and the potential leader watches. This should cover any or all of the activities needed to lead an effective group. These include praying for each group member daily and contacting them weekly. It also includes leading the aspects of the group meeting: welcome, worship, Word, works, and witness (see chap. 15).

These ministry activities may come easily for you now, but they are intimidating to a potential leader. By modeling them, you help the apprentice overcome these fears. Let them *see* you doing it. *Show* them how it is done. Let them see how you do, and ask questions afterward. I usually have my apprentice(s) come early and leave late. That way, I can tell them what I am planning to do beforehand, and we can talk about how it went afterward.

2. The Apprentice Does It; the Disciple Maker Watches

After you show the rising disciple how to do the activity, step back and let them do it as you watch. Afterward, give them encouragement and helpful feedback. Always offer at least two positives for every negative.

Do not have them lead the whole thing their first time out. Give the apprentice pieces and parts. Maybe they will lead the welcome part this week and the worship part next week. Let them do each part a few times before giving them the whole thing.

3. The Apprentice Does It on His Own; His Apprentice Watches

Once the rising disciple can lead without the direct supervision of the multiplying leader, he is ready to launch out on his own. At this point the group multiplies. One group has become two. The disciple-making apprenticeship has produced a new leader who now takes a few others with him and launches a new group.

It is best if at least one of those going with the new group has already been earmarked as a new apprentice. In fact, there is wisdom in waiting to start a new group until the new leader has identified their new apprentice. This ensures that the process of multiplication continues.

At this point the new group leader has become a disciple maker. Those in their new group are their disciples. Their apprentice is in training to lead a future disciple group. Also, at the point of sending out the new group, the original disciple-group leader should have also identified their new apprentice. In this way, it will not be very long until the two groups multiply and become four groups.

Deploying Multiplying Disciple Makers

Set Them Up for Success

While we cannot guarantee or control the success of another, we can do all we can to ensure they do succeed. You will not experience real discipleship and multiplication unless several factors are in place *before* the new disciple-group leader has launched.

INDICATORS FOR NEW LEADER READINESS

1. *Belief and Baptism*: They have repented and believed the gospel and have followed the Lord in believer's baptism.

2. *Freedom Encounter*: They have participated in a Freedom Encounter to the extent that they are no longer hindered by crippling hurts, habits, or hang-ups.[2]

3. *Disciple*: They are striving to live out the requirements of discipleship as given by Jesus in the Gospels.

4. *Disciple Group*: They have been actively involved in a disciple group long enough to understand its values and what it means to live in community.

5. *Apprenticeship*: They have been effective at on-the-job training in leading a disciple group under the mentorship of a group leader.

6. *Apprentice*: They have at least one good apprentice planning to join them as they launch the new group.

7. *Place*: They have a good place for the new group to initially meet. Preferably, they have secured a good host/hostess home.

8. *Time*: They have a good day and time for the new group to meet.

It is ideal to be able to check off each of these eight indicators. Obviously, the more indicators there are in place, the greater will be the odds of success. As I look back over our ministry, those leaders with the most indicators have had the most success.

As you mentor your apprentices, let this checklist serve as a guide for things to consider as you help them move through the development process. Try to have as many indicators as firmly in place as possible *before* you send them out. If there are gaps before they are sent out, they rarely get filled in after they are leading. Get those gaps filled in first. If it means you send out fewer leaders, then that is all right. It is better to send out a few really good ones than several weak ones. The good ones will lead healthy, growing groups that multiply. The weak ones will probably close their groups before long, if they even get them going.

MULTIPLYING SUGGESTIONS

Part of setting them up for success is preparing the group for its eventual multiplication. There are several ways to do this effectively:

1. *Keep your disciples focused on the words of Jesus.* If you have a group of "consumer Christians," you will struggle to ever experience real discipleship and multiplication. The best way to break "American Dream Christianity" is to keep your disciples reading, studying, and living the words of Jesus. Keep the focus on the Great

Commandment, the New Commandment, the Great Commission, and embracing the Cross.

2. *Talk about multiplying early and often.* Start from the very first week. Describe the fact that one of the purposes of the group is to make disciples who will make disciples. It exists to raise up leaders who will be sent out to lead new groups. At least monthly, pray in the group about the new groups to be birthed from this group. Remember, people are down on what they are not up on. Keep the group informed of the plans and progress of each step along the way.

3. *Talk about multiplying in positive terms.* Do not speak of "breaking up" the group, "splitting" the group, or "dividing" the group. Instead, talk about "making disciples," "birthing" new groups, "launching" new groups, "multiplying" groups, and "raising up" new groups and leaders.

4. *Talk about multiplying in terms of the big picture.* For example, in Las Vegas, out of a population of 2 million people, there are 1.91 million lost people. Every new group that is born lowers the number of unreached people. When we talk about birthing new groups, we talk about reaching more of the 1.91 million lost people. I find that when we begin to speak of multiplying, people often resist. Therefore, ask them questions like: "How many of you were not in church or our group a year ago?" "What if the people who were in our group a year ago had been unwilling to give up their place in this group? Where would you be now?"

5. *Pray about the best timing for multiplying.* It is possible to make the right decision at the wrong time. Maybe the group is ready to multiply, but the new leader(s) are not. Or maybe the new leader(s) are ready, but the group is not. Or maybe it is a poor season to launch. Usually groups launch best at natural times in the school calendar, like fall and January. For us, summer is usually not a good season to launch. Pray about finding the best timing for multiplication.

6. *Set a date for multiplying.* Setting a date for multiplying is essential in achieving the dream of multiplying your group. According to Joel Comiskey's survey of seven hundred multiplying cell leaders, "Cell leaders who know their goal—when their groups will give birth—consistently multiply their groups more often than leaders who don't know. In fact, if a cell leader fails to set goals the cell members can clearly remember, he has about a 50-50 chance of multiplying his cell. But if the leader set goals, the chance of multiplying increases to three of four."[3]

7. *Celebrate the new birth.* When the disciple group is ready to give birth, invite friends and have a party with lots of food. This may be a great time for testimonies. People who are staying with the original leader can share what the new leaders have meant to them. Those going with the new leader can share what they are hoping God will do through them and the new group. Some churches have the church's small-group pastor or discipleship pastor come to preside over a special time of prayer, sending out the new group(s) and leader(s). It is a great opportunity to recast the vision for multiplying.

Send Them Out

A powerful testimony of support for new leaders is a commissioning service. You can have a special time at the end of a worship service to make a visual statement of their priorities and vision. It is a chance to give public recognition and support for the task they are accepting. It is an opportunity to ask for God's special anointing on their new responsibility. A commissioning service is a time to recognize God's call on the life of the new leaders. It is an opportunity to recognize the new leaders by name. You also might want to recognize the other members of the new group.

The service involves having the new leaders come before the church to receive prayer. The prayer should be for God's anointing on their new responsibility and the new group, and for asking God to protect them and their families. It asks God to give the group growth, health, and multiplication. By faith, it thanks God for the many lives to be touched through the ministry of the group and its leaders. It might include giving each new leader a gift, perhaps a good book on leadership, disciple making, or small groups or, perhaps, a gift certificate to a Christian bookstore or restaurant.

Continue Coaching

Once a new disciple maker has begun to lead a new group, the task is not complete. We must stay with them until they have multiplied their group by training up a new leader of their own. This will not occur without continual coaching.

Once a new disciple-group leader is in place, they still need a steady dose of the same things that got them to this point. This includes the Word of God, relationships with others at the same level, accountability, and the challenge to continue to live life on mission.

I do consulting with nearly a dozen churches every year regarding their small-group systems, leadership training, and coaching. Not once have I seen one that is experiencing true disciple making and multiplication without some sort of steady coaching of the disciple-group leaders. Without continual coaching and accountability, your disciple-group leaders will not continue to make disciples, let alone multiply. Let me repeat: *Without continual coaching and accountability, your disciple-group leaders will not continue to multiply.*

There are a variety of ways to coach leaders. I have seen two that are particularly effective for multiplication. The first is more centralized, with the disciple-group leaders meeting with the pastoral staff in a large weekly meeting. This was the model used by Paul Cho in South Korea. All of the cell leaders met with him or one of his staff each week to be motivated and trained.

The second is less centralized. The G12 system created by César Castellanos in Bogota, Columbia, (see chap. 12) keeps the new leaders meeting each week in a cell with other disciple makers and with their original disciple maker. I use a modified version of G12 meeting with a dozen of those I have mentored every other week in a disciple makers group. They meet with their disciple makers on the alternating weeks.

We discuss disciple-making systems more in the next section. Remember, the system is not as significant as the fact that it insures long-term success, real disciple making, and multiplication. Disciple-group leaders must receive continual coaching and accountability or they will not continue to multiply.

Stay in Touch and Stay out of the Way

Parenting adult children is a high-wire act of staying in touch, being available to help, but staying out of the way. In the same way, when you mentor a new leader, it is easy to go to one of two extremes. Either you get too involved with the new group and leader, or not involved enough. Successful deployment requires the right amount of involvement and freedom.

1. *Be available*: New leaders need someone (ideally the disciple maker who mentored them in the first place) to be available to listen, advise, encourage, and support them.
2. *Pray*: Pray for the new leader. They are still your disciple. They need your prayers now more than ever. Ask God to give them wisdom and grace in leading the new group. Be like Jesus; pray for their spiritual protection and ongoing sanctification (John 17:15, 17).
3. *Visit the new group*: Let the new leader know before you are coming and drop in on the group session. Remember that you are a guest, not

the leader. Be highly supportive of the new leader and how God is using the new group.

4. *Celebrate every success the new group experiences*: Do not be jealous of their success or competitive with the new group leader. In a sense, their success is your success. Let their success thrill your soul.

5. *Challenge the new leader to keep the dream of multiplication before their new group*: It is easy for a new leader to be so focused on the health and growth of the new group that they lose sight of the dream of multiplication. Gently remind them of the dream. Speak to them of how they are working with their apprentice in preparing them to multiply another new group.

6. *Consult on any issues in which the new leader may seek advice*: Do not give advice that is not asked for, but do be ready to offer advice when requested. Do not be a know-it-all, but on the other hand, do share what God has taught you through your experience.

7. *Stay out of the way*: The goal is the independence of the new leader. They need to be able to lead without you. This means keeping your distance so they can grow and develop on their own. The best way to learn to stay out of the way is to do it *as* you develop them. In other words, when they are a relatively new apprentice and you give them a portion of the group meeting to lead, like the icebreaker, let them do it. Do not jump in and correct, or amplify, or edit everything they say. While they are leading, stay out the way. Otherwise they will never learn. If you prayerfully selected a good potential leader, they will surprise you with how well they lead.

Disciple making is developing and deploying new disciple-group leaders. The goal at this point is for you to find an apprentice and begin training them to lead their own disciple group. Then send them out successfully.

— Questions to Ponder —

1. What are you training your followers to do?
2. Are you intentionally coaching them as they experience on-the-job training under your leadership?
3. Have you set a date to multiply your group?
4. Look over the multiplication suggestions and note two or three that you need to work on.
5. Why is multiplication so important to the mission?

Notes

1. This definition and many of the ideas in this chapter were adapted from Dave Earley, *Turning Members into Leaders* (Houston, TX: TOUCH Publications, 2003), chap. 8.

2. A Freedom Encounter is a concentrated opportunity for a believer to experience the truth and power of the gospel as they address past issues and deal with them through thorough repentance of sin and renunciation of the enemy. This can occur either in a group seminar or retreat setting, or through a series of discipleship counseling sessions. I suggest using Neil Anderson's *Seven Steps of Freedom* (Ventura, CA: Gospel Light, 2004); *The Bondage Breaker* (Eugene, OR: Harvest House, 2006); and *Discipleship Counseling* (Ventura, CA: Regal, 2000).

3. Joel Comiskey, *Home Cell Group Explosion* (Houston, TX: TOUCH Publications, 1999), 46.

18

Focusing on a Multiplied Harvest

Dave Earley

When John Wesley died in 1791, he left behind a church of 100,000 members and 10,000 discipleship groups. The Methodist church movement traces its beginning to a small accountability group at Oxford University, Wesley's vision for the masses, and his belief in the power of multiplication. Of Wesley's vision for the harvest, Howard Snyder writes:

> Wesley put one in ten, or perhaps one in five, to work in significant ministry. And who were these people, not the educated or the wealthy with time on their hands, but laboring men and women, husbands and wives, and young folks with little or no [formal] training, but with spiritual gifts and eagerness to serve. . . . *Not only did Wesley reach the masses; he made leaders of thousands of them.*[1]

You and I only have one shot at this life—one. Very soon it will be over and we will be standing before Christ giving account of all we have been given. I cannot speak for anyone other than myself, but on that day I want to hear Him say to me the words: "Well done good and faithful servant." According to Jesus, the condition to hearing those words of commendation is multiplying what we have been given (Matt 25:14–30). We conclude this section on disciple-making methods with a few final observations about the biblical concept of the harvest and its relationship to disciple making.

The Conditions for a Multiplied Harvest[2]

Several years ago, I wanted to see my evangelism and disciple-making ministry expand and explode. I did a simple Bible study of the concept of the spiritual harvest. As a result, I was challenged by the promises and conditions for greater fruitfulness and multiplied harvest. Interestingly, these biblical requirements for multiplied ministry are the same characteristics found in transformational, multiplying disciple makers.

1. Focused Vision on the Harvest

One day as Jesus and His disciples travelled through Samaria, He taught them an important lesson about the role of vision in realizing a spiritual harvest. They had just returned from getting lunch to find Him evangelizing a Samaritan woman. In their minds, evangelization was to be limited to the Jews. The thought of reaching Samaritans had never occurred to them. When they asked Him about it, Jesus made an interesting comment about having a vision for the harvest:

> "Don't you say, 'There are still four more months, then comes the harvest'? Listen to what I'm telling you: Open your eyes and look at the fields, for they are ready for harvest." (John 4:35)

Jesus told His disciples that in order to reap a harvest they have to "open [up their] eyes and look at" it. The harvest was there, if only they would "see" it.

Successful farmers have to "see" a harvest even when it's just an empty field. In similar fashion, successful disciple makers must have spiritual vision to "see" opportunities where others see obstacles. They "see" future leaders where others do not. They "picture" potential and possibilities where others only see hindrances and hopelessness.

"I GET MY VISION FROM THE LORD"

Recently, I had the opportunity to have lunch with Pastor Sunday Adelaja. He is a man of vision who is the founder and senior pastor of The Embassy of the Blessed Kingdom of God for All Nations in Kiev, Ukraine. Sunday is a Nigerian-born leader in his mid-thirties who is known as a dynamic communicator and church planter. He is a G12 cell church pastor. He is widely regarded as the most successful pastor in Europe, with more than twenty-five thousand members as well as daughter and satellite churches in more than thirty-five countries worldwide.

I asked him where he got his vision for such a remarkable ministry. His face lit up in a beautiful smile as he said, "I get my vision from the Lord. I spend one week every month alone with the Lord and His Word. It is there that He gives me His vision."[3]

Most of us will not be able to spend a week per month alone with the Lord, but we can still apply Pastor Sunday's approach. What if we spent an afternoon or at least a focused hour each week alone with the Lord specifically seeking His vision for our lives and groups?

SET GOALS FOR MULTIPLICATION

If you want your disciples to make disciples, you must keep the vision of multiplication before them. Joel Comiskey studied eight churches that were exploding in growth through evangelistic discipleship cell groups. In his study, he discovered the power of goal setting for cell multiplication. He writes, "Cell leaders who know their goal—when their groups will give birth—consistently multiply their groups more often than leaders who don't know."[4] He continues:

Here's my advice to anyone leading a small group or considering such a responsibility: First, be crystal clear about your goal—cell multiplication. The successful cell churches around the world are focused on growth. They don't waver on this point. Second, you must make leadership development your chief priority. Successful small group leaders view each member as a potential leader, and the genetic code of cell multiplication is instilled in each believer from the onset.[5]

Gail Matthews has also researched the power of goal setting. She discovered that "those who wrote their goals *accomplished significantly more* than those who did not write their goals."[6] Her study revealed that writing one's goal enhances one's achievement especially when it is coupled with a written action plan and some sort of weekly accountability regarding progress.

2. Abiding in Jesus

Jesus promised to bear fruit through His disciples *if* they met the condition of abiding in Him. Consider again John 15:4–5:

Remain in Me, and I in you. Just as a branch is unable to produce fruit by itself unless it remains on the vine, so neither can you unless you remain in Me. I am the vine; you are the branches. The one who remains in Me and I in him produces much fruit, because you can do nothing without Me.

This promise continues today. He will do His part, but we must do ours. There are many ingredients for an intimate relationship, including honesty, openness, communication, sharing, trust, conflict resolution, shared experiences, acceptance, availability, and time. Yet, the most important might be time, because the others do not occur without it. In order to be fruitfully connected to God, we must spend time with God.

SEVEN TIMES A DAY!

At the age of twenty-five, Adoniram Judson was the first Protestant missionary sent from North America to minister in Burma (now known as Myanmar). He waited six years for his first convert. Although it took time, he eventually saw a multiplied harvest as he planted churches and translated the Bible into Burmese. Sometime after his death, a government survey recorded 210,000 Christians, 1 out of every 58 Burmese!

Judson discovered a secret that enabled him to continue to abide in Christ. Pray seven times a day!

> Endeavor seven times a day to withdraw from business and company
> and lift up thy soul to God. . . . Begin the day by rising after midnight
> and devoting some time amid the silence and darkness of the night to this
> sacred work. Let the hour of opening dawn find thee at the same work.
> Let the hours of nine, twelve, three, six, and nine at night witness the
> same. Be resolute in thy cause. Make all practical sacrifices to maintain it.
> Consider that thy time is short and that business and company must not
> be allowed to rob thee of thy God.[7]

3. Dependence on God

Disciple making is a spiritual activity. Disciples are only made as we cooperate with God's Spirit as He works in their lives. In and of ourselves, we are inherently incapable of producing true spiritual change in another person's life. Multiplying disciple makers is a God-sized task. In our strength, we cannot save anyone's soul. We cannot transform their life and set them free. We cannot make them effective multiplying leaders. God can. He will, *if* we trust Him.

In order for spiritual fruitfulness to occur, we must put all of our trust in the Lord. In order for spiritual fruitfulness to perpetuate, we must continually depend upon God. Consider Jer 17:5–8:

> This is what the LORD says: The man who trusts in mankind, who makes
> human flesh his strength and turns his heart from the LORD is cursed. He
> . . . dwells in the parched places in the wilderness, in a salt land where no

one lives. The man who trusts in the LORD, whose confidence indeed is the LORD, is blessed. He will be like a tree planted by water: it sends its roots out toward a stream, it doesn't fear when heat comes, and its foliage remains green. It will not worry in a year of drought or cease producing fruit.

The Lord promises a life of fruitfulness. Trusting in human resources leads to barrenness, but depending upon the Lord yields a lifestyle of fruitfulness.

Randall Neighbour is a veteran cell group leader and publisher. He describes the size of our task and the need for dependence in fruitful ministry:

From a human perspective, it does look like a mountain of responsibility to move with a spoon, doesn't it? But that's not reality if you are called of God to be a cell leader; you will be drawing from an energy source much greater than yourself. It is miraculous how God works through us when we are working within our calling and at the pace He desires for us.[8]

ONE HOUR A DAY IN PRAYER

My friend Daniel Henderson often says, "Prayerlessness is a declaration of independence from God." A primary way to express our dependence on God is through prayer. Paul Cho, pastor of the largest church in the world and the spiritual "father" of tens of thousands of disciple makers, has said, "The most important thing in our lives is prayer."[9] His dependence upon God is clear when he says, "I am not able to do all I have been called to do without spending the minimum of one hour a day in prayer every morning."[10] He continues, "One of the greatest lies of Satan is that we just don't have time to pray. However, all of us have enough time to sleep, eat, and breathe. As soon as we realize that prayer is as important as sleeping, eating, and breathing, we will be amazed at how much more time will be available to us to pray."[11]

4. Sacrifice

There is no multiplication without sacrifice. Consider the words of Jesus in John 12:24:

I assure you: Unless a grain of wheat falls to the ground and dies, it remains by itself. But if it dies, it produces a large crop.

In this passage, Jesus observes that in the physical world, death was the key to a single kernel being multiplied to many. He then applied this to the multiplied fruit that would abound out of His own death:

The one who loves his life will lose it, and the one who hates his life in this world will keep it for eternal life. If anyone serves Me, he must

follow Me. Where I am, there My servant also will be. If anyone serves
Me, the Father will honor him. "Now My soul is troubled. What should
I say—Father, save Me from this hour? But that is why I came to this
hour. (John 12:25–27)

Disciple makers who see genuine multiplication are those who sacrifice all for
Jesus. Martin Luther King stated, "If a man hasn't discovered what he will die
for, he is not fit to live."[12] If you are not ready to sacrifice, you will not multiply.

Randall Neighbour writes, "[Disciple-group leadership] is earned through
servanthood and prayer. When you love people by laying down your life for
each of them and love them just where they are in life, they will respect you
and follow you."[13]

Multiplying disciple makers know they must "die" to many *good* things
in order to accomplish the *best* things. They are willing to "die" to spending
their lives following selfish pursuits in order to achieve kingdom business
and multiplied results. They know that it is the time spent outside the group
meeting—praying, inviting, contacting, and mentoring—that makes the
difference in group growth and multiplication.

Another element of dying that is essential for multiplying is getting out of
the way. Some of us enjoy ministry so much that we don't know how to get out
of the way to let others have their chance. This attitude blocks multiplication.
We have to "die" to our need to be needed and get over our insecurities if we
ever hope to raise multiplying leaders.

SACRIFICE IS SPELLED T-I-M-E

Multiplying disciple makers do not dabble in following Jesus and living
for the Great Commission. They are actively sold out to it, and it shows in
their weekly schedule. Some of the best multipliers in the world are at ICM
in Bogota, Columbia, a church that exploded to sixteen thousand discipleship
groups in a twelve-year period. Joel Comiskey's analysis of their effectiveness
revealed, "One secret of ICM's success is the high level commitment of the
leadership. ICMers are sold out to the Lord's work, and their time commitment
reflects that fact."[14]

The ICM disciple-group leaders participate in church every Sunday
morning, and they attend a disciple group with their mentor every week. In
addition, they either lead a disciple group or lead a group for their disciple
makers every week or both. On top of that, they spend time in personal
devotions each day, and many of them attend the church's prayer meeting each
morning. Beyond that, they take leadership courses offered through the church.

5. Persevering Labor and Hard Work

The harvest follows hard work and making disciples is the result of diligent labor. Galatians 6:9 states, "So we must not get tired of doing good, for we will reap at the proper time if we don't give up." Comiskey's research confirms this biblical principle. He writes, "I discovered that the potential to lead a healthy, successful cell group does not reside with the gifted, the educated, or those with vibrant personalities. The answer rather is hard work."[15]

Watchmen Nee was a Christian leader, church planter, disciple maker, author, and teacher during the early twentieth century. After thirty years of very fruitful church ministry, he was imprisoned for his faith until his death twenty years later. His writings are a fresh approach to Scripture and a simple approach to discipleship and disciple making. In a series of talks given to young disciple makers, he discussed the character qualifications of a fruitful Christian worker. First on his list was diligence. He states,

> It seems superfluous to say so, but is in fact essential to say with emphasis, that a Christian worker must be a person who has a will to work. . . . Have you ever known an effective Christian worker who was indolent? No they are all diligent and always on the alert lest they squander time or strength. They are not always looking for an opportunity to rest, but rather buy up every opportunity to serve the Lord.[16]

Multiplying disciple makers comes from working hard and doing the right thing over and over and over again, even when you are too tired, too busy, and do not feel like it anymore. Too often leaders start down the path of multiplication with great enthusiasm only to give up too soon. We must not grow weary in the hard work of making disciples if we want to reap a harvest.

6. Patient Effort

Adoniram Judson labored in Burma for *six years* before seeing his first convert. Yet at the end of his life, the number had multiplied to 210,000. Great fruitfulness comes through great patience. James 5:7 states, "Therefore, brothers, be patient until the Lord's coming. See how the farmer waits for the precious fruit of the earth and is patient with it until it receives the early and the late rains." Farmers must be patient. They plow the soil, plant the seed, fertilize it, water it, and weed it. Then they have to wait and wait and wait for the seed to mature and yield a harvest. Great harvests do not come overnight. They take time.

Multiplying disciple makers takes time and patience. You must keep on praying, keep on dreaming, and keep on investing. Yet, the results are worth the time and effort. The slow, painful process of the true spiritual multiplication of disciple makers is the fastest way to reach the most people.

⚊ Questions to Ponder ⚊

1. Would you like to hear Jesus say to you one day, "Well done good and faithful servant"?
2. Are you willing to meet the conditions of a multiplied harvest?
3. Are you maintaining a focused vision on the harvest?
4. Which of these conditions are you already doing well?
5. Which ones do you need to seek improvement?

Notes

1. Howard Snyder, *The Radical Wesley* (Downers Grove, IL: IVP, 1980), 57, 63, italics added.

2. Some aspects of this chapter were adapted from Dave Earley, *Turning Members into Leaders* (Houston, TX: TOUCH Publications USA, 2003).

3. Sunday Adalaja at a lunch meeting in the executive dining room of Liberty University, Lynchburg, VA, 2007.

4. Joel Comiskey, *Leadership Explosion* (Houston, TX: TOUCH, 1999).

5. Ibid.

6. Gail Matthews, "Written Goal Study," Dominican University, http://cdn.sid savara.com/wp-content/uploads/2008/09/researchsummary2.pdf (accessed February 12, 2012), italics in original.

7. Adoniram Judson, as quoted by E. M. Bounds, *Power Through Prayer* (Grand Rapids, MI: Zondervan, 1962), 40.

8. Randall G. Neighbour, *Answers to Your Cell Group Questions* (Houston, TX: TOUCH, 2005), 33.

9. Paul Cho, *Prayer: Key to Revival* (Nashville, TN: W Publishing Group, 1984), 15.

10. Ibid., 18.

11. Ibid., 12.

12. Martin Luther King quoted in *Great Quotes from Great Leaders* (Franklin Lakes, NJ: Career Press, 1990), 13.

13. Neighbour, *Answers*, 31.

14. Joel Comiskey, *Groups of 12: A New Way to Mobilize Leaders and Multiply Groups in Your Church* (Houston, TX: TOUCH, 1999), 34.

15. Comiskey, *Leadership Explosion*, 34.

16. Watchman Nee, *The Normal Christian Worker* (Los Angeles, CA: The Stream Publishers, 1965), 11–12.

Part 4

Disciple-Making Models: Pastoral Leadership and the Local Church

In part 1, we looked at the biblical and theological foundations for disciple making. In part 2, we covered the basics of the disciple-making process. In part 3, we discussed several disciple-making methods. In this last section, we will examine the context for making disciples.

Being a disciple and making disciples occurs in a context of believers who are passionately following Jesus Christ. This context is most commonly called the "church." Jesus predicted in Matt 16:18, "I will build My church!" From this prediction the church was born on the day of Pentecost (Acts 2), and since that time the church of Jesus Christ has been in the business of declaring the gospel, developing disciples, and then deploying the disciples to accomplish the mission.

In these final chapters we will describe some characteristics of a healthy church and explore some of the current models and church structures. The goal of this examination is not to be critical of the church models, but to encourage all churches everywhere to develop healthy disciples, powerful leaders, and reproducing churches.

19

Realizing the Importance of the Body

Rod Dempsey

Dumb Move

I finished playing the basketball game, but I knew something was wrong. My right arm was numb, and now I was headed to my doctor's office. The game had gotten pretty intense, and I have always been very competitive. Growing up, I was the smallest kid in my class and had to get by on determination. This time my competitiveness had gotten the best of me.

The game was on the line, and this guy was driving the lane hard. He was a very good player, and I could see that he planned on winning the game by driving down the middle and finishing with a dunk for the last two points. Unfortunately, I was in the lane. I made up my mind that he was not going to be dunking over me. He jumped. I jumped. We collided in midair. He had momentum. I did not. The good news was that he missed the dunk attempt. The bad news was that I was now flying through the air backwards. I stretched out both of my arms behind me, bracing for impact.

What was I thinking? I was almost forty years old playing a pickup game, outside, on asphalt! I was married, had two dependents, full-time employment, and yet here I was picking myself up off the pavement with scrapes, bruises, and a very sore elbow.

Diagnosis before Prescription

I told my doctor what had happened, minus a few details, and he immediately ordered an X-ray of the elbow. The X-ray would reveal if I had fractured the elbow or not. After a few minutes, the doctor came back in, looked at the picture, noted where the fracture had occurred, and I was off with the nurse to begin the process of mending the damage. In just a few minutes, I went from perfectly healthy to "broken" and in need of repair.

In this story, the progression from healthy to unhealthy happened quickly. There was a part of my body that was injured, and the rest of my body was definitely going to suffer as a result. In our physical lives, however, the digression from healthy to unhealthy may occur over many months and sometimes even years. My story illustrates that a skilled doctor is concerned with assessment and diagnosis before prescription.

Insofar as this story illustrates assessment and diagnosis, it helps us address the relative health of a local church. For example, one day the church is healthy, but perhaps because of a poor decision by its leadership team, it suddenly goes from healthy to unhealthy. Or a church may gradually slide into unhealthiness due to many poor choices that occur over a long period of time. Whether the digression occurs rapidly or gradually, the point remains that it is usually due to questionable choices.

As a result of poor choices, a church can become "unhealthy." Unhealthy churches do not make good environments for disciple making to occur. Developing disciples needs to occur inside a healthy, active local body of believers. We would be unwise to attempt to make disciples inside an unhealthy representation of the body of Christ because the individual disciple is nurtured, cared for, and developed by the surrounding joints and ligaments (Eph 4:16) of the local body.

Healthy Body, Healthy Church

The question, however, is whether we can assess the health of a local church. We can, and must, work towards this end. Consider the letter to the seven churches in Revelation. Here we have seven different illustrations of churches in need of some advice from the greatest physician of all time. You are probably familiar with the basic storyline. Jesus is walking amongst the churches, and He is evaluating the health of seven churches in and around Asia Minor. In most of the cases He gives a brief description of some things they are doing well, and then He moves onto a couple of things that need to be addressed.

Likewise, you may go to the doctor, and he or she may say, "You're doing a good job with this area, but you need to make some adjustments to this other area." The same is true here. Jesus is evaluating the health of His body. He refers to things like "I know your works" and "I know your tribulation." Jesus even says to one church, "I know where you live" (Rev 2:13). Now that was probably not used in the same way we use it today, yet it demonstrates that Jesus knows the condition and health of every one of His churches.

You have probably heard about the four words every husband hates to hear. They are . . . "We need to talk." In each of the letters to the seven churches, Jesus is basically saying to the church, "We need to talk." Jesus is evaluating the health of His church. He is giving a diagnosis on the health of a local manifestation of His body, an actual local church.

What Are the Vital Signs?

We can measure the health of the body of Christ much in the same way a physician measures the health of the human body. For example, when you go to a doctor for your annual exam, one of the first things they do is a basic assessment of certain baseline measurements. The doctor wants to check your "vital signs."[1] How much do you weigh? How tall are you? What is your body temperature? What is your at-rest heart rate? What is your blood pressure? Do you have any allergies? Do you smoke? Are you on any medication? Is there a need for blood work or an EKG?

The point here is that the medical profession over hundreds of years has developed certain baseline measurements that reveal to the doctor where there may be an area in which the body is out of alignment. The human body is an amazing organism that has up to eleven different systems that work in harmony and cooperation with all the other parts to create health. If one system, or one part, is not working, then you are going to negatively feel the results. In the same way, I believe we can measure the "vital signs" of a church (the body of Christ) and determine whether or not it is healthy.

Take Care of the Body and the Body Will Take Care of You

The illustration above is appropriate given the fact that when Jesus describes the church, He refers to it as His body. Consider what the apostle Paul said about the church to the church at Ephesus: "And *He put everything under His feet* and appointed Him as head over everything for the church, which is His body, the fullness of the One who fills all things in every way" (Eph 1:22–23). Jesus is not merely saying that His church is *like* a body; it *is* a body. What's more, the church "is *His* body."

In a similar passage, Paul says that we are "one body in Christ and individually members of one another" (Rom 12:5). Further, in Eph 3:6, Paul said that "the Gentiles are coheirs, members of the same *body*, and partners of the promise in Christ Jesus through the gospel."

The Body of Christ

You may ask, what body is that? The answer is . . . the body of Christ. This same thought is illustrated in 1 Cor 12:12–13 where Paul says, "For as the *body* is one and has many parts, and all the parts of that *body*, though many, are one *body* — so also is Christ. For we were all baptized by one Spirit into one *body* — whether Jews or Greeks, whether slaves or free — and we were all made to drink of one Spirit." Again, the apostle Paul says that the body is Christ.

When we receive the gracious gift of salvation, we are baptized by the Spirit into the universal church, which is the body of Christ (1 Cor 12:13; Eph 4:5). In Ephesians 4, Paul gives perhaps the clearest explanation of the inner workings of the church, stating, "And He personally gave some to be apostles, some prophets, some evangelists, some pastors and teachers, for the training of the saints in the work of ministry, to build up the *body* of Christ" (Eph 4:11–12). He continues in verse 16, "From Him the whole *body*, fitted and knit together by every supporting ligament, promotes the growth of the *body* for building up itself in love by the proper working of each individual part."

This passage is saying that the church is the same thing as the body of Christ. They are synonymous. In addition, Paul points out that the body of Christ is to be built up and that it grows strong by "the proper working of each individual part." Stated negatively, if there are parts in the body that are not working "properly," the body will not be healthy. The chart that follows on page 189 illustrates the importance of all the parts working together.

Again I ask, "How many parts of your body do you want working?" We take great care to look after our bodies. At the slightest indication that something is not working properly, not only do we notice it, but we go to a doctor to try to find out what is wrong. When we receive a diagnosis by the doctor, we are usually very meticulous about following through and doing whatever is necessary to experience health once again.

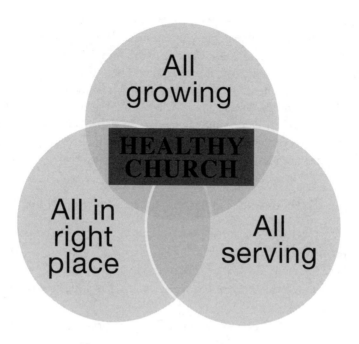

What Are You Passionate About?

Generally speaking, we are passionate about the health of our bodies. We should be just as passionate about the health of the body of Christ. Jesus wants all the parts of His body working. The apostle Paul devotes an entire chapter to this idea in 1 Corinthians 12:

> Now there are different gifts, but the same Spirit. There are different ministries, but the same Lord. And there are different activities, but the same God activates each gift in each person. A demonstration of the Spirit is given to each person to produce what is beneficial: to one is given a message of wisdom through the Spirit, to another, a message of knowledge by the same Spirit, to another, faith by the same Spirit, to another, gifts of healing by the one Spirit, to another, the performing of miracles, to another, prophecy, to another, distinguishing between spirits, to another, different kinds of languages, to another, interpretation of languages. But one and the same Spirit is active in all these, distributing to each one as He wills. For as the *body* is one and has many parts, and all the parts of that *body*, though many, are one *body*—so also is Christ. For we were all baptized by one Spirit into one *body*—whether Jews

or Greeks, whether slaves or free—and we were all made to drink of one Spirit. So the *body* is not one part but many. If the foot should say, "Because I'm not a hand, I don't belong to the *body*," in spite of this it still belongs to the *body*. And if the ear should say, "Because I'm not an eye, I don't belong to the *body*," in spite of this it still belongs to the *body*. If the whole *body* were an eye, where would the hearing be? If the whole were an ear, where would the sense of smell be? But now God has placed each one of the parts in one *body* just as He wanted. And if they were all the same part, where would the *body* be? Now there are many parts, yet one *body*. (vv. 4–20)

This passage teaches us several things about the health of the body:

1. Every Christian has at least one "manifestation of the Spirit" (spiritual gift)
2. There are many different types of spiritual gifts
3. Even though the body of Christ has many parts, there is only one body.
4. All parts of the body are important, not just the external (visible) but also the internal (invisible parts).
5. Just because a part is not seen, it is still a part of the body.
6. God has placed the parts in the body "just as He wanted."
7. Where would the body be if there were only one part?
8. All the parts work together to form one body.

Putting It All Together

Here, the apostle Paul is explaining to us the proper function of the body of Christ. It is an organic system where all the parts work together. In a local church, we need to understand that in order for it to be healthy, all the parts need to be working "according to the proper working of each individual part." The most important "vital sign" for the church is the degree to which all the parts of the body of Christ work together. Greg Ogden emphasizes the importance of the body, saying,

> As we rediscover the church as a living organism, the body of Christ, church members have been called out of the audience to become players on the stage. Everyone has a part in this play. Every believer is a necessary part of the drama God is producing, the drama of salvation history. We are on stage together, pastors and people alike. There is no longer a select, professional union of actors. In the body of Christ, all the

"actors" have a direct connection to the Producer, the Creator, and the Choreographer of History.[2]

Let me ask you a very important question: have all the believers in your church discovered their spiritual gift, and are they using their spiritual gift the way the Master intends?

No longer is it just the pastor's job to "feed the flock." Listen to Aubrey Malphurs: "Do you want to know if your church is effective? Look for disciples! While the Great Commission includes pastoral care, it's much broader than that."[3] The pastor's main job is to "equip" or "train" the members to grow spiritually and use their gift in the proper way in the body. When all the parts are working "just as He wanted," then the body is healthy. Disciple making is about helping individuals develop to their full potential for Christ and His kingdom. This happens best in a healthy body where all the parts are functioning the way He intended.

In summary, disciple making is not easy, but it is possible if we remain focused on keeping the body healthy. It is clear from the letters written to the seven churches in Revelation that Jesus is evaluating His church. He has an intense desire for His church to be healthy. There are no perfect churches. They all have weaknesses because they are made up of imperfect people. However, the goal of a healthy church is a worthwhile goal.

To understand health in the church, it is important to understand that the primary illustration given in the New Testament of the church of Jesus Christ is a body. The church of Jesus is the visible manifestation of His body. The human body is a wonderful and complex system of interrelated parts (1 Corinthians 12). In this regard, the church is an organic collection of systems that form an organization. Unfortunately, we have often ignored this organic element. We are more concerned with the health of the organization and less concerned with the health of the individuals that makes up the organization.

Sick Members = Sick Church

The starting point for most pastors is to measure the health of the organization, not the health of the individual. I believe the starting point for a healthy church is the health of the individual. Our focus, as pastors, is to get all the parts healthy (spiritual growth/"being") and to get all the parts working (spiritual activity/"doing"). When all the parts of the organism are healthy, then the organization (body) will be healthy. A healthy body of Christ is the perfect environment for disciple making. Christians maturing in word, thought, attitude, and action is the goal.

To measure health in the human body, medical doctors spend many years studying science and many more years perfecting their art. There are many different perspectives about how to measure a church's health. Some people measure health by the attendance on Sunday morning. Some would seek to find out how many buildings the church has. Some would like to see the church's bank account or balance sheet.

The world tries to measure health by externals. Jesus is looking deeper. He is looking inward to see the condition of the body. In reality, the body of Christ stays healthy in much the same way as the human body. The human body is healthy and stays healthy as each part works the way it was designed to work. The body of Jesus is healthy, and stays healthy, as each disciple grows strong and fulfills his or her role in the body of Christ. Make no mistake, Jesus, like a wise and experienced physician, is analyzing and measuring the health of His body. We would be wise to follow His example.

～ Questions to Ponder ～

1. In Eph 1:23, how does Jesus relate to the church?
2. How is the health of the church related to the health of each individual part of the body?
3. Do you know your spiritual gift?
4. How are you using your gift to strengthen the body of Jesus?
5. Why is it important to get every disciple using his or her gift in the proper way in the body?

Notes

1. See http://www.uihealthcare.com/topics/generalhealth/ghea4577.html (accessed October 12, 2012).

2. Greg Ogden, *Unfinished Business: Returning the Ministry to the People of God* (Grand Rapids: Zondervan, 2010), Kindle location 355–59.

3. Aubrey Malphurs, *Strategic Disciple Making: A Practical Tool for Successful Ministry* (Grand Rapids, MI: Baker, 2009), 157.

20

Disciple Making Is . . .

Comprehending Spiritual Leadership

Rod Dempsey

Cold Hard Facts

I had been married for a few years before I realized I was not a very good husband. Now I am not proud to admit this, but it is the truth. Don't get me wrong; I was not doing anything questionable or immoral. My wife and I both had attended a Christian college, had good teaching and good examples. Besides, I had a couple of Christian counseling courses and a leadership course in seminary, and I naively thought I was "prepared" for marriage. The harsh reality of being married is that it exposes who you really are.

Being married is like looking into a "character mirror." If you are selfish and immature before you marry, then you will be selfish and immature after you marry. I agree with Martin Luther, who "viewed marriage as a school of character, whereby God uses the hardships of daily family life to sanctify us."[1] I also believe this is why the apostle Paul told Timothy in 1 Tim 3:4–5 that an overseer needs to be the "husband of one wife" and a person "who manages his own household competently, having his children under control with all dignity. (If anyone does not know how to manage his own household, how will he take care of God's church?)" Paraphrasing this passage would sound something like this: "To be a leader in the church, you must be a leader at home.

If you cannot lead your wife and family, then forget about leading the church." In the last chapter we discussed the importance of the body in the disciple-making process. Yet, the mission and ministry of the body are facilitated by godly pastoral leadership. In this chapter, we will explore the nature of spiritual leadership.

God's Proving Ground

Within the confines of the marriage covenant, God teaches us to sacrifice, putting the needs of others ahead of our own needs. This is what Paul says in Eph 5:25: "Husbands, love your wives, just as also Christ loved the church and gave Himself for her" (NKJV). Becoming a better husband means you must learn to sacrifice. You must learn to put the needs of your wife and family ahead of your own desires. This requires character. My goal as a husband and father is to help my wife and children grow and develop to reach their full God-given potential. My goal as a husband and a father is that my wife and children will hear from Jesus, "Well done, good and faithful slave" (Matt 25:23). Likewise, putting others ahead of your wants and needs is the essence of Christian leadership, but it will not happen if we are spiritually immature.

This idea of character building and sacrifice is important if one is to understand *Christian* leadership because Christian leadership is different from secular leadership. Henry and Richard Blackaby comment on the importance of character, "The first truth in leadership development is this: God's assignments are always based on character—the greater the character, the greater the assignment (Luke 16:10)."[2] At the very core of Christian leadership is the idea that I am here to help you grow and develop. Without character, we will not sacrifice for, or serve, others. Jesus sacrificed for us, and in order to lead like Jesus, we must sacrifice to develop God's children. In the same way that we are to serve and develop our family, we are to serve and develop His church.

My Goals, God's Goals

As a Christian leader, I am here to help you grow and become all God has in mind for you to become. The motivation in secular leadership is that you are here to help me make the organization successful. The health of the organization is the highest goal. Furthermore, as a leader I am here to make the organization successful, and the person is viewed as a resource. The motivation in Christian leadership, however, is that I am here to help you become a healthy (mature) and productive part of the body. The result will be that the body (organism) will be healthy. The starting points, therefore, are different.

The starting point in Christian leadership is the health of the individual. It is not the health of the organization, but the health of the organism. Nevertheless, a true Christian leader is still concerned about the health of the organization, though it is not the primary motivation. The health of the organization is a result of the individual members maturing and ministering according to their role in the body. It is similar in the family. All family members must fulfill their roles to have unity and purpose.

Making disciples is a developmental process. Bill Hull describes the process this way: "We call this process spiritual transformation. In spiritual transformation, we move from the person we are, and continue to change by degree into the image of Christ."[3] As disciples grow and develop within the body, the natural progression is that Great Commission leaders will begin emerging. Defining and developing Great Commission leaders is the topic we will examine next.

Christian Leader: The Person

To study the topic of becoming a Christian leader, one approach that I have found helpful for my students is to examine many different definitions of a concept and identify recurring themes. Once those themes have been identified, I then encourage my students to create a definition incorporating the three or four concepts they feel are most important. I have done this exercise many times in my classes, and each time I am amazed at how quickly my students are able to synthesize the concepts and develop a personal and powerful definition.

I have approximately sixty-five different definitions of "leader" and "leadership" in my personal files. Several recurring words and phrases emerge from these definitions. Some distinguish between what it means to be a leader (the person), and others on the nature of leadership (the process).

Leader Foundations

In looking at the definitions of Christian leadership, here are some recurring themes:

1. *Influence through solid character.* This idea is repeated in almost half of the definitions. The general idea is simply this: a leader will persuade or influence other people to follow either their example or follow the stated vision by their character. Without character, people

will question the leader's motives and will ultimately not follow the leader's vision.

2. *Vision or direction.* The leader has an idea of where to go, and they also have an idea of how to get there. A leader has a clear mental image of a preferable future, and they are passionate about getting there.

3. *Development.* The general idea here is that a leader is not only concerned about getting people to do what they want but also about empowering the people to grow and develop to reach their full potential.

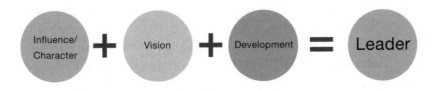

Influence = Leader

The first repeated concept in all the definitions is "influence." It is important to realize that a leader will influence others. There are many ways to influence others. We can influence others by our own spiritual growth. We can influence others through our speech. We can influence others through our character. We can influence others through using our gifts and talents.

For the Christian leader, we can influence others through our prayers. We can influence others by exhorting them in the Word of God. Fundamentally, being a leader means you will influence and impact others.

Vision and the Secret Place

The second word that we notice is the idea of *seeing* the way or having *vision.* Seeing the road and knowing the path is critical to being a leader. Being able to see further, farther, and clearer is an important responsibility for the Christian leader. When we spend time with God in His word and we spend time in His presence, we begin to hear His voice clearly.

Jesus said in John 10:27, "My sheep hear my voice, I know them, and they follow Me." In fact, Jesus Himself often spent time alone with His Father to ascertain His will. This starting point sets apart the Christian leader. The secular leader will spend time crunching numbers and analyzing statistics in order to determine the health of the organization. The Christian leader spends time with God. Blackaby comments on this point: "The secular world ignores God's will, so nonbelievers are left with one alternative—to project their own vision. Christians are called to a totally different approach. For Christians, God alone sets the agenda."[4] As a result, he or she cultivates the art of listening to God to the point where God reveals to them the secrets of the kingdom (Matt 13:11; Luke 8:10). Proverbs 3:32 says, "For the perverse person is an abomination to the LORD, but His secret council is with the upright" (NKJV). When we spend time with God, we become friends, and friends share with each other their secret dreams and hopes. Let me ask: are you spending time with God and listening for His voice?

Catch and Release

The third idea from the definitions is the idea of *developing* and *enabling* people to become who God created them to be. I believe the central task of the Christian leader is to encourage, equip, and empower individuals to grow and become what God intends them to be. I agree with Warren Bennis, who says, "Becoming a leader is synonymous with becoming yourself. It is precisely that simple, and it is also that difficult."[5] As one grows and develops in Christlikeness, they are also encouraged to discover how God has gifted them and what they should be doing in the kingdom. Ephesians 2:10 says, "For we are His creation—created in Christ Jesus for good works, which God prepared ahead of time so that we should walk in them." God has saved us, not *by* works (Eph 2:8–9), but He has saved us *to* work. The Father has something in mind that He wants us to do. If a person has accepted King Jesus, then that person has a kingdom destiny.

God expects every one of His children to know and use the gift He has given to them. When this occurs, God is the one who gets the credit because it is not based upon a person's natural ability or talents. A Christian leader understands that it is his or her responsibility to prepare God's people to stand before Christ and not be ashamed. In fact, we should make it our goal for every believer to stand before Christ and personally hear from Him, "Well done, good and faithful servant" (Matt 25:23 NKJV).

Definition of Leader

With these three ideas in mind, let us formulate a definition that synthesizes the reoccurring concepts and describes what it means to be a Christian leader:

A Christian leader is a person of influence. He or she follows God's
vision for his or her life, and influences others to follow God's plan for
their lives.

From this definition we can help the Christian leader to see that his or her
responsibility is to develop each of God's children to reach their full potential.
This is also the same model that God has established for the family. As parents,
we are here to help our children grow and develop and become fully functional
citizens of society. The same concept is true for God's family. We are here to
help individuals grow and develop and become fully functional members of
God's kingdom.

Christian Leadership: The Process

Whatever defines the Christian leader should also define Christian
leadership. That is, they should have similar words and concepts while allowing
for one major difference: one deals with the person, and the other deals with
the process. With this in mind, let me share some common ideas related to the
process of leadership:

1. *Influence*: All leadership comes down to the ability to influence
   others.
2. *Vision*: Leaders have a specific direction of where to go and how to
   get there. They have a vision of a preferred future.
3. *Development*: Leaders are not only concerned about getting people to
   do what they want, they are also concerned about developing people
   to reach their full potential.

Leadership Foundations

The first concept I notice from all the definitions is the idea that leadership
is about influencing people. J. Oswald Sanders said, "Leadership is influence,
the ability of one person to influence others to follow his or her lead."[6]

Influence is by far the most common phrase used in any definition.
The idea is this: a leader influences the people toward accomplishing certain
objectives. The goals of the organization are paramount, while the people in
the organization are there to aid and assist in that mission. In many cases,
extrinsic motivational techniques are employed in order to motivate people to
accomplish the organizational goals.

The next phrase is the idea of having a vision. It is a forward-looking
concept. Without a vision there is no clear-cut direction of where a ministry or

organization is heading. George Barna suggests that vision is a "clear mental image of a preferable future."[7] This is perhaps the simplest and clearest explanation for vision. Leaders have the ability to see things that others do not see.

The third phrase is the focus on the development of the individual. Developing individuals to reach their full potential is what God has in mind for His body. I believe Harvey Firestone got it right when he said, "The growth and development of people is the highest calling of leadership."[8] To return to the family analogy, God's design for the family is all about developing our children to mature and become highly functioning members of society. The same is true of God's design for the church. His children should be encouraged, equipped, and empowered to mature and become highly functioning members of His kingdom. Christian leaders are passionate about developing a healthy body. The way to develop a healthy body is to develop healthy members.

Christian Leadership Defined

In a human body, healthy appendages are the result of being used and exercised. For instance, if you never used your left arm, how strong would your left arm be? In addition, if you never used your left arm, how effective would your body be? God wants all the parts of His body working, so Christian leadership is about developing every individual member to become and do all God desires. Now let's take a look at a definition that incorporates all three elements:

> Christian leadership is the *process* of influencing individuals to follow God's plan for their lives and become all they can be for Christ and His mission.

Christian Leadership Applied

This definition of Christian leadership is almost exactly the same as Christian leader (see p. 197). The person (leader) and the process (leadership) are inseparable elements of spiritual leadership and, as such, should be similar. You could shorten the definition of Christian leader this way: "A Christian leader influences individuals to follow God's plan for their lives." Then, you could let the leadership definition explain the process. Either way, the focus of the leader needs to be on the growth and development of the individual because the way to grow the body is to grow the individual. This is what Christian leaders do.

It is the same with parents. We nurture and develop our children to grow up and become all they can be for God's glory. There is continuity between parenting and Christian leadership in God's kingdom. The goals of being a parent concern the growth and development of our children, and the goals of being a spiritual parent (disciple-making leader) concern the growth and development of God's children. It is crucial for those who attempt to make disciples to understand that our job as a leader is to steward the growth and development of His children.

～ Questions to Ponder ～

1. What does marriage teach us about ourselves?
2. What is the goal of Christian leadership?
3. What are 3 components of being a Christian leader?
4. What are the 3 components of Christian leadership?
5. What do you need to work on from each area?

Notes

1. See http://thegospelcoalition.org/blogs/tgc/2011/08/03/martin-luther-on-marriage-as-a-school-of-character (accessed October 12, 2012).

2. Henry Blackaby and Richard Blackaby, *Spiritual Leadership: Moving People on to God's Agenda*, rev. and exp. ed. (Nashville, TN: B&H, 2001), 288.

3. Bill Hull, *The Complete Book of Discipleship* (Colorado Springs, CO: NavPress, 2006), Kindle location 1789.

4. Blackaby and Blackaby, *Spiritual Leadership*, 69.

5. See http://quotationsbook.com/quote/22784 (accessed October 12, 2012).

6. J. Oswald Sanders, *Spiritual Leadership* (Chicago: Moody, 2007), Kindle location 517–18.

7. George Barna, *The Power of Vision* (Ventura, CA: Regal, 2009), back cover.

8. See http://www.brainyquote.com/quotes/authors/h/harvey_s_firestone. html (accessed October 12, 2012).

21

Reproducing Missional Leaders

Rod Dempsey

Leaders Lead

In the previous chapter, we discussed several common characteristics between a Christian leader (the person) and Christian leadership (the process). Let's review the definition of a leader:

> A Christian leader is a person of influence. He or she follows God's will for their lives and influences others to follow God's plan for their lives.

It is clear from this definition that a leader influences others to follow God's plan for *their* lives. Notice it does not say "influencing people to follow the needs of the ministry." Notice also that the definition does not say "influencing people to follow plans that you select for them." It is important to note also that this definition does not specifically say that a leader "influences people to meet the needs of an organization."

The primary job of a leader is to help individuals discover and accomplish God's will *for their lives.* That is what leaders do, period. In following God's will, there is a progression that moves from an individual going from not knowing Jesus to accepting Him as the Lord and Savior. The individual then grows spiritually strong. This process is called sanctification in the Scriptures (1 Thess 4:3), and it is God's will for every believer. In the process of sanctification, a believer grows by investing time and effort in certain spiritual habits or disciplines that connect them to the grace of God. Habits like hearing, reading, studying, memorizing, and meditating on the Word of God enable believers to have the "mind of Christ." Jesus talks about the need to "continue" (reading, studying, memorizing, and meditating) in John 8:31–32:

> So Jesus said to the Jews who had believed Him, "If you continue in My word, you really are My disciples. You will know the truth, and the truth will set you free."

Continuing in Christ's words helps the disciple grow from a baby in Christ to a mature and strong disciple who is being set free from the entanglements of the world, the flesh, and the devil (1 John 2:15–17). As we grow stronger, we begin to serve in the body of Christ and, as a result, discover and use the "spiritual gifts" God has predetermined for us to use. Consider 1 Pet 4:10–11 again:

> Based on the gift each one has received, use it to serve others, as good managers of the varied grace of God. If anyone speaks, it should be as one who speaks God's words; if anyone serves, it should be from the strength God provides, so that God may be glorified through Jesus Christ in everything. To Him belong the glory and the power forever and ever. Amen.

It is abundantly clear from this passage that God has given to every believer at least one spiritual gift He intends to be used for His Glory. When a person is correctly using the gift God has given to them, he or she bears spiritual fruit to the glory of God. Jesus talks about this ultimate goal in John 15:8, stating, "My Father is glorified by this: that you produce much fruit and prove to be My disciples."

Our job as Christian leaders is to help individuals grow, develop, and serve the King and His kingdom. We lead people as we share the truth with them and help them discover and accomplish His will. Ultimately, they become "fruitful" as they grow in Christian character (by walking in the Spirit) and discover and use the gifts God has entrusted to them. By following this plan and approach, God is the one who gets the glory. This is the essence of Christian discipleship. In disciple making, there is a personal dimension to spiritual growth, and there is a public expression of the individual serving the kingdom as well. Christian leaders develop disciples, and the disciples accomplish the mission of Christ. If you have any view of Christian leadership other than winning people to Christ, helping them grow and develop to the point where they are fruitful for the kingdom, then you need to seriously reexamine what you are doing. In the previous chapter we noted some general principles and characteristics of Christian leadership. This chapter will expand on those fundamentals, noting their relationship to the disciple-making process.

Be Careful

For far too long we have substituted activity in church events and called it discipleship. Organizational activity is no substitute for personal involvement. Christian leaders oversee the development of disciples. From a growing number of disciples, Great Commission leaders will emerge. Christian discipleship and Christian leadership are inexorably linked.

Without an effective discipleship system, you will not have leaders for the mission, and if you do not have Christian leaders, you will not have reproducing discipleship. Christian leaders help people come to know Christ, grow in Christ, and develop to their full potential for Christ and His mission. That is what Christian leaders do. When this intentional and individual pursuit is occurring in sufficient quality and quantity, the natural by-product is emerging harvest leaders.

The Purpose of Christian Leadership

Do you know the difference between secular leadership and Christian leadership? As we noted in the previous chapter, secular leadership is concerned with the health of the organization. Many times individuals are viewed as a means to an end. Christian leadership is concerned about the health of the individual. If we equip and empower all the individuals, then the organization (body) will be healthy. Consider our definition for Christian leadership from the previous chapter:

> Christian leadership is the process of influencing individuals to follow God's plan for their lives and become all they can be for Christ and His mission.

As we noted earlier, this definition is very similar to the definition of Christian leader, the major difference being that this definition relates to the *process* of developing the individual.

I have been involved in the process of winning people to Christ and helping them to grow and develop now for more than thirty years. I have been involved in disciple making in a variety of contexts and traditions, and I am here to tell you that disciple making occurs best inside the confines of a relational environment like a small group. This conclusion has been supported and put into practice many times throughout church history.[1]

The Power of Love

The leaders of the early church certainly believed in and developed disciples in churches that met in homes (Acts 2:46; 5:42; 12:12; 16:40; Rom 16:3–5, 23; 1 Cor 16:19; Col 4:15). One reason the early church may have followed this practice was because Jesus had stated clearly that His disciples were to love one another. As a result of that love for fellow brothers and sisters, the unbelieving world would know the followers of Jesus Christ. Consider the clear teaching of Jesus:

1. "I give you a new commandment: *Love one another.* Just as I have loved you, you must also *love one another*" (John 13:34).
2. "By this all people will know that you are My disciples, if you have *love for one another*" (John 13:35).
3. "This is My command: *Love one another* as I have loved you" (John 15:12).
4. "This is what I command you: *Love one another*" (John 15:17).

From these passages we may conclude that where no visible expression of mutual love exists, there is no witness to the unbelieving world. The apostles certainly picked up on this theme. Throughout the New Testament there are forty different "one anothers" scattered in the letters to the churches. The reason we see the "one another" phrase repeated so often, and by so many authors, is because they were explaining to us how to live out our love for each other. Take a look at the different ways we are exhorted to practice the "one anothers," and it will become clear that if we practice the "one anothers," we will certainly be showing how to live in Christ's love:

1. "Love one another" (Rom 13:8).
2. "Show family affection to one another with brotherly love" (Rom 12:10).
3. "Outdo one another in showing honor" (Rom 12:10).
4. "Be in agreement with one another" (Rom 12:16).
5. "Let us no longer criticize one another" (Rom 14:13).
6. "Accept one another, just as the Messiah also accepted you" (Rom 15:7).
7. "Instruct one another" (Rom 15:14).

8. "Have the same concern for each other" (1 Cor 12:25).
9. "Serve one another through love" (Gal 5:13).
10. "Carry one another's burdens" (Gal 6:2).
11. "We must not become conceited, provoking one another, envying one another" (Gal 5:26).
12. "With patience, accepting one another in love" (Eph 4:2).
13. "Be kind and compassionate to one another" (Eph 4:32a).
14. "Forgiving one another" (Eph 4:32b).
15. "Speaking to one another in psalms, hymns, and spiritual songs" (Eph 5:19).
16. "Submitting to one another in the fear of Christ" (Eph 5:21).
17. "In humility consider others as more important than yourselves" (Phil 2:3).
18. "Do not lie to one another" (Col 3:9).
19. "Accepting one another" (Col 3:13).
20. "Forgiving one another if anyone has a complaint against another" (Col 3:13).
21. "Admonishing one another" (Col 3:16).
22. "Encourage one another" (1 Thess 4:18; 5:11; Heb 10:25).
23. "Build each other up" (1 Thess 5:11).
24. "Encourage each other daily" (Heb 3:13).
25. "Be concerned about one another in order to promote love and good works" (Heb 10:24).
26. "Don't criticize one another" (Jas 4:11).
27. "Do not complain about one another" (Jas 5:9).
28. "Confess your sins to one another" (Jas 5:16).
29. "Pray for one another" (Jas 5:16).
30. "Love one another earnestly from a pure heart" (1 Pet 1:22).
31. "All of you should be like-minded and sympathetic" (1 Pet 3:8).
32. "Have fervent love for one another" (1 Pet 4:8 NKJV).
33. "Be hospitable to one another without complaining" (1 Pet 4:9).
34. "Based on the gift each one has received, use it to serve others" (1 Pet 4:10).
35. "Clothe yourselves with humility toward one another" (1 Pet 5:5).
36. "Love one another" (1 John 3:11, 23; 4:7, 11–12; 2 John 5).

The Christian leader involved in the process of leading people to follow Christ must encourage, empower, and illustrate how to live in Christ's love. The small-group environment (relational discipleship) provides the most effective context for demonstrating love for God and neighbor (the Great Commandment) and for one another (the New Commandment).

Share the Load, Reap the Benefits

The Christian leader must be committed to being the paradigm. He or she is committed to spending time with other brothers and sisters and sharing life together. Further, the Christian leader also seeks to involve as many people as possible in the functions of the group. We seek to share the load and the responsibilities (see Exodus 18) of leading God's people. Here are some different ways to involve people in the life of the group:

1. Leading the icebreaker portion of the group
2. Leading the group's prayer time
3. Recording and keeping track of the group's prayer requests and sending email updates
4. Sending cards and letters to absentees
5. Planning the group's refreshment schedule
6. Planning the group's fun activities
7. Planning the group's outreach efforts and activities
8. Hosting the group
9. Leading the group discussion
10. Praying about starting a new group in the future

One of the greatest benefits of this type of involvement in the group is that, as they serve, people will begin to discover their spiritual gift(s) in a natural way. In addition, as we share our lives together, we also become aware that God has brought us together, not just to have fun and fellowship, but to labor in the harvest fields. The Lord of the Harvest desires us to be active in His mission. That is why we must keep multiplication and reproduction of new groups at the forefront of group members' minds.

Motivation for Multiplication

Behind this drive to develop new leaders and start new groups is the conviction that we are doing this not for the people who are currently here, but for those *who are not here yet*. The Christian leader is intimately involved in the process, looking for those who have the potential to say to others, "Follow me as I follow Christ." As we pray for laborers to be sent into the harvest, and those people begin to emerge from the group, we prayerfully select (even before the group begins) one, two or three individuals or couples to begin sharing in the tasks of leading others spiritually.

Dave Ferguson talks about the importance of developing future leaders when he says, "Apprenticeship is not about finding people who can help us do tasks more effectively. We're not talking about preparing people to simply replace us so we can move on to something else. At the heart of biblical apprenticeship is a mindset of reproduction: reproducing our leadership so the mission will be carried on to future generations."[2] Reproduce new groups to reach new people!

As disciples are developed, new leaders will emerge from the body. As new leaders emerge, we must help them see that God's will for them is to reach out to people who do not know Christ. Here are some suggestions for the group leader to keep in mind as he or she focuses on group health and reproduction:

1. The leader must believe in, and be committed to, the following:

   a. *Prayer*: Sets apart approximately an hour a day to pray for self, family, group, church, lost.
   b. *Evangelism*: Has an outward focus and leads the group toward reaching out to the lost.
   c. *Goal setting and growing*: Is not afraid to set some God-sized goals, and prays and works hard at accomplishing them.
   d. *Equipping others*: Primarily trains his or her assistant to lead a group in just a few months.
   e. *Multiplication*: Is not satisfied until reproduction of the group has taken place.

2. The leader intentionally selects at least one apprentice leader and possibly two. It is important to have a clear-cut strategy to eventually birth a new group. If you start your group without an apprentice, it is very possible that your group will never plant a new group.

3. The leader seeks to involve as many people as possible in the healthy functioning of the group. As the individual grows and develops, he or she discovers their spiritual gift and begins using it. The body grows strong and healthy "according to the proper working of each individual part" (Eph 4:16 NASB).

4. The leader prepares for the lesson and leads the discussion, trying to involve everyone. The leader knows where the group is going and how they are going to get there.

5. The leader meets with his/her coach on a regular basis (at least monthly). In a multiplying model, the coach is keeping his or her eyes on some very important vital indicators to see if the group is moving in the right direction.

6. The leader attends all training/equipping sessions and turns in weekly attendance reports. In order to be effective, leaders need additional training and equipping.

7. The leader leads the group in service or ministry projects. The tendency of most groups is to turn inward and develop an "us four and no more" mentality. Service and ministry projects keep the group focused on others. Alan Hirsch calls this "communitas."[3]

8. The leader guides the group toward reproduction of another group in twelve to eighteen months. The leader keeps an eye on the horizon toward the highest goal of group life, which is healthy spiritual multiplication.

As the leader focuses on and practices these habits, disciples will grow and develop. Dave Kraft observes, "Today the crying need is for more leaders. To grow by addition, you recruit more followers. To grow by multiplication, you add more leaders."[4] Our goal is to develop a multiplication movement that will reach the world. That means we need a discipling movement, where leaders naturally emerge and lead in the Great Commission.

As disciples grow and develop, leaders will be the result. As leaders emerge, we then give them additional responsibilities and encourage them to think about starting a new group in the future. We encourage them to leave the current group and start a new group, or they stay in the existing group and we go out to start a new group. Either way, we must stay focused on reaching the lost.

Look Out upon the Fields

We must keep the focus on the harvest fields that are "ready for harvest" (John 4:35). If we do not stay focused on the harvest fields, the group will adopt an inward focus. As we focus on the harvest fields, reproduction of new leaders and new groups should be a natural by-product. When our focus turns inward, however, the result is not so pretty. The world is growing at an exponential rate, and we need exponential strategies to reach the world. Multiplication of disciples, leaders, groups, and churches is our only hope.

— Questions to Ponder —

1. What is the purpose of Christian leadership?
2. What is the normal progression for a disciple of Jesus?
3. Why is love so important to accomplishing the mission of Christ?
4. Look over the list of the "one anothers" and pick out two or three that you need to work on.
5. From the list of ten suggestions, how can you get more people involved in group life and relational discipleship?

Notes

1. Bill Hull, *The Complete Book of Discipleship* (Colorado Springs, CO: NavPress, 2006), chap. 3.

2. Dave Ferguson and Jon Ferguson, *Exponential: How to Accomplish the Jesus Mission* (Grand Rapids: Zondervan, 2010), 62.

3. Alan Hirsch, *The Forgotten Ways* (Ada, MI: Brazos Press, 2007), Kindle location 241.

4. Dave Kraft, *Leaders Who Last* (Wheaton, IL: Crossway, 2010), 138.

22

Creating
a Healthy Church

Rod Dempsey

In this section, we have discussed the context for making disciples, first noting the importance of the body of Christ (chap. 19). Next, we explored several general principles of spiritual leadership (chap. 20) followed by a more in-depth look at the purpose of leadership: multiplying missional leaders (chap. 21). We return in this chapter to the shape of a healthy church and its role in the disciple-making process.

Healthy Body . . . Healthy Church

In the simplest terms, a healthy church looks like and acts like a healthy body. The apostle Paul makes it clear that the church is to be considered the body of Christ (Eph 1:23). The human body is an amazingly complex arrangement of organic systems. When all of the parts are working properly, the body seems to grow and develop without any effort. Ray Stedman, in his seminal work *Body Life,* observes, "When we think of the church as a body, then Ephesians 4 presents us with an anatomy lesson, a view of the physiology and structure of the body: how the various organs function together, how the parts of the body are coordinated to accomplish the purpose of the body."[1] In this chapter, I want to take this analogy one step further. I want to describe what some of the "systems" look like and how they could operate. As much as possible, I want to connect the system to a scriptural command or principle. If possible, I would suggest that you take an assessment of the health of the church you are either leading or attending.

In the same way one ascertains the health of the human body, it is possible to gain an idea of the health of the body of Christ. This assessment does not serve as any person's or any church's judge. This is offered as a possible exercise to help your church, or any church, grow healthier.

I have developed twenty descriptions of what a healthy church either looks like or does. My goal is to show from the Scriptures the importance of each area. After this initial description, I encourage you to rate the area on a scale from 1 to 5 (1 being nonexistent and 5 being fully practiced). After each area is evaluated, you can then add the twenty areas to create an overall score (20 areas times 5 possible points per area = 100 total possible points). This inventory will quickly reveal the lowest area and give you some direction on what areas need to be addressed first. To begin, let me give you the twenty statements that could possibly indicate health in the body of Christ.

A healthy church is:

1. Where the gospel is being proclaimed by word and deed
2. Where new believers are baptized
3. Where new believers are growing in their ability to surrender and sacrifice for the kingdom
4. Where new believers are intentionally and individually nurtured and developed
5. Where believers are willingly investing their financial resources in the kingdom of God
6. Where the "whole counsel of God" is being taught with a view toward application even to the point of church discipline
7. Where the leaders see their role as equipping and empowering the saints
8. Where the saints are growing in maturity (connecting them to Jesus through the disciplines—spiritual formation)
9. Where the saints are growing in unity and love for one another
10. Where the saints are encouraged to discover their spiritual gifts
11. Where a majority of the saints are using their gifts "properly" (according to God's design)
12. Where relational groups are intentionally developed and members are growing in their love for one another (the "one anothers" are happening)
13. Where relational groups are lovingly sharing their lives and the gospel

with unbelievers (living on mission in community)

14. Where passionate prayer is continually being offered up for the lost and for laborers

15. Where leaders for the Great Commission are intentionally being developed

16. Where relational groups are multiplying new leaders and new groups

17. Where worship occurs at the individual level and it is powerfully manifested when the body gathers together

18. Where the poor and "least of these" is intentionally being ministered to

19. Where the mission of Christ is being accomplished locally, regionally, nationally, and globally by members from within the local body

20. Where new churches are being planted as a result of effective discipleship and effective leadership development

A healthy church is a representation of the people of God coming together to accomplish the mission of God for the glory of God. As a caveat, the twenty statements above are not meant to be exhaustive. You could create twenty more. However, they should have scriptural support and justification in order for the exercise to have meaning.

Suggested Healthy Church Assessment

Now let's go through all twenty statements with scriptural support and justification. A healthy church is . . .

1. *Where the gospel is being proclaimed by word and deed.* Luke describes the mission of Jesus this way: "He also said to them, 'This is what is written: The Messiah would suffer and rise from the dead the third day, and repentance for forgiveness of sins would be proclaimed in His name to all the nations, beginning at Jerusalem. You are witnesses of these things'" (Luke 24:46–48). We are to preach the gospel (1 Cor 15:1–4) to every creature, and any church not proclaiming and showing this message is not healthy.

2. *Where new believers are baptized.* Jesus made it very clear in the Great Commission (Matt 28:19–20) that in our going, we are to make disciples. One of the most important ways to develop a disciple is to "baptize them in the name of the Father and of the Son and of the Holy Spirit." The person who accepts Jesus as Savior also accepts Him as Lord (Rom 10:9–10), and the evidence of this submission and

surrender is baptism. The church that does not baptize new believers
is not healthy.

3. *Where new believers are growing in their ability to surrender and
    sacrifice for the kingdom.* Jesus also made clear in Luke 9:23–24 that
    "if anyone wants to come with Me, he must deny himself, take up
    his cross daily, and follow Me. For whoever wants to save his life
    will lose it, but whoever loses his life because of Me will save it."
    You cannot follow Christ without surrendering everything to Him.
    All He wants is everything. The church that compromises on total
    surrender to Christ cannot be healthy.

4. *Where new believers are intentionally nurtured and developed.*
    The Bible illustrates salvation with the visual picture of being
    "born again" (John 3) and becoming a new creation (2 Cor 5:17). In
    keeping with this analogy, when a person comes to know Christ as
    Lord and Savior, they are like a baby who needs nurture and care
    to grow spiritually strong (see Heb 5:12–14). A healthy church will
    intentionally devote time and loving care to new believers (see also
    1 Thess 2:7–9).

5. *Where believers are willingly investing their financial resources in the
    kingdom of God.* Jesus made this principle very clear when He said,
    "Don't collect for yourselves treasures on earth, where moth and rust
    destroy and where thieves break in and steal. But collect for yourselves
    treasures in heaven, where neither moth nor rust destroys, and where
    thieves don't break in and steal. For where your treasure is, there your
    heart will be also" (Matt 6:19–21). The apostle Paul has much to say
    about this topic (1 Cor 16:1–4; 2 Cor 8:1–5; 9:6–8). A healthy church
    teaches its members to invest financially in God's kingdom.

6. *Where the "whole counsel of God" is being taught with a view toward
    application, even to the point of church discipline.* The apostle Paul,
    speaking to the Ephesian church in Acts 20:25–27, says, "And now
    I know that none of you, among whom I went about preaching the
    kingdom, will ever see my face again. . . . Therefore I testify to you
    this day that I am innocent of everyone's blood, for I did not shrink
    back from declaring to you the whole plan of God." James takes this
    even further when he says that we should "be doers of the word and
    not hearers only, deceiving yourselves" (Jas 1:22). A healthy church
    teaches the Word for the purpose of obedience. When someone
    is intentionally disobeying the Word of God, the church takes it
    seriously and calls the sinning persons into account (Matt 18:15–17).

7. *Where the leaders see their role as equipping and empowering the saints.* The apostle Paul makes this clear when he explains in Ephesians 4:11–12 that Christ "personally gave some to be apostles, some prophets, some evangelists, some pastors and teachers, for the training of the saints in the work of ministry, to build up the body of Christ." In a clergy-driven church, the pastor sees his role as doing the work of the ministry. In a healthy church, the pastor sees his primary role as equipping and training the saints to do the ministry.

8. *Where the saints are growing in maturity (connecting them to Jesus through the disciplines).* Ephesians 4:15 is again our guide for this principle when the apostle Paul says that we are to speak "the truth in love, let us grow in every way into Him who is the head—Christ." Believers are to grow from immaturity to maturity. The essential method of this growth is connection to the head (Christ) through reading the Scriptures and prayer (see John 15).

9. *Where the saints are growing in unity and love for one another.* Jesus told us very plainly in John 13:34–35: "I give you a new command: Love one another. Just as I have loved you, you must also love one another. By this all people will know that you are My disciples, if you have love for one another." The test of whether or not people will know that we are His disciples will be from our love for one another. A healthy church creates this loving environment.

10. *Where the saints are encouraged to discover their spiritual gifts.* The apostle Paul devoted three entire chapters to this subject (Romans 12; 1 Corinthians 12; Ephesians 4). A church that desires to be healthy is intentionally encouraging the members to discover the special gift given to them by Christ. I believe one of the highest goals of a church should be the goal of helping every believer discover and use their gift in the body according to God's design. Further, it serves as an assessment tool. If, for example, a church has 80 percent of the body using their gifts, then it is 80 percent healthy. Conversely, if the church only has 30 percent of the body functioning, it is safe to say it is not healthy.

11. *Where a majority of the saints are using their gifts "properly" (according to God's design).* Again Eph 4:16 is helpful here: "From Him the whole body, fitted and knit together by every supporting ligament, promotes the growth of the body for building up itself in love by the proper working of each individual part." Christ not only wants His children active, He also has a specific plan in mind for them (see Eph 2:10).

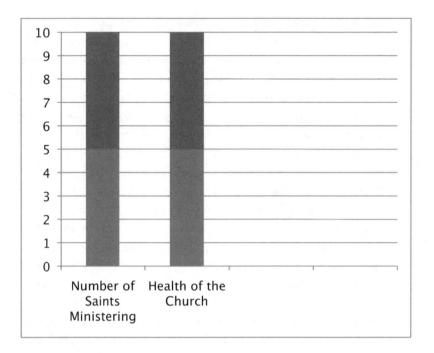

12. *Where relational groups are intentionally developed and growing
    in their love for one another (the "one anothers" are happening).* I
    believe the early church, in response to the commands of Jesus to love
    one another (John 13:34) and to love our neighbor as ourselves (Matt
    22:39), developed a strategy that would accomplish both of those
    commands in a single structure. The place where this occurs most
    naturally is in and through the homes of believers. We cannot practice
    the "one anothers" without close interaction. Believers gathering in
    homes is the obvious choice.

13. *Where relational groups are lovingly sharing their lives and the gospel
    with unbelievers (living on mission in community).* The early church
    is the example here (Acts 2:42–47). Not only are believers gathering
    together in homes, but they are living on mission together. They are
    not only intentionally sharing and living in close fellowship, they
    are also intentionally praying for, and sharing their lives with, their
    friends, neighbors, and coworkers. A healthy church is encouraging
    evangelism to occur naturally in the context of relationships.

14. *Where passionate prayer is continually being offered up for the lost and
    for laborers.* In Luke 10, Jesus instructs His disciples, "The harvest is

abundant, but the workers are few. Therefore, pray to the Lord of the harvest to send out workers into His harvest. Now go; I'm sending you out like lambs among wolves" (vv. 2–3). The healthy church is consistently looking out toward the harvest fields and passionately praying for laborers to go into the harvest fields.

15. *Where leaders for the Great Commission are intentionally being developed.* The apostle Paul told Timothy to "be strong in the grace that is in Christ Jesus. And what you have heard from me in the presence of many witnesses, commit to faithful men who will be able to teach others also" (2 Tim 2:1–2). A healthy church will not just be developing growing and maturing disciples . . . a healthy church will develop leaders for the mission as well.

16. *Where relational groups are multiplying new leaders and new groups.* In the book of Genesis, the original mandate to Adam and Eve was simply, "Be fruitful, multiply" (Gen 1:28). We mentioned in the last chapter that the world is growing at an exponential rate. A healthy church has an exponential disciple-making strategy to accomplish the mission.

17. *Where worship occurs at the individual level and it is powerfully manifested when the body gathers together.* Romans 12:1–2 is helpful here: "Therefore, brothers, by the mercies of God, I urge you to present your bodies as a living sacrifice, holy and pleasing to God; this is your spiritual worship. Do not be conformed to this age, but be transformed by the renewing of your mind, so that you may discern what is the good, pleasing, and perfect will of God." A healthy church understands that the ultimate form of worship is living for God 24 hours a day, 7 days a week, 365 days a year.

18. *Where the poor and "least of these" is intentionally being targeted for the gospel.* The mission statement of Jesus should be our guide. If it was good enough for Jesus, it should be good enough for us. "The Spirit of the Lord is on Me, because He has anointed Me to preach good news to the poor. He has sent Me to proclaim freedom to the captives and recovery of sight to the blind, to set free the oppressed, to proclaim the year of the Lord's favor" (Luke 4:18–19). Because of our love, a healthy church will minister to those who cannot repay.

19. *Where the mission of Christ is being accomplished locally, regionally, nationally, and globally by members from within the local body.* Acts 1:8 states, "But you will receive power when the Holy Spirit has come on you, and you will be My witnesses in Jerusalem, in all Judea and

Samaria, and to the ends of the earth." We can see clearly from this verse that the Lord wants us to go locally and globally. A healthy church is working on a plan to accomplish this goal with the disciples who are in the local church.

20. *Where new churches are being planted as a result of effective discipleship and effective leadership development.* Jesus said in Matt 16:18, "I will build My church, and the forces of Hades will not overpower it." For almost two thousand years now, the church has been the force of world evangelism. The church of Jesus Christ is the best way to spread the gospel and make disciples. Ultimately, the test of whether or not a church is healthy is whether or not it is reproducing new churches. A healthy, growing, maturing church (body) should be birthing new churches.

What Needs Attention?

At this point, I suggest assessing the church you lead or attend along the lines of these twenty marks of a healthy church. Rate each item on a scale from 1 to 5 (1 being low and 5 being high) and then add all twenty scores to form an overall score. Take note of two or three of the lowest scores and the two or three highest scores. The lowest scores are, of course, the first areas that need attention.

1. What is the overall score?
2. What is the lowest score?
3. What is the highest score?
4. Which area do you think needs the most attention right away?
5. What is your plan to increase the health in that area?

In the same way a physical doctor can determine the health of the human body, we can have an idea of the health of the body of Christ. We do this by examining how His body is functioning in some key areas.

In a sense, we are "doctors" of the body of Christ. We are constantly encouraging the practice of good healthy habits. We are constantly exhorting people to "exercise" their gifts. We are concerned about matters of the heart. We desire for the body of Christ to be healthy so that it grows and matures. As it matures, it will reproduce new life: new disciples, new leaders, and new churches.

— Questions to Ponder —

1. What does Ray Stedman say about Ephesians 4?
2. How can we help the body of Christ become healthy?
3. From the list of twenty suggestions for church health, what are your strongest areas (2–3)?
4. From the list of twenty suggestions for church health, what are your weakest areas (2–3)?
5. What are two or three things you can do right now to promote health in the body of Christ?

Notes

1. Ray Stedman, *Body Life* (Grand Rapids, MI: Discovery House, 2011), Kindle location 1351–53.

23

Disciple Making Is . . .

Maintaining
a Tight Focus

Rod Dempsey

Determination and Focus

Despite my small stature, I was very active in sports growing up. Almost every day after school I was involved in whatever sport was in season at the time. Typically, we would gather somewhere to play basketball, football, or softball, and a couple of people would pick teams. As expected, the strongest and the fastest were selected first. Now if you happened to be the smallest, weakest, and slowest, this could be a very embarrassing time. For a long time, I was the last person chosen because I was so much smaller than the other kids.

This can be a difficult thing to go through. Yet, I determined that whatever sport I participated in, I was going to be the hardest-working person on the field or on the court. I was single-minded in my approach to the sport. I would practice for hours and hours to gain the necessary skills to excel in the activity. Eventually, I was no longer the last person chosen, in spite of the fact that I was still the smallest person in the pool of candidates. I was chosen because I was determined. I had skills and I had focus. This type of focus enabled me to letter for four years in high school basketball, play one year in community college, and win the championship in intramural competition at my university. All through my passionate pursuit of sports, I was still usually the smallest person on the court or field, but I was able to perform at a high level because of determination and focus.

Pressure or Priorities?

Let me ask: In your ministry, what do you focus on the most? What takes most of your time and attention? Out of the 168 hours in a week, if you were to do a time analysis, what would the time analysis reveal? What takes up the biggest chunk of your time? Would the time analysis reveal that your focus and attention is on making disciples?

In most churches, you must concentrate on many things. Personal study and prayer, teaching, meetings, calendar planning, programs, visiting the sick, recruiting volunteers, counseling, budgets, and overseeing the staff are a few of the multiple priorities that vie for our attention. Charles Hummel wrote about this problem in his book called *Tyranny of the Urgent*. The issue, Hummel said, is not so much a shortage of time as a problem of priorities. He recalls: "An experienced factory manager once said to me, 'Your greatest danger is letting the urgent things crowd out the important ones.'"[1] Noticeably absent from the conversations I have with leaders in churches about priorities is the discussion about making disciples.

To be sure, we say we want to make disciples, but for the most part we are busy with activities and developing programs, not developing people. Somehow the focus of making disciples has shifted from personally investing in people to managing the events and activities of an organization. Eric Geiger draws this conclusion: "After hundreds of consultations with local churches and a significant research project, we have concluded that church leaders need to simplify. They are constantly asking, 'How can we make all this work?'"[2] The ministry has shifted from personal attention to impersonal programs. It has shifted from simple to complex.

Executive or Equipper?

Many times in church life, leaders and pastors function like corporate executives. For example, in a smaller church, the pastor is normally the person in charge and responsible for everything. He is at the top of the organizational chart, and everyone and everything ultimately reports to him. In a medium-size church, the flow chart is still the same, but the pastor has hired some specialized experts in their field. These experts are there to assist the pastor in developing programs and ministries to aid the pastor to minister to the families in the church.

In a larger church, the senior pastor is viewed as the chief executive, and all staff and their departments report to him through the executive pastor. The executive pastor meets with the pastor and manages the paid staff persons. The paid staff person oversees or manages a department. The departments have a specialized function, a team (full-time or part-time employees with volunteers), a budget, and designated space in the buildings or campus.

How Do You Measure Success?

In these large churches, success is typically measured either by the number of people involved in the program or the events, or by the church's budget, or the value of its property and building. Some people refer to this as "bodies, bucks, and buildings." In order for this organization to function efficiently and effectively, it requires leadership and management of people and resources. It requires exceptional leadership skills to keep all the professional staff and volunteers moving in the same direction at the same time. The senior pastor is incredibly busy and has a tremendous amount of responsibility.

Because the load is so great and so diverse, the senior pastor often does not feel a sense of fulfillment. He is removed from the actual ministry of disciple making and life transformation, which often leads to loneliness and isolation. Being in the ministry is many times reduced to overseeing buildings, budgets, meetings, and problems.

Beware of the Ministry Treadmill

In this environment, the ministry is like being on a treadmill. We all know how a treadmill operates. On a treadmill there is not a lot of exciting things going on. You get on the treadmill, turn it on and start walking. After a while, you gain a little confidence and increase the speed to the point where you are jogging. This is all well and good, but in the ministry, it seems like the speed continues to increase. You start out at a casual walk, but before long, you realize someone or something has increased the speed of the machine to such a point that you are in a flat out, lung-burning sprint for survival.

You want to get off the treadmill, but you do not know how, or you are afraid. To make matters worse, everyone is watching what you do on the treadmill. They may be the ones needing the exercise, but you answered the call. You feel exhausted, and yet the machine keeps running. You are sweating, your legs are aching, and you begin to think to yourself: *How am I going to continue?* At this point, many pastors will just gut it out and continue running, but they are running on empty. After a while, physical, emotional, and spiritual exhaustion sets in, and the pastor eventually "trips" on something and falls.

He or she will fall for many reasons, but the result is the same. Maybe this illustration has just described how you feel about the ministry. You are running, but getting nowhere. In fact, in addition to being exhausting, the ministry (if you were honest) is, perhaps, even a little boring. You want to shout to the machine, "Stop" or "Reduce speed." You know the machine will not respond, you have tried that before. For some reason, the machine does not respond to any of your commands. You may want to put your feet out to the sides and just rest for a little while, but you are also a little nervous about what might happen. Here are some things you may be thinking if you stop or change things:

- What will people think?
- What will people say?
- What if I make some changes and the people do not like the changes?
- What if I am asked to resign or leave? After all, I am getting paid to run, whether it is slow or fast. I am still getting paid to run.
- There has got to be another way of doing ministry that doesn't culminate with me being exhausted and falling down.

How to Get Off the Treadmill

To make disciples, you must maintain a tight focus on the Great Commission. You must develop and implement effective discipleship systems and environments. Dave has written extensively about what that looks like, and I have described how disciple making should occur in the context of relationships and small groups. The church of Jesus should move away from complex corporate models of organization toward a biblical model of discipleship. Dave Browning observes, "Many how-to books for church leaders suggest things for the leaders to do (in addition to what they are already doing) to improve the effectiveness of their church. Unfortunately, many pastors are already experiencing diminishing returns (or burnout) from attempting too much."[3] The biblical model of discipleship should occur in the context of relationships. Disciple making does not happen by the senior pastor or the leadership team in a dead run for their lives while the saints are on the sidelines watching the drama unfold. There has to be another way.

From Eph 4:11–16 we understand the pastor's main job is to "equip" the saints to do the works of service (NKJV). We make disciples by helping others growing in Christlikeness and helping them to do what God has gifted them to do (v. 16). This is the long and short of the whole matter. I believe this happens most naturally in a small group where every person can exercise his or her gift and build up the body in love. Read Eph 4:16 again:

From Him the whole body, fitted and knit together by every supporting
ligament, promotes the growth of the body for building up itself in love
by the proper working of each individual part.

The "proper working of each individual part" depends on the person discovering and using the gifts God has given to them. This is why getting disciples into groups is so important. Inside the group, the leader can give personal attention to each disciple, challenging them to experiment and discover their own gifts. In the group, one person with the gift of mercy may volunteer to keep track of prayer requests. Someone with the gift of administration may plan the next group outreach activity. Another person with the gift of exhortation may send cards of encouragement to absent group members. One person with the gift of teaching may want to lead the discussion for the evening (although you do not need the gift of teaching to make a good small-group leader).

There must be some reason why God has given to every believer at least one spiritual gift. Greg Ogden observes, "We are to be stewards of the unique design and motivation that God has placed on our hearts. Instead of filling a church slot as defined by the institution, an organism seeks to have each person play the part for which he or she was created. A church's ministry takes the shape of the gifted people instead of forcing the people into preexisting niches that act like a confining straitjacket."[4] Every Christian has been given a gift, and the exercise of that gift is critical to the body becoming and doing everything that God has in mind. I exhort my students regularly to figure how to help every disciple discover and use their gift. We have tried that exercise many times and consistently come to the conclusion that a relational small-group environment provides the best opportunity for every disciple to get involved and use the Lord's gift. Read 1 Pet 4:10–11:

> *Based on the gift each one has received, use it to serve others,* as good
> managers of the varied grace of God. If anyone speaks, it should be as
> one who speaks God's words; if anyone serves, it should be from the
> strength God provides, so that God may be glorified through Jesus
> Christ in everything. To Him belong the glory and the power forever and
> ever. Amen.

Important Questions

Implementing and maintaining this focus on the development of God's saints will require the ability to say "stop" or "end program." Here is where the rub comes. The way to accomplish the goal of making disciples inside a small-group environment may mean that we redefine what the ministry looks like, and it may redefine how we spend the 168 hours that we have in a given week. There are many programs inside a typical church that could be reduced or even eliminated. To make this transition requires that the leaders of the church come to an agreement on many issues, such as:

- What is the purpose of the church?
- What is the Great Commission?
- How did the early church make disciples?
- How do we make disciples?
- How do we "equip" the saints?
- What does "works of service" mean?
- How do we help every Christian discover their spiritual gift?
- How do we help every Christian use their gift in the way God intends?
- How do we prepare every person to stand before Christ and hear from Him, "Well done, good and faithful servant"?

Important Mission

Perhaps the starting point in this journey is to answer each of the questions above for your own personal life. You can then work through them with the leadership team of the church. Finally, you can develop a simple mission statement for the ministry or church. The mission statement could sound something like this:

_____ Church exists to win the lost to Christ, to equip them to grow spiritually, and to empower them to accomplish His mission for His glory.

After developing a simple biblical mission statement, you need to then look at the existing ministry structures and systems and evaluate whether or not they are accomplishing your church's mission. Over time the leadership team needs to create a "stop doing" list, or at least "do not resuscitate list." A "DNR" list means that you are going to allow the ministry or program to continue but without the necessary resources to sustain it. You are not going to give it attention, money, space, or anything that would allow it to grow. In fact you are going to allow the program to die so that relational disciple-making groups can emerge from the over-programmed church.

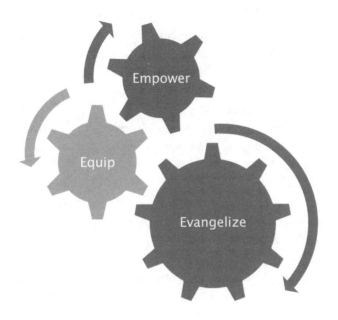

It requires exceptional leadership skill and determination to allow something to die in order that new life can emerge. Tony Morgan adds: "It takes a confident yet humble leader to follow God's calling in his or her own life while also considering the interests of others around them. We have to live in that tension in order to experience God's design for the church. That's how we accomplish His purposes."[5] The job is not for the fainthearted. Those opposed will make it very clear what you need to do and what you are not doing. Yet they have not been entrusted to oversee the body of Christ. You have. If you allow others to set the agenda and control the outcome, then you do not have a calling; you have a career.

Important Choices

Another way to make progress in the transition to become a relational, disciple-making church is to lead by example. "Be the paradigm" is a good piece of advice. Whatever you expect of the average member in your church, you should be willing to do. You should lead by example. You are not superman. If you try to do everything, the saints will not grow up. They will remain spiritual babies, and you will constantly be giving them the milk of the Word and cleaning up their messes.

The goal is to reach the world with the gospel and to make disciples. In order to accomplish that mission we must maintain a tight focus on winning people to Christ, helping them grow to their full potential, and then sending them out to join the mission of Christ. Unfortunately, the church today often resembles a corporation that is concerned with managing and maintaining. We need *an equipping, empowering, and releasing model.* In order to reach the world, all of God's children must follow Jesus into His mission. The small-group model that focuses on developing every person has the best chance of accomplishing the mission.

The challenge for developing and maintaining a tight disciple-making focus is knowing what to emphasize and what to de-emphasize. You need a clear vision, core values, concise views, clean vehicles, and concrete verifiers. In most churches you may need to clarify the purpose of the church. You may need to reduce the complexity of the model. You may need to lead by example and do what you ask your congregation to do. You may need to stop doing some things. As you do this over time and you begin emphasizing a simpler, more natural way of making disciples, you will begin to see life transformation happen in the lives of ordinary people. Ordinary people can then begin to do extraordinary things for the kingdom and glory of God!

— Questions to Ponder —

1. What is the "tyranny of the urgent"?
2. How does the "ministry treadmill" work?
3. How is success measured in the typical church (three Bs)?
4. What is your church or ministry's purpose statement?
5. How does Eph 4:11–16 help us to get off and stay off the "ministry treadmill"?

Notes

1. Charles Hummel, *Tyranny of the Urgent* (Downers Grove, IL: IVP, 1997), 10.
2. Eric Geiger and Thom S. Rainer, *Simple Church* (Nashville: B&H, 2009), 4.
3. Dave Browning, *Deliberate Simplicity: How the Church Does More by Doing Less* (Grand Rapids: Zondervan, 2009), Kindle location 420–22.
4. Greg Ogden, *Unfinished Business: Returning the Ministry to the People of God* (Grand Rapids: Zondervan, 2010), Kindle location 451–53.
5. Tony Morgan and Ben Stroup, *Developing a Theology of Leadership* (np: LiberWriter.com, 2012), Kindle location 70–71.

24

Disciple Making Is . . .

Evaluating Different Church Models

Rod Dempsey

Methods or Models

When you think of the word "model," what comes to mind? When I was a child, one of my favorite activities was constructing model cars. I had a '67 Mustang fastback, a '69 Camaro SS, and many others. It was a great thrill not only to purchase the replica of the actual car but also to put the model together and enjoy the finished product for years to come. Models enable us to look at something from several different angles and appreciate the symmetry of the architect's vision.

The dictionary defines "model" in this manner: "a small object, usually built to scale, that represents in detail another, often larger object."[1] Another definition is: "a schematic description of a system, theory, or phenomenon that accounts for its known or inferred properties and may be used for further study of its characteristics."[2] The second definition is the one that I want to focus on in this chapter. "Model" refers to a description of a "system," or a "phenomenon." The church of Jesus Christ from the day of Pentecost has been a phenomenon, and we need to study how it works, and then design models that reflect the inherent properties of the system. There is a basic DNA of church structure, and if we can examine a strand of healthy DNA, we can perhaps create models to replicate it.

I believe God has a basic model in mind for His church. The model is fashioned after a body. Ray Stedman comments, "When Paul speaks of the church as a body, he makes it clear that no one joins that body except by a new birth, through faith in Jesus Christ. There is no other way into this body. Once a person becomes a part of that body, every member has a contribution to make. As each member works at the task God has given him to do, the whole body functions as intended."[3] This body is made in God's image, and it is wonderful to behold. So the topic of church models is a very important one. Further, God desires His body to be healthy, maturing, and reproducing. The closer we get to the image that God has in mind for His church, the more we will experience His favor and blessing.

In chapter 22, I summarized twenty scriptural principles that characterize the habits and practices of healthy churches. This chapter will briefly survey the four prevalent models of church structure and, in the remaining four chapters, I will analyze and critique each model as it relates to disciple making. In so doing, I seek to offer a personal summary and critique of the models as I see them. The four prevalent church models are: traditional, attractional, organic, and hybrid (see the chart at the end of the chapter for a summary of all the models).

The Most Common Model: The Traditional Church

As you travel around the US, you will often notice the rising steeple of a church situated prominently in the center of a small town. Here are a few things that come to mind when I see such churches:

1. I wonder how many people attend this church.
2. I wonder what the pastor is like.
3. I wonder how the church got started and how a group of people decided to build this church.
4. I wonder if the church is growing in health. Are new people being reached with the gospel?
5. I wonder if disciples are being developed in this church.

This church is most likely a "traditional" church. That is, if you go to this particular church and then to another down the street or across the country, there would be striking similarities. Below are some general observations of the traditional church model.

This model normally has a senior pastor who oversees the programs and ministries of the church. Most of the activities of the church occur in and around the physical building. The organizational structure is not complex. The senior pastor assumes most of the leadership of the church, yet sometimes the deacons or several influential families retain this role on some level. Evangelism is not as central, but members are concerned with "soul winning." Discipleship is taught from the pulpit but is limited, primarily, to that which occurs during the Sunday school hour.

The church members are supportive of the pastor yet often resist or are suspicious of change. The pastor is viewed as the "professional," and the saints are the "lay people." The leadership philosophy is codependent: the people need the pastor to minister to them. Consequently, the pastor and/or staff do most of the ministry while the members support and fund the ministries and programs of the church. As a result, spiritual gifts are not elevated to a prominent place in the life of the church.

The pastor preaches two or three times per week, and the focus is directed more exclusively toward the needs of the congregation. Giving is a priority. The offerings are used primarily for staff salaries and to maintain the facilities. Worship occurs every week promptly at 11:00 a.m. Prayer meetings are held at the church, often during a midweek gathering. Given this larger group structure, prayer tends to be more surface in nature.

The pastor understands, and normally embraces, his role as a spiritual caregiver to a sometimes aging congregation. Training is minimal, and there are few emerging leaders from the congregation primarily because the model does not need leadership development. If the pastor does have an assistant, the role is more clerical in nature. The traditional church often has a narrower Great Commission perspective. To be sure, the members are mission minded, but with the exception of an occasional short-term mission trip, support is funneled through foreign mission boards. There is little vision for church planting, in large part because the model is ultimately based upon addition and not multiplication.

Come and See: The Attractional Church

The attractional model is perhaps better known by the term *seeker church*, and its philosophy characterizes what some might refer to as the "mega" church. Below are some general observations and characteristics of this model.

Because most seeker churches have a focus on evangelism, they can become quite large. More recently, Alan Hirsch has described this type of church as the "attractional church."[4] That is, this church attracts unbelievers to "come and see" what God is doing in their church. The church members practice a method of evangelism called "invest and invite."[5] This approach encourages church members to be intentional about spending time with their lost friends and inviting them to come to their church and hear their pastor. The building is, likewise, the primary location where programs and events occur.

This model boasts of significant new conversions, yet it also attracts members from other churches in the area. Due to this rapid, and often sustained, influx of new people, the church sponsors routine "membership" classes. Individuals are encouraged to get involved in serving in the Sunday morning ministries of the church. Since the church is attractional by nature, ministry involvement often varies relative to one's commitment level. Prayer takes on a more personal and introspective dimension and occurs normally within a small-group setting.

The pastor's role resembles a corporate executive, and there may even be an executive pastor overseeing the details of the ministry to free the senior pastor to focus on the weekend services. He is usually extremely polished and charismatic. People want to listen to him. People want to be around him. He has an attractive and winsome personality. The staff runs the church, and the main focus is the weekend services. This model values leadership development, and there are many opportunities for specialized training given the logistics necessary to plan and implement a weekend service. The primary goal of an attractional church is evangelism done through the gifted communicator. New satellite churches are being developed around the pastor's gifts and his passion for evangelism.

Go and Be: The Organic Church

Currently there are many authors and church practitioners speaking about the need for a return to the ethos of the early church. Some of the more prominent advocates writing about and experiencing *Church 3.0* are: Alan Hirsch (*The Forgotten Ways; Right Here, Right Now; Untamed*, etc.); Ed Stetzer (*Breaking the Missional Code; Transformational Church; Viral Church Planting; Missional Churches*); Hugh Halter (*The Tangible Kingdom: Creating Incarnational Community; Sacrilege: Finding Life in the Unorthodox Ways of Jesus*); Frank Viola (*Pagan Christianity; Finding Organic Church; Reimagining Church*); Dennis McCallum (*Organic Disciple-Making: Mentoring Others into Spiritual Maturity and Leadership; Members of One Another: How to Build a Biblical Ethos into Your Church*). Additionally, well-known author and pastor

Francis Chan (*Crazy Love*) is speaking and acting on the need to transform the church from "come and see" to "go and be."[6]

The organic church is a term used to describe a simpler, more relational way of doing church. The organic church is usually led by a team of elders. It has a much flatter leadership structure. There are teaching elders and small-group or house-church leaders. That is pretty much it. The church is not organized around age-group ministries or even purpose-driven ministries. It is organized around incarnational relational groups living on mission in the community. The church may gather on Sunday morning, but the primary expression of the church is lived out in relational groups. Members gather in small groups (some are called house churches or missional communities), and the groups serve as the basis for all disciple making. The saints are encouraged to use their gifts in their house church or missional community.

The groups do meet corporately, but when they do, they are taught from one of the elders, and the teaching is designed to encourage and equip them in their group life. Worship is a lifestyle expressed in obedient living and on mission. Prayer is important and focuses on those people who do not know Christ. The role of leadership is viewed as equipping, empowering, and releasing God's children to discover and use their spiritual gift in the body (to create health). As the body grows healthy, it becomes loving and attractive to those who do not know Christ. The goal is healthy disciples who develop into healthy leaders who develop new healthy churches to reach new people. Multiplication is the stated goal of the model.

Both . . . And: The Hybrid Church

The hybrid church model combines elements from both the attractional and the organic church to form a model that is both attractional and missional. It is both "come and see" and "go and be." The hybrid church is usually led by a senior pastor and a professional staff. It is primarily Sunday morning and building focused. It is also extremely complex. The hybrid church believes in making disciples, but it goes about this task in a variety of ways. In short, the hybrid model has taken a small-group system and laid that system on top of an existing traditional/attractional model.

The hybrid model seeks to take the best from all the models. The challenge is that there is no real effort to reduce any of the complexity of the models. Everything is thrown together. The saints are encouraged to get involved, but there are so many things going on in this model, it is hard to focus on exactly *what* they are supposed to be doing. The church's calendar is full of activities, and the professional staff members are there to make sure there are no empty dates on the calendar as a result of its complexity. It is easy for the average member to slip between the many cracks because this system has a lot of places to hide.

The pastor is multitalented and multigifted. That is, he is a shepherd, a counselor, a preacher, a CEO, and a friend. He is omnicompetent and very personable. He reminds me of Moses before Jethro showed up in Exodus 18. The pastor understands servant leadership, but he still needs many people to run the weekend services. There is an extensive staff who do a lot, but their efforts are divided between the competing philosophies of "come and see" and "go and be." Training is emphasized throughout the model, but again, there is confusion regarding sorting out the multiple priorities. There is talk of reaching the harvest fields and planting new churches, but since there are a multitude of programs and ministries, there is a great need for people to run the Sunday morning ministries. Consequently, the people are developed, not primarily for the Great Commission, but to run the Sunday morning programs.

As I see it, these are the four current models of church structure that are being practiced today. There could be variations of one model or another, but these seem to be the prevalent church structures that dominant the landscape. Look over the four broad categories mentioned in this chapter and try to identify the category your church/ministry would most closely resemble.

Qualifying Questions

In summary, the way you answer several important and clarifying questions will directly influence what approach you choose:

1. How do you view the church?
2. How do you view the pastor's role?
3. How do you view the responsibility of the saints?
4. How do you view evangelism?
5. How do you view the mission of the church?

If you view the church as a place, then it will impact the way you do church. If you view the pastor's job as the professional minister, then it will influence how you view the ministry. If you view the saints as sheep who are weak and need constant care, then you will not call them to higher involvement. If you view evangelism as something done by the professionals at the building, then that will become your method. If you view the mission of reaching an exponentially growing world with quiet skepticism, then you will not lean into the mission with bold faith and aggressive action.

Critical Decisions

So which approach should you take? That depends. Are you starting a church or are you assuming a church? Can you start from scratch or do you already have a model in place? If you are starting from scratch, I would definitely recommend starting simple and staying simple. If you do not have that luxury, then you need to have wisdom and skill to transition toward a healthy disciple-making church. In the next chapter, we will look at the traditional church in more detail and try to determine whether or not disciples can be developed in that model.

⁓ Questions to Ponder ⁓

1. How does Ray Stedman paraphrase the apostle Paul's definition of church?
2. What are the four prevalent church models that we see today?
3. Of the four models, which one most closely resembles your church?
4. Of the four models, which one, in your opinion, has the strongest scriptural support?
5. Regardless of the model, what can you do to help your church become more healthy?

Notes

1. See http://www.thefreedictionary.com/model.
2. Ibid.
3. Ray Stedman, *Body Life* (np: Discovery House Publishers, 2011), Kindle location 1341–43.
4. See http://missionalchurchnetwork.com/attractional-or-extractional-church-cultural-distance (accessed October 15, 2012).
5. See http://store.northpoint.org/invest-and-invite.html (accessed October 15, 2012).
6. See the Relevant Magazine article for a fuller explanation, http://www.relevantmagazine.com/god/church/features/24816-the-crazy-mission-of-francis-chan (accessed October 15, 2012); see also Jeff Vanderstelt's video from SOMA communities, http://www.somacommunities.org/mcvideo/ (accessed October 15, 2012).

VIEW/PRACTICE	1. TRADITIONAL	2. ATTRACTIONAL	3. ORGANIC	4. HYBRID
1. CHURCH STRUCTURE	Single pastor/deacon led or congregation led	Single elder	Multiple elders	Single elder with deacons or elder board
2. CHURCH LOCATION	Building	Building	Incarnational—lived out in the community	1, 2, and 3 but building focused
3. COMPLEXITY	Simple	Complex	Simple	Extremely complex
4. EVANGELISM	If at all—"soul winning"	"Come and see" or "invest and invite"	"Relational missional groups"	Mainly "come and see"
5. DISCIPLESHIP	From the pulpit—hearing	Classes—curriculum driven: learning	Mainly small groups—learning & mentoring	1 and 2
6. SMALL GROUPS	No small groups	"Of" small groups	"Is" small groups	"With" and "of" small groups
7. CHANGE ATTITUDE	Change is not needed: resistant	Change is accepted b/c of evangelism	Change is constant due to missional living	Change is tolerated but not well received
8. SPIRITUAL FORMATION	If it happens . . . it happens at church	Attender is encouraged to become a self feeder	Intentional mentoring in community	Both personal and community
9. GIFTS	Not needed	Outward gifts needed	All gifts needed	Needed for the programs
10. PREACHNG	For the congregation	Toward the seeker	For the believer	1, 2, and 3 but light
11. GROWTH ENGINE- What drives the church? or How is success measured?	Maintenance/Survival	Evangelism	Mission/Discipleship	Activity
12. BUDGET	Limited for the preacher	Support the staff, property and buildings	Aimed toward the mission	2 and 3 and complex

13. WORSHIP	On Sunday morning	On Sunday morning	Through the people in the community	2 and 3 but mainly Sunday focused
14. PRAYER	At the church	Personal	Body life	Personal
15. LEADERSHIP PHILOSOPHY	Codependent leader—the people need me to minister to and for them	Hierarchical—the people are there to accomplish the leader's goals	Equipping leadership to develop the people to reach their full potential	Understands equipping leadership but manages a complex organization
16. LEADERSHIP DEVELOPMENT	No leaders developed	Leaders developed for the programs	Disciples developed; leaders emerge for the mission	2 and 3 but limited
17. SENIOR PASTOR	"Preacher"	Charismatic CEO	Equipper/ Teacher	Multitalented
18. STAFF	Limited staff	Paid staff to run the Sunday programs	Can be paid, but also bi-vocational	Extensive paid staff
19. SAINT'S ROLE	Watch and pay	Watch and cheer	Involved and active	Watch, pay, cheer, and limited involvement
20. SAINT'S ATTITUDE	"Watcher"	"Consumer"	"Kingdom Citizen"	1, 2, and 3 but limited
21. TRAINING	No training	To run the programs	To lead the missional groups	2 and 3 but divided
22. PERSONAL GOAL	Be faithful	Meet my needs	Fulfill my role in the mission	Both emphasized, but the default is meet my needs
23. MISSIONS	Foreign missions board	Local (satellites) and international	Local, national, and international through church planting	Local (satellites) and international
24. MULTIPLICATION	Not Applicable	Addition b/c of leadership philosophy	Multiplication oriented	Addition b/c of leadership philosophy
25. CHURCH PLANTING	Not applicable	Add satellites/ campuses	Multiply churches	2 and 3 but limited

<table>
<tr><td>

25

</td><td>

Disciple Making Is . . .

Weighing the
Traditional Model

Rod Dempsey

</td></tr>
</table>

In the previous chapter, we surveyed four different church models: traditional, attractional, organic, and hybrid. In these last few chapters, we will evaluate these church models more closely in an effort to establish the most effective disciple-making system. In this chapter, we will consider the traditional model, but before we get there, let's quickly review the ground we have already covered in order to set a context for our evaluation.

Check Your Mirrors

One of the most important parts on your vehicle is the rearview mirrors. You remember your first car driving lessons and how you were exhorted to "check your mirrors" every few seconds. You were likely instructed to adjust your mirrors before operating the vehicle. Without the rearview mirrors, we would constantly be swerving into vehicles making their way into our "blind spots." We have blind spots in our lives and our ministries as well. As we look back, in this book we have covered disciple-making philosophy, disciple-making basics, and disciple-making methods. Let's review these briefly.

We have considered the motivation for disciple making—the glory of God—suggesting that the way to bring God glory is by helping others grow and develop to the point where they bring forth "fruit" (John 15:8). We have defined a biblical disciple and suggested that making disciples is a matter of cooperating with the Spirit in His work. We have argued that disciples are best developed in the context of a community of believers: a local church as the visible body of Christ. We have examined both the biblical expectation of *being* a disciple as well as *making* a disciple. From the commands of Jesus and the ministry of Paul, we argued that a disciple must declare Jesus as Lord and Savior and be developed and deployed for Christ and His mission. We discovered that the church of Jesus Christ *is* His body. Consequently, if the body (made up of healthy individual parts) is healthy, the church will be healthy as well. We discussed more than twenty potential marks that characterize a healthy church. We have explored the importance of growing in our comprehension of spiritual leadership in the process of disciple making. We have looked into the power of multiplication and its implications for accomplishing the mission of Christ. Finally, we analyzed how to establish and maintain a tight focus on disciple making.

Principles Should Guide Our Models

The principles above help us form a solid, scriptural foundation. While all of these principles should guide our disciple-making model, I want to highlight two that are particularly significant, yet countercultural: love and leadership. First, the foundation for disciple making is love, a virtue not highly prized in our culture. Love for God will produce a love for our neighbor. Jesus taught us that in addition to loving God and loving people, we must love one another. In fact, He said it was *the* way to show that we were His followers. As we grow and mature, we begin to exercise our gifts and thereby show our love for one another (Eph 4:16). The world takes notice and is convinced that Jesus is among us. When this is occurring, we are then able to share the good news of the gospel of Christ in the context of transformed lives. It is not only believable, but powerful.

Second, biblical leadership looks much different than secular leadership. Typically, we look at leadership like the world does. Stronger, bigger, smarter are characteristics we like to see in our leaders. Ken Blanchard in *Lead Like Jesus* observes, "In one sense, the leadership model that people often experience is summarized by the popular opinion: 'It's all about me.' In all kinds of organizations and institutions, the rewards of money, recognition, and power increase as you move up the hierarchy."[1] Biblical concepts like humility, equipping, empowering, and serving are not words we usually ascribe to our leaders. As a result of our worldly view of leadership, we want leaders to "take charge" and "organize" and "give direction." Yet, the emphasis in Scripture is many times antithetical to the world's methods (Matt 20:26).

Leaders in God's kingdom have a different starting place. We start with His will. We start with an understanding that the growth and development of God's people is our most important undertaking (Eph 4:11–16). Biblical leadership is not just about the health of the organization, but more about the health of the individual (Col 1:28). Biblical *leadership* is driven by *love*. These few principles show the other-worldliness of the kingdom of God. Consequently, the systems and structures that we develop in the local church should be a reflection of the nature and character of God's kingdom.

Characteristics of a Traditional Church Model

As I mentioned earlier, making disciples is normally approached in the context of one of four church structures: the traditional church, the attractional church, the organic church, and the hybrid church. I have some experience with all four models. I am most familiar with the traditional model but have some experience with the attractional and, by extension, the hybrid model as well. I have experienced the organic model in a cell-church setting. In this chapter, I am going to examine and critique the traditional model. Any critique may be painful for some to accept. My motivation is to challenge certain assumptions and practices in order to help the body of Christ become healthier (see chap. 22).

Based upon my observation and experience, below are a few characteristics of a typical "traditional church" (see also chart on pp. 236–37 for more detail):

1. Hierarchical in nature (The church is ruled or governed by one pastor or by one group of people.)
2. Building focused
3. Sunday focused
4. Preaching focused
5. Worship is Sunday morning function
6. Professional staff ruled
7. Addition based
8. Little passion for evangelism
9. More concerned about maintenance
10. Little training or development
11. Views other churches as competition
12. Views leadership from top down not servant leadership

Mathematical Problems

Eighty percent of all churches in North America have reached a plateau or are declining.[2] This is a crisis in our time. Yet, seemingly, we continue to try and solve the problem with the same approaches that caused the crisis in the first place. This situation reminds me of the United States' debt crisis. Currently, the United States owes more than 16 trillion dollars. What is our answer? Borrow money from foreign governments and raise more taxes without curbing spending. We keep trying to solve the same persistent problems with the same solutions that are only compounding the problem.

In the same way, the traditional church model struggles to develop solutions that address its challenges, one of the greatest being the failure to multiply. The world is growing at an exponential rate (we just crossed over the 7 billion population mark). How do we try to answer this mathematical problem? The traditional church, by and large, is not a multiplication model, and yet the world's population is multiplying. How many of you took basic algebra in high school or college? Trying to solve a multiplication problem with an addition-based solution will never work. Reaching the world for Christ demands that we approach this challenge with a solution that will address the mathematical problem.

Another challenge in the traditional church is that it is trying to reach the world almost exclusively through paid professionals. I call this the bottleneck problem. You have seen what happens in a bottleneck: there is a constriction that limits the amount flowing through a container. The mission of the church cannot and should not be limited to only a few professional clergy who are the "ministers." All God's children need to be committed to, and involved in, accomplishing the Great Commission.

Watch the Definitions

This raises another area of concern regarding the identity of the people of God and the rigid categories of "professional" and "laymen." It is not just that the professionals in this scheme do all the ministry. Beyond that, the laypeople are not really expected to do anything. Consequently, in many churches the 80/20 rule applies.[3] That is, 20 percent of the people do 80 percent of the work in the church. This practice overlooks the fact that every believer has been given a supernatural gift by God to advance the kingdom. I do not want anyone to stand before Christ ashamed and embarrassed when He asks them, "What did you do with what I gave you."

Further, it seems we have changed the way Jesus defined "disciple." Instead of someone willing to sacrifice all ("take up your cross and follow Me"), we prefer Christians who do not get too carried away with that religious stuff. We have also redefined the word "church." It seems we are saying that "church" is a location where people go to "worship." We corral believers into a big room and talk about how we should be reaching the world, but do not equip and empower the individual members to go across the street to their neighbor.

Yet another term that needs to be redefined is the imbalanced view toward "Bible study" that seeks deeper truths, but not necessarily the goal of application. Stated negatively, it seeks not the obvious interpretation and application of Scripture, but deeper theological truths of the Word—so deep that we argue and wrangle about peripheral doctrines and then look down on people who do not share our level of understanding and knowledge. Another challenge is the way we do evangelism. We have shifted from "they went out and preached everywhere" (Mark 16:20; Acts 8:4) to "let the pastor handle it." This approach persists even though Jesus is the one who stated in His mission statement (Luke 4:18–19):

> The Spirit of the Lord is on Me, because He has anointed Me to preach good news to the poor. He has sent Me to proclaim freedom to the captives and recovery of sight to the blind, to set free the oppressed, to proclaim the year of the Lord's favor.

Jesus was going to go to the poor and the oppressed because He was sent by His father. What about you? Will you go and take the gospel to the poor and the oppressed in your community?

How Did We Get Here?

Albert Einstein's reflection on insanity is apropos here: "Insanity is to continue doing the same thing over and over again and expect different results."[4] What are we doing? Why are we stuck in this approach when it is so obviously not working? How did we get so far away from the simplicity of making disciples who make disciples, to a model that does not equip, empower, and release God's children for His mission?

Ultimately, the reason this model is so challenging is because it is not an equipping and empowering structure. This model is largely based on a business, or corporate, structure. The chart below shows the senior pastor at the top of the model, and everyone and everything reports to him (not that there is

anything wrong with having a senior pastor). The staff positions in this model
are volunteer, part-time, or full-time positions.

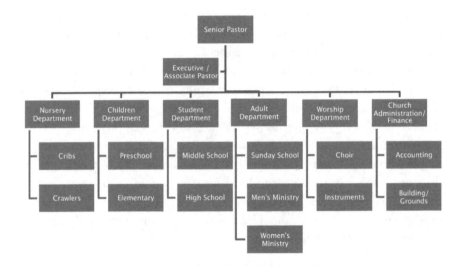

This model does not expect the individual to do significant ministry in
the kingdom. Further, this model is not designed for multiplication, but for
maintaining the status quo or adding to the current structure. As such, it is
a "command and control" model: controlling the property, controlling the
building, controlling the staff, controlling the budget, controlling the direction,
and worst of all, controlling the people. In a healthy model, God's people are
not saved by works, they are saved to work (Eph 2:10). As a result, they should
be equipped, empowered, and released to the mission.

The traditional model characterizes the majority of churches across North
America. Again, the model does not encourage the releasing of God's people to
God's mission. We need to be in the business of releasing God's people to do
the "works" He has in mind for them. Ed Stetzer and Warren Bird conclude,
"As we watch churches who are initiating multiplying movements, they are,
if nothing else, aggressive in reaching out to new people. Their leaders bore
easily of ministry that is preservation focused or lacking in challenge. In fact,
they are driven to the edge of insanity by maintenance mode. Leaders of
great movements are those driven to find new people and carry them into a
new future."[5] Finding new people (evangelism) is one thing; developing and
releasing them to the mission (discipleship) is the challenge of disciple making.

Career or Calling

Any model that discourages or prevents God's people from becoming and doing all that God has in mind is not only harmful but unbiblical. The way to reach the world with the good news of Christ is by mobilizing all the members of Christ's body. I am not saying that the leaders of traditional churches are doing this intentionally (unless they know the truth). I believe most leaders of traditional churches are good people with good motives, but the result is still the same: God's people are not encouraged and mobilized to fulfill their God-given purpose.

Since this mind-set is so prevalent, I often encourage students to plant new churches that will win people to Christ, develop disciples, and deploy new leaders who will ultimately reproduce new churches. God's plan is to reach the world. Why should we be satisfied with anything less? This leads me to one final observation: there is no reason for excuses. If your church is not structured to win the lost to Christ, grow them up in their faith, and send them out for the mission, then change it. If you are unable change it, for God's sake (and yours, too), do not reduce your calling to a career decision.

Transforming Effect

The church should be a place where the gospel is being powerfully proclaimed in word and witness. Followers of Jesus Christ should be "growing up in all aspects" and maturing to the point where they want to serve others. As they model and share the gospel, the unbelieving world takes notice and is convinced of their lack of peace, power, and purpose. They realize they need this new way of living. Instead of the miracles being performed by the apostles, the miracles are the lives being transformed by the gospel from self-centered, selfish living to lives that are following the King of kings and Lord of lords. At the end of the day you cannot argue with a transformed life. Transformed lives are sharing the good news with friends and neighbors. The gospel must become a personal conversation with friends and neighbors.

For example, in the book *House Church*, Steve Atkerson gives some suggestions on how ordinary Christians can interact with unbelievers. He states, "We need to regularly seek to put ourselves in places where we can interact with non-Christians. We can join a neighborhood watch program, civic group, or square dancing group to meet people. We can open our homes during the holidays and invite our neighbors in. We can invite unbelievers into our homes for dinner. We can start an investigative Bible study for any of our unsaved friends who are open to learning what the Bible has to say. We can ask our unbelieving friends what we can be praying for in their lives."[6] If we do not allow unbelievers to see our lives, they cannot see Christ's body in action. Invite the lost into your world. Become a friend of sinners.

In conclusion, in Matthew 16 Jesus is having a conversation with His disciples, and He asks them a question: "Who do people say the Son of Man is?" (v. 13). The disciples were caught a little flat-footed with this question. They replied, "Some say John the Baptist; others say Elijah; and still others, Jeremiah or one of the prophets" (v. 14). Let me paraphrase that answer for you: "Well, Lord, there is a variety of opinion about Your identity, and the jury is still out regarding the verdict." Then Jesus turns the question around and makes it personal when He asks, "But you . . . who do you say I am?" (v. 15). One of the disciples (Peter), who just could not contain himself any longer, blurted out, *"You are the Messiah, the Son of the living God."* (v. 16). This is not only the foundation for the gospel, it is also the foundation for a mystery that Jesus is about to reveal about the future of His ministry. Jesus answers Peter with this statement:

> Simon son of Jonah, you are blessed because flesh and blood did not
> reveal this to you [that Jesus is the Messiah and Son of God], but My
> Father in heaven. . . . I will build My church, and the forces of Hades will
> not overpower it. (Matt 16:17–18)

This new entity—the church—was a revelation from the heavenly Father. This new community (the body of Jesus) was to have a transforming effect not only on individuals but also on the entire world. By God's grace, let us not prevent the church of Jesus Christ from transforming individuals, who transform families, who transform communities, who transform a secular society into the Kingdom of God. If the traditional model is not cultivating this reality, it is time for a change.

— Questions to Ponder —

1. What is the foundational principle for making disciples?
2. What should leaders do in a disciple-making church?
3. What are two or three characteristics of a traditional church?
4. What are two or three challenges of a traditional church?
5. How should transformation take place in society?

Notes

1. Ken Blanchard and Phil Hodges, *Lead Like Jesus: Lessons from the Greatest Leadership Role Model of All Time* (Nashville: Thomas Nelson, 2006), 3.

2. See http://www.simplechurchathome.com/Why.html (accessed October 15, 2012).

3. See http://management.about.com/cs/generalmanagement/a/Pareto081202. htm (accessed October 15, 2012).

4. See http://www.brainyquote.com/quotes/quotes/a/alberteins133991.html# ixzz1e71sb2tu (accessed October 15, 2012).

5. Ed Stetzer and Warren Bird, *Viral Churches: Helping Church Planters Become Movement Makers* (Hoboken, NJ: John Wiley and Sons, 2006), 54.

6. Steve Atkerson, *House Church: Simple, Strategic, Scriptural* (Atlanta: New Testament Restoration Foundation, 2008), Kindle location 3388–91.

26

Analyzing the Attractional Model

Rod Dempsey

Historical Perspective

The late Billy Hornsby wrote a book titled *The Attractional Church: Growth Through a Refreshing, Relational, and Relevant Church Experience*. In this book he states, "A growing movement of churches is offering people a refreshing, relational, and relevant church experience. Because of their ability to attract large numbers of people to their places of worship, these churches have been defined as attractional."[1] The idea of attractional church has been around for a while. In fact, Michael Hamilton, in an article in *Christianity Today*, noted that churches seeking to attract people from their community have been around since the 1920s.[2] He states:

> The churches (in that era) began by listening to their new neighbors. What did they need? What might get them to come to church? In response to what they heard, they built churches that didn't look like churches. Many looked like warehouses; St. Bartholomew's Episcopal in New York was a nine-story building with a rooftop garden.
>
> They didn't look like churches because they included new kinds of facilities for new kinds of ministry—gymnasiums, swimming pools, medical dispensaries, employment centers, loan offices, libraries, daycare centers, and lots of classrooms. Critics invariably complained that their

worship spaces seemed to be an afterthought, but these buildings were designed for seven-days-a-week service.

This is one of the most common trends in church architecture. Buildings resemble corporate businesses, and church property has a definite campus feel. Gone are the ornate churches with high steeples and stained glass windows. The article went on to describe more changes made in the 1920s that sound strikingly similar to today's attractional churches:

> They held services in several languages. Some dispensed with hymnals and projected song lyrics on the wall. They taught English, hygiene, home economics, and work skills. They showed movies, held lectures, and sponsored concerts.
>
> Shaping ministry programs around the needs of their neighbors made some of these churches huge. St. Bartholomew's employed 249 paid workers and 846 volunteers serving nearly 3,000 members and countless local nonmembers. Russell Conwell's 3,000-member Baptist Temple in Philadelphia built a hospital and a university (Temple University) as well as a large new church. And William Rainsford's St. George's Episcopal in New York City had over 6,600 people involved in its parish ministries.[3]

The article described several megachurches across the country seeking and attracting thousands of needy people. This may sound vaguely familiar to the megachurch movement of our day, which seeks to attract nonbelievers to their services. Such a movement is to be commended for its passion for evangelism. "Seeker driven" or "seeker sensitive" churches are at least seeking to save that which is lost.

It reminds me of a story I heard a long time ago of someone opposed to D. L. Moody's emotion-stirring altar calls for people to be saved from their sins and the fires of hell. When confronted directly, Mr. Moody was reported to have said he did not much like his method either, but was curious to know whether or not he had another approach to recommend. The curt answer was something to this effect: "Well, Mr. Moody, I do not have a method for evangelism." To which Mr. Moody replied, "Well, in that case, . . . I like my method better."

Who's Who?

Perhaps most famous of the modern megachurch movement might be Bill Hybels's Willow Creek Church located outside of Chicago, Illinois. Here is a description of the range, scope, and size of the churches that are members of the Willow Creek Association (WCA) of churches:

For nearly 20 years, the WCA has developed a respected history of excellence and innovation in serving local churches and their leaders. In that time, the WCA has inspired and trained more than one million church leaders and has created and distributed millions of church resources into tens of thousands of churches representing more than 90 denominations. With more than 10,000 Member Churches in 35 countries, WCA leadership training events are now held in more than 250 cities in 50 countries each year.[4]

This is what you might call an influential church. At the core of their mission is a "deeply held belief that God's ordained plan to redeem and restore this world for Christ is through the church. In fact, we believe that it is the hope of the world."[5] It is evident that churches like Willow Creek passionately desire for people to come to know Christ. Consequently, any criticism should be carefully measured, especially if your technique is not working. The attractional model looks and functions like a funnel (see diagram below). The worship or celebration service is at the top of the funnel, and everything in the model starts with attracting people to that service.

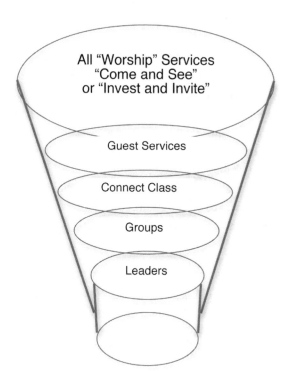

Personal Experience

It seems the passion to evangelize is the engine that drives attractional churches. I have attended several conferences at Willow Creek and know from personal experience that they are committed to reaching the lost for Christ. Another key value of an attractional church is their commitment to excellence. They are going to make sure they are ready for "company." They look at every aspect a guest would experience when they visit the church in order to ensure that all guests have a pleasant experience. Again, there is nothing wrong with this type of thinking. I have learned many things in regard to attractional ministry philosophy from Willow Creek Church.

In fact, I experienced, firsthand, the attractional model during my time as an assimilation pastor and a membership pastor at New Life Church in Columbus, Ohio. I was a founding pastor at New Life with Dave Earley and a team of Liberty University graduates, and I served there for almost twenty years. New Life, like many churches, has gone through several major transitions. We went through the "worship wars" of the early 1990s and came out on the other side with a contemporary-worship-styled service. The second transition entailed a move toward being intentionally "seeker sensitive." The third transition included the development of a small-group ministry (see chap. 28 on the hybrid church).

As a team, we talked through these transitions and agreed that we needed to reach lost people and wanted to involve our members in the "invest and invite" strategy. That is, we wanted our members to build relationships with their friends, coworkers, and neighbors and invite them to come to church. During this season in New Life's history, we became a "seeker sensitive" church. Like Willow Creek, we fervently wanted to reach the lost for Christ, and we believed we could create a workable strategy to improve our evangelistic efforts. As a result of attending several conferences at Willow Creek, we developed a three-step strategy to focus on attracting and retaining guests from our community. Step one focuses on encouraging people from the community to come to the church:

Step One: Attract Them
Advertising, Marketing, Mailings, Radio, TV Spots, Cinema Ads, Quality Celebrations, Dramatic Presentations, Special Events

Step two focuses on getting the guest from the community into the new-members class:

Step Two: Convince Them
Greeters, Ushers, First-Time Guests, 7 Touches of Love, Bread Patrol, Phone Team, 101, 201 Calls and Recruitment, Quality Membership Class

Step three focuses on connecting the new member into the ministries and programs of the church:

Step Three: Connect Them
New-Member Interviews, Connection Center Staffed, Small-Group Network, Leader Identification and Training, Group Multiplication

Additional Components

Here are some additional things we developed to become more attractive to our community:

1. We made sure that our parking lot was consistently maintained and freshly striped.
2. We made sure that our signage was visible and readable to visitors.
3. We recruited greeters to welcome guests and stationed them throughout the building.
4. We made sure our nursery rooms were impeccable and staffed with friendly volunteers.
5. We invested a significant amount of money in a welcome center with a full coffee bar and breakfast items.
6. We revamped our worship service to make it friendly to unchurched/de-churched guests from our community.
7. We eliminated any "awkward moments" for guests during the worship service. For instance, we stopped recognizing guests from the platform, and we mentioned during the offering that if you were

visiting, please don't feel obligated to put any money in the offering plate.

8. We made sure to explain any terms that may be confusing to guests.

9. We brainstormed on every sermon series and tried to pick topics that would be meaningful and relevant to guests.

10. We took time in our service to explain everything: the welcome, the announcements, the offering, the guest card, the invitation, and baptism to make sure our guests felt included.

11. We trained our members to invite their friends at the start of every new sermon series.

12. We implemented something called the five-foot rule and five-minute rule. That is, if someone comes within five feet of you, make sure you say "hello" or "good morning." We emphasized that during the first five minutes after the service, you should try to go and talk with people you do not know.

Is Evangelism the Goal?

We tried to make everything a guest might experience comfortable and convenient for them and their family. We wanted them to come and enjoy their experience, and we wanted them to return again and again. After attending for a while and consistently hearing the gospel and experiencing God's presence among His people, we believed the person would become convinced of their need for Christ. We saw many people come to know Christ through this process. Again, it is hard to criticize a model that is seeing some impressive evangelistic results. Many churches would be wise to adopt most, if not all, of the elements from the list above out of common sense.

What's the Problem?

The components above are not the problem with the attractional model. The real problem is that the emphasis is not on disciple making. The emphasis in this model is on evangelism. The other problem with this model is that it sends a message to the unbelieving world that the church is here to serve "me." This creates a consumer mentality. The first message, and subsequent messages, the visitor receives (consciously or subconsciously) is that this church cares about "me" and "my" sensibilities. For instance, below are some feelings some people may have about church:

- I'm uncomfortable hearing churches talk about money, and this church understands that and doesn't do it.
- I'm not a big fan of in-depth Bible teaching (some of that stuff is hard to understand). This church presents relevant information for me.
- I like to listen to music that sounds like the music I grew up with, and what do you know? This church is jammin'.
- I enjoy messages that touch my heart and stir my emotions, and this church has a dramatic presentation during the church service. Or, I like to watch video clips on YouTube, and this church has a video clip almost every Sunday.
- I like to remain anonymous when I go to church, much the same way I attend a movie theater, and this church doesn't recognize me or put me on the spot.
- I like the functional, practical office environment where I work, and this church looks like a corporate office complex.
- I am comfortable in the corporate world with a corporate structure of leadership and management, and this church's organization seems very similar to where I work.

Consumer or Kingdom Warrior?

First, the overall model is founded on a consumer mentality. A consumer mentality runs counter to the ethos of being a follower of Jesus Christ. Disciple making is clearly about helping the individual discover that Jesus is King of the universe and must be King in their life as well. We covered this information back in chapter 2, but I will briefly review it here to contrast kingdom concepts with attractional church concepts:

1. A disciple of Jesus has counted the cost and is willing to sacrifice for the cause of Christ.
2. A disciple of Jesus lives in close fellowship and community with other believers.
3. A disciple of Jesus is undergoing a total transformation of core values, habits, and purpose.

As you can see, a casual reading of these scriptural concepts runs counter to the overall attitude of an attractional church. If an attractional church is going to remain faithful to the teaching of Jesus regarding discipleship, then at some point the conversation must turn from "What's in it for me?" to "How can I serve Jesus and His church?" This is a difficult transition to make, and to the person who only knows the attractional church model, it may feel like a "bait and switch." That is, the person may feel like this: "I came to Christ because I felt He could help me in my life, and now I am understanding that Jesus is asking me to surrender everything and be willing to die if need be to advance His kingdom—I'm not sure if I like that."

You can see the tension created in this system. Jesus calls for total surrender, yet in our presentation, we are not holding up the same standard. Is this person a disciple if they are not willing to surrender all? Are they even saved? In our passion to see people come to know Christ, have we unwittingly and unknowingly caused a tension that is difficult to resolve?

Discipleship or Attendership?

The attractional model is good for evangelism but not so good for discipleship. In fact, Willow Creek's own "Reveal Study"[6] showed some dissatisfaction among its members after they had attended the church for several years. A summary of the key findings from the study revealed:

1. Church activity has limited impact on spiritual growth. "We found that those who were the most active in the church did not necessarily report higher levels of spiritual attitudes ("love for God and others") and spiritual behaviors (evangelism, tithing, etc.) than those who were less active."[7]
2. Many have stalled spiritually. "The highest percentages of people who say 'I have stalled spiritually' fall in the Exploring Christ and Growing in Christ segments. This means that becoming stalled is much more likely to occur at the earlier stages of spiritual growth."[8]
3. There is dissatisfaction with what members perceived to be the church's role in spiritual growth (17%). Consequently, there was a correlation between this dissatisfaction and church drop out (41%).[9]

The study also revealed a progression of spiritual growth and satisfaction as member's moved through a continuum from:

1. Exploring Christ
2. Growing in Christ
3. Close to Christ
4. Christ-centered living[10]

Willow Creek is to be commended for attempting the attractional model in the first place. Yet, the progression of spiritual maturity, and the corresponding aspect of spiritual satisfaction, is the most important discovery of the entire study. The results showed increased levels of satisfaction as a member matured in their walk with Christ. Our goal as disciple makers is to help people come to know Christ, grow in Christ, develop for Christ, and produce fruit (other disciples) who will reach the world with the good news of the gospel. Ultimately this will bring the most glory to God. When all of His children are growing, maturing, and involved in His mission, He is glorified.

Again, the attractional church is to be commended for their zeal for evangelism. However, their zeal for evangelism may be at the expense of developing disciples who are involved in the mission. If you are not developing "fishers of men," you are not developing disciples of Jesus. This does not necessarily imply poor leadership, but a deficiency in the system itself. However, we do need to be aware that leaders have the power to change the system. Leaders can make significant changes to the model to reorient the emphasis toward developing disciples who develop disciples.

⏤ Questions to Ponder ⏤

1. What is an early example of an attractional church?
2. What is a contemporary example of an attractional church?
3. What are some characteristics of an attractional church?
4. Overall, what is a strength of the attractional model?
5. What are some challenges of the attractional model?

Notes

1. Billy Hornsby, *The Attractional Church: Growth Through a Refreshing, Relational, and Relevant Church Experience* (Nashville: Hachette Book Group, 2011), 1.

2. See http://www.christianitytoday.com/ct/2000/november13/5.62.html (accessed October 15, 2012).

3. Ibid.

4. See http://www.willowcreek.com/about (accessed October 15, 2012).

5. Ibid.

6. See http://www.revealnow.com (accessed October 15, 2012).

7. See http://www.revealnow.com/key_findings.asp (accessed October 15, 2012).

8. Ibid.

9. Ibid.

10. See http://www.revealnow.com (accessed October 15, 2012).

27

Interpreting the Organic Model

Rod Dempsey

Organism or Organization?

When you hear the word *organic,* what image comes to mind? In our "farm to table" culture, the word usually has the idea of fresh, harvested locally, not genetically modified, and pesticide free. In the United States, a food can be labeled as organic if it contains a minimum of 95 percent organic ingredients.[1] When it comes to the Christian community, the term *organic* bespeaks of living, simple, natural, healthy, and reproducing. At the same time, the term *organic* is being shaped by several different groups and camps in relation to disciple making.

Granted, disciple making will ultimately occur in the context of a local church and, as I have argued, will normally find expression in one of four models (see chart on pages 236–37):

1. A traditional church (chap. 25)
2. An attractional church (chap. 26)
3. An organic church (chap. 27)
4. The hybrid model (chap. 28)

This chapter will explore the many different uses of the term *organic* as it relates to church models and disciple making. The organic church attempts to keep the church model very simple and basic. In this regard it is very similar to a cell church structure (see chart below). Joel Comiskey observes, "In the cell church, the cell group is the backbone, or center, of church ministry. Cell ministry replaces the need for many traditional programs."[2]

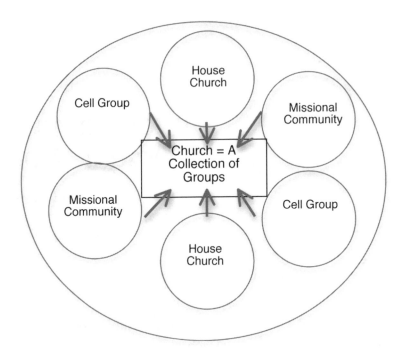

Compared to other models, the organic model is much simpler. The church is basically a collection of groups that meet out in the community. The terms *house church*, *missional community*, and *cell group* are used interchangeably. Similar to a human body, the church grows healthy as the cells are healthy. Healthy cells equal a healthy body. The cell or house church fulfills all the functions of the church. It does relational evangelism, follow up, and discipleship of new believers. It enables the believers to discover and use their spiritual gifts in the context of the body. It serves and meets the needs of the members in the group (hospital visits, grief care, benevolence). It does basic biblical counseling for the body. It does hands-on development of Great Commission leaders. It is in essence the "farm team" for developing new works and churches. It has the ability to accomplish the Great Commission, the Great Commandment, and the New Commandment at the same time. This is organic church in a nutshell. What follows is a synthesis of several concepts into a few principles that will hopefully capture the essence of what disciple making looks like inside an organic church. Before we get there, however, I will survey a few key advocates of the organic model, with some brief biographical information to guide further investigation. They are in no particular order.

Neil Cole is cofounder of Church Multiplication Associates (http:// www.cmaresources.org) and the Greenhouse Movement, which has grown to thousands of churches in fifty states and forty-plus nations. He has authored many books, including *Church 3.0*, *Organic Church*, *Organic Leadership*, *Search and Rescue*, *Cultivating a Life for God*, and *TruthQuest*. I have met and spoken with Cole. He is devoted to developing healthy disciples, leaders, churches, and movements from the place where you are planted and finishing at the ends of the earth.[3]

Alan Hirsch is the founding director of Forge Mission Training Network, and he leads an innovative learning program called Future Travelers that helps numerous megachurches become missional movements. He is the author of *The Shaping of Things to Come* (with Michael Frost), *The Forgotten Ways*, *ReJesus*, and *Untamed* (with his wife Debra).[4] I have interacted with Hirsch. His passion is to see the church of Jesus Christ rediscover its "missional ecclesiology" and become the most potent force for transformational change the world has ever seen.

Frank Viola is a pioneer in organic missional church life. He has written many books, including *From Eternity to Here*, *Jesus Manifesto* (co-authored with Leonard Sweet), and *Pagan Christianity* (co-authored with George Barna).[5] I have not met Frank in person, but we have corresponded by e-mail. According to his own blog, he has but one objective: *"To absolutely steal every believer for Jesus Christ. To blow their minds to the heavenlies and bring them into those intangible things of Christ and the deeper things of God."*[6] His contribution to the discussion of organic church has both breadth and depth.

Tony and Felicity Dale are active church planters. They founded *House2House* magazine and have authored several books, including *The Rabbit and the Elephant*, *Simply Church*, and *Getting Started*, a manual on planting house churches. Though not technically associated with the term *organic*, this couple has been influential in the propagation of organic principles, which they term "simple church." They believe that the New Testament church was simple from the beginning, and we should return to the original intent for disciple making in the context of "house churches."[7] I have never met them, but I am very familiar with the house-church structure from my time in Columbus, Ohio, especially Xenos Church led by Dennis McCallum and Gary DeLashmutt.[8]

Agreement in Philosophy

All of the aforementioned authors are in agreement on fundamental elements of the organic-church model. For example, everyone agrees that a church building is not necessary and is, in fact, often detrimental to the model.

They all agree that there should be no separation between the clergy and the laity since everyone is called to join God on His mission. All agree that love for one another should be one of our highest goals and aspirations. All agree that every member of the body of Christ should be actively using their gift in the way that God intends. All agree that the church of Jesus should function less like an organization and more like a family. All agree that the organized church should be simplified and more reliant on the leading of the Holy Spirit expressed through the gifts of the members in the group or house church.

In addition, they all share the conviction that convenience, comfort, and consumerism are a plague upon the institutional church and that leadership should naturally emerge from within the body. All maintain that the church contains a basic DNA (operating principles) that needs to be restored, although they have different views on what that DNA consists of (e.g., Cole has three elements and Hirsch has six elements).

They all agree that Jesus should be at the center of each and every church, with every member living under the lordship of Christ. Consequently, the way the church allows Him to be the head will necessarily impact the structure of the meeting time. Finally, all agree that the communion meal, in the context of the home, is an important practice of the organic church.

Slight Disagreements

Nevertheless, there are some differences specifically related to priorities. Neil Cole, for example, emphasizes multiplication more than Frank Viola.[9] Viola believes the leaders of the church should not receive a salary. Alan Hirsch advocates the fivefold ministry of Ephesians 4 and believes it is essential to the church's function.[10] Cole believes that in addition to the house church, there should be another smaller meeting he calls "Life Transformation Group," involving Bible reading and accountability.[11] Viola would also place more emphasis on the "seasonal nature" of group life.

Tony and Felicity Dale emphasize receiving visions from the Lord. They believe this to be an important part of Jesus being the head of His body.[12] As a result, listening to the Lord is a very important element of "simple church."

Viola believes the primary job of church leadership is to teach a congregation how to have open-participatory worship, with less doctrinal concern for issues such as the "millennium" and the "rapture."[13] Hirsch, however, believes the primary job of leadership is to bring various systems into meaningful connection and community.[14] While all believe in the importance of home gatherings, Hirsch adds the element of "communitas," reinforcing the need to be on mission together (adventure) in a way that builds community.[15]

Where Did It Come From?

Now that we have an overview of the general philosophy of the organic model, it might be helpful to clarify a few issues and fill in a few gaps before offering a critique of the organic model as it relates to disciple making. Disciple making, as we have argued, occurs best in the context of a local church. Consequently, the church should have a *practical* ecclesiology. With this in mind, the organic-church model seems to be a reaction against certain forms of ecclesiology. While this makes the model a bit suspect at the outset, nevertheless, the reaction is warranted insofar as it exposes, and addresses, the failure of the modern Western church to make disciples effectively. We are not seeing disciples getting involved in the Great Commission, and if this is the case, then we are not really developing disciples. Generally speaking, we are not seeing traditional or even attractional churches produce churches. Why is this not happening? Ed Stetzer has quipped that "if the church is designed to reproduce, and it is, then the church must be on some powerful birth control, because it is not reproducing."[16]

I suggest the main reason is that disciples, defined as sacrificial sold-out followers of Jesus, are not being developed. The organic model is reacting against those traditional and attractional models failing to produce the type of disciple who is committed to the mission of Christ. Yet, this is not a knee-jerk reaction. The people who are speaking and writing on this subject have zeal and knowledge and, consequently, must be taken seriously.

Challenges for Organic Church

Nevertheless, every model has room for improvement. With this in mind, I suggest four challenges with the organic-church model:

1. *Training.* If the movement is producing disciples and leaders from within, then is there sufficient training to "accurately handle" the

Word of God? Although some have developed effective training components (for example, Xenos church in Columbus, Ohio), overall I sense that training could be a weakness for the organic church. Granted, I am not looking for training at the seminary level. Yet, basic theological training is imperative.

2. *Leadership/Oversight.* Most all of the adherents of the organic church speak of decentralized leadership and are anti-hierarchical in their approach to leadership. The motivation behind this is to encourage the headship of Jesus over His church. However, this does not necessarily mean that the church does not have undershepherds who are seeking to connect the members to the head. In some of the literature, this point has been taken to the extreme with any centralized leadership perceived as unbiblical.

3. *Teaching.* If 1 Corinthians 14 is taken as the rule and is the normative expression of church life (Frank Viola), then there is going to be extensive "sharing" about the Scripture, with little formal teaching. This is an extension of body life taken to the extreme. While I am not in favor of the current "sit down, be quiet, and do nothing" approach common in many traditional churches today, much harm could result without a careful exegesis and explanation of the text. This does not mean that everyone sharing in the gathering needs to be seminary trained. I have met many people who are careful students of God's Word yet have no formal seminary training. It is important to see the church developing disciples and leaders to lead new churches from within their own ranks. Perhaps questions could be encouraged at the end of a "teaching," or the teaching could be the basis of a good home group (house church) discussion.

4. *Evangelism.* Will relational, incarnational evangelism work in a consumer-driven society where people want what they want, when they want it, and how they want it? Is 1 Cor 9:19–23 a description of how to tailor our evangelistic efforts (to blend it with the present culture)? Is 1 Cor 9:19–23 a description of how Paul approached his apostolic mission? Will we be able to retrain a generation of consumer-driven disciples in lifestyle evangelism that goes on 24/7? Will we be able to convince every believer that they should live as missionaries to their culture?

Keep It Simple

Overall, I do believe that there needs to be a simpler approach to doing ministry. Specifically, disciple making needs to be done in a church that is:

1. Christocentric—a focus on His headship (praying and listening)
2. Simpler—less focus on buildings (incarnational)
3. Relational—a focus on love (serving)
4. Missional—a focus on the harvest (sharing)
5. Healthy—a focus on everyone using their gifts (participation)
6. Maturing—a focus on equipping (developing)
7. Reproducing—a focus on church planting (multiplication)

The above principles are rooted in the biblical idea of discipleship and need to find expression in a simple church model that naturally reaches people with the gospel, empowers them to grow, equips them to serve, and releases them to the mission of Christ. The "model" is not as important as obedience to Christ's command to make disciples who look like, think like, and act like Jesus.

~ Questions to Ponder ~

1. What is the basic idea of an organic-church model?
2. How does an organic church function like a cell church?
3. Who are some of the advocates and practitioners of the organic-church model?
4. What are some challenges in the organic model?
5. What are some key principles in the organic church?

Notes

1. See http://en.wikipedia.org/wiki/Organic_food (accessed October 15, 2012).

2. See http://www.joelcomiskeygroup.com/articles/churchLeaders/CellChurch Definition.htm (accessed October 15, 2012).

3. See www.cmaresources.org/files/NeilColeBio.pdf (accessed October 15, 2012).

4. See http://www.theforgottenways.org/alan-hirsch.aspx (accessed October 15, 2012).

5. See http://frankviola.org/biography (accessed October 15, 2012).

6. See http://frankviola.org/about (accessed October 15, 2012).

7. See http://www.site.house2house.com/about-us/welcome (accessed October 15, 2012).

8. See http://www.xenos.org (accessed October 15, 2012).

9. See http://www.cmaresources.org/article/organic-church_n-cole_f-viola (accessed October 15, 2012).

10. See http://www.theforgottenways.org/apest (accessed October 15, 2012).

11. See http://www.cmaresources.org/article/organic-church_n-cole_f-viola (accessed October 15, 2012).

12. See chap. 17 of Tony Dale, Felicity Dale, George Barna, *The Rabbit and the Elephant: Why Small Is the New Big for Today's Church* (Carol Stream, IL: Tyndale House, 2009).

13. Frank Viola, *Reimagining Church: Pursuing the Dream of Organic Christianity* (Colorado Springs, CO: David C. Cook, 2008), Kindle location 1146.

14. See http://www.theforgottenways.org/apest (accessed October 15, 2012).

15. Alan Hirsch and Leonard Sweet, *The Forgotten Ways: Reactivating the Missional Church* (Grand Rapids, MI: Brazos, 2007), 217.

16. Ed Stetzer, "Helping Church Planters Do Global Missions," Exponential Conference, Orlando, FL, 2010; see also Ed Stetzer, "Have Churches Forgotten How to Reproduce?" at http://outreachmagazine.com/features14627-have-churches-forgotten-how-to-reproduce.html (accessed January 15, 2013).

28

Investigating the Hybrid Model

Rod Dempsey

The hybrid model, as the name implies, seeks to blend elements of the traditional, attractional, and organic models. Usually, the hybrid model overlays a new small-group model on top of an existing traditional, or even attractional, church model. One of the main challenges in the hybrid model is that the church leadership often does not reduce any of the existing ministries and programs. As a result, there is considerable complexity with the model. I would venture that most churches that have attempted to transition to small groups or cell groups could be categorized as some variation of the hybrid model.

Personal Experience #1

I am very familiar with the hybrid model. I graduated from college in 1982 with a bachelor of science degree in pastoral studies from Liberty University. I finished my master of religious education degree two years later, this time graduating from Liberty Baptist Theological Seminary. While in college and seminary, I met Dave Earley. Dave was my dorm resident assistant. Periodically, he would come into my dorm room at night and ask my roommates and me a rather personal question: "What did you get out of the Word today?" Funny how a simple question like that can impact your life. The first time he asked me, I was embarrassed to say, "I haven't been in the Word today, so I got nothing out of the Word." The next day Dave came by and asked the same question. Again, I gave the same answer. On the third day I decided I was going to get in the Word for myself to avoid the embarrassment of not having read God's Word. That was thirty years ago, and to this day I still follow the "One Year Bible Plan" of reading through the Bible each day. I have recommended this simple approach to thousands of people, and I recommend it to you as well.

From this foundational building block of discipleship, Dave began to meet with several young men in our dorm. We began to discuss what we were going to do after graduation. The focus at Liberty during those days was to graduate, go and plant a church somewhere, and then "capture a town for Christ." Church planting was definitely the "in" thing to do. The expected model, however, was to go out as a husband and wife and plant the church "solo," that is, without a team. As we studied the Scriptures together, we became convinced that the best, and biblical, way to plant a church was as a team. So we began talking about planting a church in the Columbus, Ohio, region as a team. Four young men with their newly married wives and one single young man agreed to plant a new church together.

One of the main passages we agreed upon as a blueprint for ministry was Eph 4:11–16. We were convinced that it was the pastor's job to "equip" the saints for the works of service. We also believed in the power of small groups. Dave was the campus pastor at Liberty and was responsible for developing the small-group system still used at Liberty to the present day. We had Ephesians 4 and small groups in our DNA as a team.

Humble Beginnings

With this vision we left Liberty as a team and started New Life Community Baptist Church in the summer of 1985. We knew about small groups and the benefit of connecting believers together to accomplish the "one anothers." We started the church that summer and began meeting in a middle school in our community. We met at the middle school on Sundays and in our apartments, scattered around the suburbs, for small groups during the week.

We did this for a number of years, but as the church grew, we struggled with developing disciples because our groups were oftentimes "overrun" with children. We developed Sunday school classes for children and adults at the middle school on Sunday morning. We eventually built a new church building and were able to gather all of our groups together and meet (without having to set up and tear down each week) in our own facilities.

This was the typical pattern for church plants at the time: meet in a school for a while, grow the church attendance, build a building, grow the church, build another building, grow the church some more, and so it goes. We did this for the better part of ten years, and the church attendance grew to more than 1,000 people. At that time we built another building that could seat 1,000 people. We had several adult education classes and were conducting two services at the same time. Our total worship capacity was around 2,000 people.

Yet our adult education/group capacity was well below that number, and we needed more space for our children and student ministries. Yet, we could not borrow any more money to build additional buildings because we were already in debt for 2 million dollars. We were faced with a discipleship challenge. We did not have enough room for our adults to continue meeting on the church property. After much discussion, we decided the best option was to move our adult groups off the property into homes across the community. This would allow our children and student ministries to continue growing. Additionally, with our adult education off the Sunday morning time slot, we could focus on the Sunday morning gathering.

Developing Small Groups

We decided to investigate small groups for our adult discipleship. Dave and I decided that I would become the point person for developing small groups across the church. I began traveling around the country to learn from ministries with successful small groups. I discovered many principles that would help us make small groups more central in our church structure.

I traveled to Houston, Texas, for a small-group conference hosted by Ralph Neighbour. Ralph is a pioneer in cell church strategy. I also traveled to Tucson, Arizona, for a conference led by Joel Comiskey. Joel has studied the cell church model extensively and is a powerful voice for developing disciples inside a "cell church." He has written more than a dozen books devoted to the topic and has been a constant resource for disciple making over the years.

Beyond that, Dave and I traveled to Baton Rouge, Louisiana, for a conference by Larry Stockstill. Larry wrote the book *The Cell Church*. His church at the time had more than six hundred cell groups and was growing like a wild fire. Around the same time, I invited Dale Galloway to come to our church and speak to our small-group leaders about how he made the transition to small groups at his church, New Hope Community Church of Portland, Oregon. Dale helped me to see, through practical wisdom, how a church can transition from a traditional Sunday school model to a small-group model. The transition was under way.

Taking the Plunge

The first year of the transition we trained and developed 7 small groups. The next year we had 25 groups. The third year we had more than 50 small groups, and the fourth year close to 80 groups. By the fifth year, we had more than 125 small groups and a coaching system with seventeen coaches. Before we made this transition, we had only 8 adult Sunday school classes with just a handful of adult teachers. After the transition, we had more than 125 groups with leaders, apprentices, hosts, and coaches with nearly 400 leaders involved in disciple making.

Our church also doubled in attendance during this time. We went from 1,000 to 2,000 in Sunday morning attendance in five years. We successfully made the transition from a church "with" groups to a church "of" groups and were very close to becoming a church that "is" groups (see next chapter). We were not able to go all the way to becoming a church that "is" groups because we were not able to change our primary mode of evangelism or the complexity of our model.

Hybrid Model by Default

We became a hybrid model. We took the best of the organic-church model, while keeping many elements of both the traditional and attractional models. The way we did evangelism was "invest and invite," and although we did reduce complexity and adjust personnel, we retained a traditional church structure. Dave Browning, in his book *Hybrid Church: The Fusion of Intimacy and Impact*, describes the model this way: "In the up-and-coming world of the hybrid church, there is unprecedented experimentation in the blending of intimacy and impact. A discernible gravitational pull is obviously taking large churches in the direction of the micro church, and vice versa. Large churches are exploring various ways in which they can break things down for greater community life."[1]

Below are some of the important hybrid model characteristics true of us (see chap. 24):

1. We continued to have a building focus.
2. Our model was extremely complex.
3. The evangelism strategy was "come and see" or "invest and invite."
4. Discipleship was important, but so was everything else.
5. We kept many of the programs that were in place before the transition.

6. Spiritual gifts were being discussed, but in the context of running the programs.
7. Preaching was topically focused on both believer and seeker.
8. Budget and ministry expenses were spread across all the areas.
9. Worship was mainly a Sunday morning experience.
10. Leadership development was for both Sunday morning (programs) and for disciple making.
11. The senior pastor was involved in every area and was spread thin due to the complexity of the model.
12. The saints were involved, but not directly in the Great Commission, and they were not strategically using their spiritual gifts according to God's design.
13. We had training for both Great Commission work and Sunday morning programs.
14. Church planting was a goal, and new churches were being started from within the body. This was due to the small-group system producing so many Great Commission leaders.

Overall, we were able to go from a fairly traditional church with an addition mindset to a church with a multiplying mindset. In the years following this transition, New Life has planted seven new churches with homegrown leadership teams. This is a testimony that making disciples and developing leaders will create new works and churches for the King. What we were not able to do as effectively was to reduce the complexity of the model itself. There were many organic principles mixed with some traditional approaches (building focused, corporate flow chart structure, "come and see" evangelism, program focus, dispersed budget, gifts not being maximized, and training but not focused on the mission).

Personal Experience #2

My second experience with transitioning a church to a hybrid model occurred when the Lord called me to go to Liberty Baptist Theological Seminary to teach. At this same time, one of my lifelong mentors, Dr. Elmer Towns, encouraged Jerry Falwell to hire me to help transition Thomas Road Baptist Church to a more "Purpose-Driven Church."[2] Dr. Falwell and I discussed the possibilities of transitioning this historic church to become a church "of" groups.

When I was hired at Thomas Road, I took an inventory of the adult Sunday school classes. We had 19 adult classes. While some of these classes were very large and had great teachers, we did not have enough people involved in the Great Commission. Nevertheless, we decided to wait to implement our small-group philosophy until we moved to a new location across town. In the meantime, I focused on developing key relationships and a disciple-making mind-set.

When we finally moved to a new location, we began new groups almost immediately. We developed groups on Sunday morning, Freedom groups on Monday night, women's groups on Tuesday morning and Tuesday night, outreach groups on Wednesday night, and groups on Thursday mornings for mothers of preschoolers. We also developed groups on Fridays for men's accountability. In just a few years, we went from 19 adult groups to almost 300 groups meeting on the property all throughout the week.

When we ran out of room for groups on Sunday morning, Jonathan Falwell (now senior pastor after Jerry Falwell's home-going) shifted our focus from groups meeting only at the property to groups meeting out in the community. As a result, we developed another 125 groups. In just five years, we went from 19 adult Sunday school classes to more than 400 groups meeting both at the church and out in the community.

During this same time, we saw a dramatic increase in evangelism. We baptized more than 3,000 people in thirty months and are still baptizing 5 or 6 people every week. The transition has occurred because we were passionate about evangelism and discipleship. It is not enough to reach people with the gospel. We are also called to make disciples.

Thomas Road has transitioned from a fairly traditional church a few years ago to a megachurch on a mission. It is a hybrid church insofar as it retains elements from all the models. We still have a building mentality, but are equipping and empowering people to go out into the fields and do evangelism. We still have many programs and ministries, but are developing new satellite churches to reach people with the gospel. We are still very complex, but we are focused on the Great Commission. We are a hybrid church with traditional, attractional, and some organic elements.

Lessons Learned

As I look back on my experiences at New Life and Thomas Road, I remember the promise from the Great Commission. Do you remember the promise in the Great Commission? Jesus said, and I paraphrase, "If you go and make disciples (preaching the gospel, baptizing them, and teaching them to obey everything I commanded you) . . . I will be with you!" If you and I determine to obey the Lord and make disciples, He has promised to be with us. I am here to testify of the truth of that promise. Trust me when I say, I am nothing without the Lord enabling and empowering me. The lessons learned in both of these transitions occurred out of a simple desire to follow the Lord's command and His subsequent blessing. We have changed many things at Thomas Road, all in an effort to win people to Christ, help them to grow in Christ, and send them out for Christ. We are in process of developing people for the King and His kingdom.

Is Good the Enemy of Great?

The hybrid model seeks to adopt the best of all models. Yet, many times it does not reduce its complexity. This complexity causes confusion in the minds of the members and uncertainty about their role in ministry. The staff is also conflicted. While tasked with the ministries and programs of the church, they are also encouraged to be in small groups and develop disciples. Disciple making in this environment is challenging because there are so many options.

Another challenge is the failure to *multiply* new churches. Most hybrid churches are starting satellite churches, but they are not *multiplying* leaders. Ed Stetzer and Warren Bird comment on this challenge: "Is the implication for churches that we need an approach to evangelism that centers on church multiplication instead of addition? As our friend Ralph Moore often says, 'It's time to stop counting converts and begin counting congregations.'"[3] Addition models will never reach an exponentially growing population.

The hybrid model is common for those churches transitioning from a traditional model to a church intentionally making disciples through small groups. The move from traditional to hybrid is to be commended. Yet I do not recommend the hybrid model for church planters who are seeking to make disciples in a simple, relational, incarnational, missional environment.

Conclusion on the Models

We are called to make disciples, and the model and structure we choose should be based upon biblical principles. The Great Commandment, the New Commandment, the Great Commission, the book of Acts, Eph 4:11–16,

1 Corinthians 12, and Romans 12 are just some of the passages that should guide us as we seek to develop disciples of Jesus Christ. Many churches are in process of transitioning from one model to another with minor changes here and there moving them further down the line. The test of whether a particular model is working, however, should be reflected in growing disciples, emerging leaders, and new churches planted for the kingdom and glory of God!

— Questions to Ponder —

1. Briefly describe the hybrid model?
2. What are some strengths and weaknesses of the hybrid model?
3. What is the personal experience number one?
4. What is the personal experience number two?
5. How does the hybrid church model intersect with other models?

Notes

1. Dave Browning, *Hybrid Church: The Fusion of Intimacy and Impact* (Hoboken, NJ: John Wiley and Sons, 2010), 72.

2. Rick Warren, *The Purpose Driven Church* (Grand Rapids, MI: Zondervan, 1995).

3. Ed Stetzer and Warren Bird, *Viral Churches: Helping Church Planters Become Movement Makers* (Hoboken, NJ: John Wiley and Sons, 2010), 43.

29

Disciple Making Is . . .

Discovering
Effective Systems

Rod Dempsey

What Did He Say?

In this last section, we have explored the proper context for disciple making. Specifically, we have argued for the importance of the body of Christ (chap. 19), the role of spiritual leadership (chap. 20), the marks of a healthy church (chap. 22), and a governing disciple-making focus (chap. 23). Finally, we surveyed and critiqued four common church models, noting strengths and weaknesses of each. In this chapter, we will draw some final conclusions regarding the best context for disciple making. Ultimately, this is a discussion about the nature and the purpose of the church. In the Great Commission, the command to "make disciples" is clear. In the final instructions from Jesus to His disciples, we have some clues about how to go about making disciples regardless of the model:

- We must be going (Matt 28:19; Mark 16:15; John 20:21).
- We must be going to all the nations (Matt 28:19; Mark 16:15; Luke 24:47; Acts 1:8).
- We must be preaching the gospel (including repentance; that Jesus is Lord) (Rom 10:9–10; Mark 16:15; Luke 24:46).
- We must die to self and be witnesses (martyrs) for Christ (Mark 16:15; Luke 24:48; Acts 1:8).

- We must be going and making disciples (Matt 28:19), which includes:
  - baptizing (Matt 28:19; Mark 16:16)
  - and teaching them to observe (obey) everything that Christ commanded (Matt 28:20).
- We must wait on the Spirit of promise to go with us (Luke 24:49; Acts 1:4).

Environment or Education

What, then, is the most effective method and context for disciple making? The answer to this question has evaded churches for centuries. Yet it is extremely important since the answer shapes how we go about making disciples. Most approaches will agree that the best place to make disciples is inside a small-group environment. There are dozens of books on the topic, including the Bible. For example, the Great Commission (teaching them to observe), the implications of being members of a body (implying close connection), the "one anothers" (more than thirty-five different injunctions for us to live out the New Commandment), and the concept that we are brothers and sisters living in a family all illustrate that the best way to make disciples is in a relational context. Christianity is more caught than taught, and to make progress in the disciple-making process, we need good examples of people who model the apostle Paul's "follow my example as I follow the example of Christ" (1 Cor 11:1 NIV) paradigm.

The best context for cultivating this kind of environment is a small group within a local church. Churches down through the centuries have wrestled with how to create relational structures that function like a family or a body. With the exception of the first three hundred years of church history, we have not done a very good job of creating that structure.

Back to the Future

Neil Cole in his book *Church 3.0*[1] argues that, historically, the church has had three operating systems. The first system was organic and functioned around the idea of a people movement. The second system rejected this system and morphed into a professional clergy-driven model. The third operating system is a return to the family/body operating system where every person is important to the health of the church.

One can trace these three systems, which Cole labels 1.0, 2.0, and 3.0 respectively, throughout church history. From the founding of the church in

Jerusalem, to Antioch, to Galatia, to Ephesus, all the way to Constantine, one may trace elements of Church 1.0. Church 2.0 spans from Constantine to the present day. Characteristics of Church 2.0 may vary, but most churches in this category function with a clear distinction between the "professional" clergy and the "lay" people. Yet this system moves away from what the early church believed and practiced, and often fails to cultivate an effective disciple-making environment. Nevertheless, the church has continued in this professional clergy mode for almost 1,700 years.

Cole and others[2] believe that the church is on the verge of a new movement, a third stage he calls Church 3.0. There are some significant differences between Church 2.0 and 3.0 which suggest an emerging paradigm shift. The chart below illustrates some of these contrasts:[3]

MODE:	CHURCH 2.0	CHURCH 3.0
Seating when gathered	Rows	Circles
Environment	Anonymous	Intimate
Leadership source	Institutions of higher learning	Harvest fields
Growth	Addition	Multiplication
Results	An audience is attracted	A spiritual army is mobilized
Ministry practitioners	The ordained	The ordinary
Resources	Imported to the harvest	Discovered in the harvest
Primary leadership role	Pastoral teacher	APEST team
Learning lab	Classroom-based education	Trench-based education
Cost	Expensive	Inexpensive
Ministry setting	The meeting place	The marketplace
Success	Full seating capacity	Full sending capacity
Church posture	Passive: "Y'all come!"	Active: "We all go"
Attractions	Felt-need programming	Obvious life transformation
Model of church life	Academic	Family

Church 3.0 is a return to first principles, but it is also an upgrade from Church 1.0. There is a return to the family/body emphasis along with advances in Scripture knowledge, technology, and leadership development.

Focus on the Individual

Advocates of Church 3.0 maintain the need to transform the church into an effective disciple-making movement. However, in order to accomplish this goal, the church will need to discover, or rediscover, some principles practiced by the early church. In particular, there is the principle that the context for making disciples is in the home (Acts 2:47; 5:42; 8:1; 12:12; 16:40; 20:20).

There were many reasons for this emphasis in the early church, but perhaps the greatest reason is the fact that the best way to "love one another" is within a smaller, intimate gathering of believers. In addition, the apostle Paul argues that all the parts of the body should use their spiritual gifts to build up the body of Christ. Ephesians 4:16, for example, states, "From Him the whole body, fitted and knit together by every supporting ligament, promotes the growth of the body for building up itself in love by the proper working of each individual part."

The body cannot, and will not, grow strong and healthy unless *all* the parts are functioning according to God's intention. Greg Ogden comments on this fact, stating, "Upon closer examination of the body, one is impressed with the unique function of the individual parts and the necessity of each part for the health of the whole. For the body to thrive, every part must operate according to its design."[4]

God has something in mind for the individual believer to do in His kingdom. Our job as leaders of His body is to help them grow in maturity and discover His plan for their lives. We help the person grow in the same way that we help our children grow . . . with individual attention. Colossians 1:28 illustrates this well: "We proclaim Him, admonishing *every man* and teaching *every man* with all wisdom, so that we may present *every man* complete in Christ" (NASB).

The focus of this verse is on the repeated phrase "every man." Our goal as Christian leaders is to help *every* individual stand before the King of kings and hear from Him: "Well done, good and faithful servant." This necessitates that we create intimate, disciple-making contexts where personal attention can be given to the individual. The best place for this to occur is in the context of a small group.

Decisions ... Decisions

Existing churches that do not have an effective discipleship system will need to make some tough decisions if they desire to develop God's children to their full potential. They will need to decide how far they are willing to go to encourage, equip, and empower the members of Christ's body to do His ministry. New church plants have an advantage in so far as they are able to start from a clean slate. However, they must also be aware of the tendency to reproduce that which they have seen and experienced in other models.

Existing churches, and new church plants, will face important theological and philosophical decisions regarding the nature and purpose of the church. This will then inform the shape of their disciple-making ministry and the degree to which small groups will play a role in that ministry. If small groups play any role, they will likely fall in one of three categories: a church "with" groups, a church "of" groups, or a church that "is" groups. These categories help identify where a given church lands on the trajectory of small-group philosophy, and the degree to which they reflect the relational environment so important for developing disciples. The church that "is" groups has the greatest potential for effective disciple making. Yet, no matter where a church may be on the trajectory, if at all, it can initiate a small-group ministry, or transition to a greater emphasis on small groups, if its leadership is willing to make some tough decisions. What follows is a survey of the "with," "of," and "is" small-group categories as well as a few insights with regard to transitioning along this small-group trajectory. Below is a chart explaining some of the key differences of each category:

"WITH" SMALL GROUPS Traditional	"OF" SMALL GROUPS Hybrid	"IS" SMALL GROUPS Organic
Professional staff run	Staff develop programs	Leaders equip the saints to accomplish the Great Commission
Senior pastor group involvement: not really involved	Senior pastor group involvement: in favor of groups along with everything else	Senior pastor group involvement: leads a group and talks about group life often
Pastor's role: shepherd taking care of sheep	Pastor's role: developing the ministries of the church	Pastor's role: developing the members of His body to reach their full potential
Building focused—"Our church meets here."	Building and community focused—"Our church meets here and we are in the community."	Community focused—"We gather on Sunday morning, but we are His body in the community."

"WITH" SMALL GROUPS Traditional	"OF" SMALL GROUPS Hybrid	"IS" SMALL GROUPS Organic
Church's goal: hang on till Jesus returns	Church's goal: preach the gospel and make disciples	Church's goal: transformed lives . . . transformed society
Preaching: toward the constituency (5 families)	Preaching: "seeker sensitive"	Preaching: toward the believer usually exegetical
Evangelism: if at all—attractional	Evangelism: attractional "invest and invite"	Evangelism: member's share their life with lost
Discipleship: 8-week course taught by the pastor (maybe once a year)	Discipleship: "base path" development composed of several classes	Discipleship: doing life together in community with other believers
Prayer: happens at the church	Prayer: focus on the individual praying	Prayer: happens in the groups for the harvest
Missions: offerings taken and shipped to a missions organization	Missions: offerings taken and short-term trips planned	Missions: people are encouraged to live as missionaries and go across the street and across the world
Growth: "outside in" focus on quantity	Growth: "outside in" focus on quantity and hope for quality	Growth: "inside out" focus on quality and plan on quantity
Gifts: not emphasized	Gifts: some important—especially for the platform	Gifts: all essential; body life emphasized
Training: not needed	Training: to run the Sunday morning programs	Training: for the Great Commission
Groups: "We have a few groups . . . I believe."	Groups: "We believe in groups."	Groups: "We are groups."
Leadership development: don't need or necessarily want leaders	Leadership development: need "leaders" to run the programs of Sunday morning	Leadership development: need "missional leaders" who care for and develop God's people
Church planting: no	Church planting: yes . . . sort of; satellites/campuses (addition)	Church planting: yes; new churches emerge from disciples developing into leaders (multiplication)
Open or closed groups: closed groups: • Accountability • Men's groups • Women's ministry	Open or closed groups: open and closed groups: • Campaign groups • Purpose-driven groups • Free-market groups • Host groups	Open or closed groups: open groups: • Cell groups • Intergenerational groups • Neighborhood groups • Missional groups

"With," "Of," and "Is" Overview

The traditional church is most often considered to be a church "with" small groups. It is by far the most common church today and, as such, reflects the small-group philosophy of most churches. The hybrid model reflects the next level as a church "of" small groups. It borrows, as we have seen, from the other two models, yet retains, at varying degrees, the hierarchical structure of the traditional model. Nevertheless, in transitioning from "with" to "of," it seeks to implement a more empowering structure even if the power and control remains with relatively few leaders. Finally, as a church that "is" small groups, an organic model seeks to empower and simplify. It has a much flatter organizational structure and seeks to equip everyone in the body to be involved in the Great Commission.

There are many factors to consider when transitioning from "with" to "of." This can be a difficult transition, affecting a church's fundamental philosophy of ministry. Nevertheless, it is possible if the senior pastor understands that his job is to "equip" the saints to do the works of service (and not just the Sunday morning services). He and his team must work to create a simple yet comprehensive mission statement that focuses on developing God's people for God's glory. Groups should be intentionally developed for mission, and leaders trained to lead those groups. The senior pastor should speak often about the importance of getting involved in a group, and staff leaders should be encouraged to participate in and lead those groups.

Moving from "of" to "is," likewise, is possible but can create some tension and uncertainty in the transition period. Specifically, given the decentralization of power, the senior pastor may be uncertain of his role as ministry shifts from being campus focused to small-group focused. His new role would encompass both leading a group and developing new leaders to multiply the groups.

Further, the ministry leaders would be expected to lead groups in their homes. This is a significant shift from a Sunday morning ministry to leading small groups and coaching leaders. Many programs would be intentionally paired down to allow for a holistic small-group strategy within which most of the ministries of the church would take place. Specifically, evangelism, discipleship, spiritual gifts, pastoral care, counseling, leadership development, and new church development would occur inside a small-group environment.

Transitioning from "with" to "is" is perhaps the most difficult given that it requires a complete overhaul of the operating system of the church. Consequently, I counsel against such a drastic change. Having said this, in cases where a traditional church is at a plateau or is near death, such a transition is possible if new leadership is able to explain the theological and philosophical reasons for such a change. Even so, statements made in earnest do not always survive painful emotional choices.

Health Is the Goal

When teaching my students, I realize many of them will begin their ministries in traditional churches with little or no discipleship system. We talk about the challenges of transitioning a traditional church, and I encourage many of them to consider planting a new church. However, I realize that there are many churches out there that can make the transition from "with" to "of," and there are some that can go from "of" to "is." It is my hope that wherever the Lord has you, you are able to help the church develop healthy disciples who grow into Great Commission leaders who plant new churches for the glory of God. Making disciples for the kingdom and glory of God requires that we passionately pursue His plan for developing His people!

⁓ Questions to Ponder ⁓

1. Whatever the model, what are some things we must be doing?
2. What is the difference between Church 2.0 and Church 3.0?
3. How do we focus on the individual?
4. What is the difference between a church "with" groups, a church "of" groups, and a church that "is" groups?
5. What are some of the dangers of transitioning from "with" to "is"?

Notes

1. Neil Cole, *Church 3.0* (San Francisco, CA: Jossey-Bass, 2010).
2. See Alan Hirsch, *The Forgotten Ways*; *Right Here, Right Now*; *Untamed*; Ed Stetzer, *Breaking the Missional Code*; *Transformational Church*; *Viral Church Planting*; *Missional Churches*; Hugh Halter, *The Tangible Kingdom: Creating Incarnational Community*; *Sacrilege: Finding Life in the Unorthodox Ways of Jesus*; Frank Viola, *Pagan Christianity*; *Finding Organic Church*; *Reimagining Church*; Dennis McCallum, *Organic Disciplemaking: Mentoring Others into Spiritual Maturity and Leadership*; *Members of One Another: How to Build a Biblical Ethos into Your Church*. Francis Chan's *Crazy Love* addresses the need to transform the church from "come and see" to "go and be." For a fuller explanation see Tyler Charles and Josh Lujan Loveless, "The Crazy Mission of Francis Chan," *Relevant Magazine* (Feb. 23, 2011), http://www.relevantmagazine.com/god/church/features/24816-the-crazy-mission-of-francis-chan (accessed 2/7/13) .
3. Cole, *Church 3.0*, 9.
4. Greg Ogden, *Unfinished Business: Returning the Ministry to the People of God* (Grand Rapids, MI: Zondervan, 2003), Kindle location 581.

Conclusion

Putting It All Together

Dave Earley

You have just read a ton of information about the Great Commission and making disciples. You have examined biblical and theological foundations for disciple making (chaps. 1–4). You have explored what it means to be a disciple of and make disciples for Jesus (chaps. 5–11). You have looked at disciple-making methods (chaps. 12–18) and investigated some common models being used to make disciples (chaps. 19–29). That is all very good, but not good enough. Let me explain. Better yet, let's have a wise pastor explain it for us:

> But prove yourselves doers of the word, and not merely hearers who delude themselves. For if anyone is a hearer of the word and not a doer, he is like a man who looks at his natural face in a mirror; for once he has looked at himself and gone away, he has immediately forgotten what kind of person he was. But one who looks intently at the perfect law, the law of liberty, and abides by it, not having become a forgetful hearer but an effectual doer, this man will be blessed in what he does. (Jas 1:22–25 NASB)

In the above text, Pastor James pointed out that hearing the Word *without* doing it leads to spiritual deception, while hearing it *and doing* it produces blessing. In other words, information *without* application leads to *spiritual deception*, while information *with application* leads to *transformation*.

Rod and I did not write this book to inform you. We wrote it to *transform* you so you can participate in God's big plan to transform the world. Therefore, we desperately hope that you apply it. We would be lousy disciple makers if we let you get away with being inspired and informed, but not changed.

So this chapter is all about application. As such, it may be the most important and transforming chapter in the entire book . . . if you do it. Take a few minutes to complete the following.

The Big Picture

Briefly complete each of the following statements.

- The one thing I liked most about this entire book was:
- The main truth I was reminded of was:
- The most significant lesson I learned is:
- The truth that will change my life if I apply it is:
- The idea I most need to implement in my ministry is:
- The chapter I want to reread first is:

The Foundations (Chapters 1–4)

Briefly complete each of the following statements.

- The one thing I liked most about this section was:
- The main truth I was reminded of was:
- The most significant lesson I learned is:
- The truth that will change my life if I apply it is:
- The idea I most need to implement in my ministry is:

The Basics (Chapters 5–11)

Briefly complete each of the following statements.

- The one thing I liked most about this section was:
- The main truth I was reminded of was:
- The most significant lesson I learned is:
- The truth that will change my life if I apply it is:
- The idea I most need to implement in my ministry is:

The Methods (Chapters 12–18)

Briefly complete each of the following statements.

- The one thing I liked most about this section was:
- The main truth I was reminded of was:
- The most significant lesson I learned is:
- The truth that will change my life if I apply it is:
- The idea I most need to implement in my ministry is:

The Models (Chapters 19–29)

Briefly complete each of the following statements.

- The one thing I liked most about this section was:
- The main truth I was reminded of was:
- The most significant lesson I learned is:
- The truth that will change my life if I apply it is:
- The idea I most need to implement in my ministry is:

In Summary

Briefly complete this statement.

- In summary, the biggest thing God did in my life through this book was:

Scripture Index

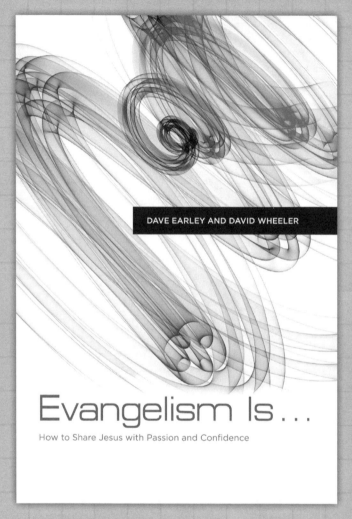

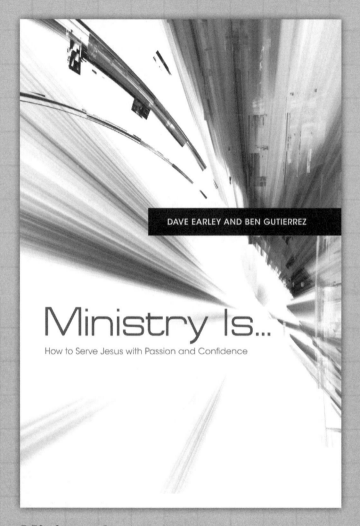